The
Little Book
— OF —
Christmas
Joy

The
Little Book
— OF —
Christmas Joy

True Holiday Stories to Nourish the Heart

Jennifer Basye Sander

PREVIOUSLY PUBLISHED AS *A MIRACLE UNDER THE CHRISTMAS TREE*
AND *A KISS UNDER THE MISTLETOE*

PARK
ROW
BOOKS

PARK
ROW™
BOOKS™

ISBN-13: 978-0-7783-8833-3

The Little Book of Christmas Joy: True Holiday Stories to Nourish the Heart

This publication contains opinions and ideas of the author. It is intended for informational and
educational purposes only. The reader should seek the services of a competent professional for
expert assistance or professional advice. Reference to any organization, publication or website
does not constitute or imply an endorsement by the author or the publisher. The author and the
publisher specifically disclaim any and all liability arising directly or indirectly from the use or
application of any information contained in this publication.

This edition published by arrangement with Harlequin Books S.A.

Park Row Books
22 Adelaide St. West, 40th Floor
Toronto, Ontario M5H 4E3, Canada
ParkRowBooks.com
BookClubbish.com

Printed in U.S.A.

CONTENTS

A Miracle
Under the
Christmas
Tree

Painted Christmas Dreams

Dee Ambrose-Stahl

———◆◆◆———

Deirdre woke early, just like every December 25. She tiptoed downstairs, hoping against hope that this would be the year her dream would come true. Her parents were already awake and seated at the kitchen table; that fact alone gave the young girl pause, as they were never downstairs on Christmas morning until much later.

"Morning, sleepy head," Ben, Deirdre's father, said. "'Bout time you rolled outa the hay!" When Nancy, Deirdre's mother, tried to hide her giggle behind her coffee cup, Deirdre knew something was up.

So began the short story—or some variation—that I wrote every year growing up. It was my dream to walk downstairs Christmas morning and find a paint horse tied outside the picture window. I, like most girls, was obsessed with horses. Usually that obsession passes like any other fad. Mine didn't. In fact, it set down roots so firm that not even marriage to a "nonhorse" man could pull them up.

Every year I wrote a similar story, "Dreaming of My Paint

Horse," and gave it to my parents, hoping that they would get the hint. It seemed they never would. Every year I looked out the picture window to find an empty yard and disappointment, a vacant space where my horse ought to be.

We were never deprived as kids, far from it. But I'd have gladly relinquished every toy, every item of clothing, even every horse statue and book for that Dream Horse.

My childhood passed, as did many of my interests. Tennis? Too much work. Knitting? Knot! Horses? Now that was the constant passion in my life. I read about them, wrote about them and even joined a 4-H club that taught about them. Of course, I also dreamed about them. My own horse, though, was always out of reach.

My two older sisters each had a horse when they were younger, but in the words of my parents, "They lost interest in the horses as soon as boys came along." How was that my fault? I didn't care about boys. Boys were dumb. This was my mantra even through my teen years, until the unthinkable happened... I met Ron.

Ron and I came from similar working-class backgrounds and became best friends shortly after we met. Ron was perfect in every way, except that he barely knew the head from the tail of a horse. This, I thought, I could deal with. I might even teach him a thing or two. We were engaged within six weeks and married a year later. Some things you just know.

We marked our fifth anniversary, then our tenth, and then suddenly we were looking forward to our twentieth anniversary. Through all the years, my obsession with horses lived dormant—below the surface of other goings-on, but it was present nonetheless. Ron dealt with this quirk of mine the way he dealt with most things: with a quiet smile and an "oh, well" shrug of the shoulders, thinking I would get over it someday. But someday never came.

The Internet, however, did, and its information superhighway allowed me access to horses. A voyeuristic approach, I admit, but one which at least gave relief to some of my desire. I discovered a myriad of websites that listed horses for sale, and I haunted them all. I searched for paint horses, torturing myself looking at horses I knew I'd never own. Until one day in December when I found a website owned by Sealite Paint Horses in Ijamsville, Maryland. I immediately searched the Foals page. There, my pulse quickened from a minor trot of anticipation to a full-blown gallop at finding so many paint foals, from weanlings to long yearlings. I was drawn to three in particular: two yearlings and a weanling, all beautifully marked and all fillies. My heart dropped into my shoes.

On impulse, I phoned Kim Landes, the owner of Sealite, although I felt as if I were doing something illicit. We chatted for nearly an hour about horses in general and her paints in particular, and I was thrilled when she invited me to visit. I told her about the fillies that had caught my eye. She said that all three were still for sale. The news was both a blessing and a curse.

As much as I wanted to be horse shopping, Realist Ron made an excellent point when he asked, simply and softly, "How could we afford a horse?"

"So we'll just go for a drive," I said, "look at pretty horses and that's all. We'll come home right after. I promise." I knew the truth, though.

A few days later, we loaded our two corgi dogs into the back of the Jeep and began the three-hour drive to Maryland, the home of my dream. Ron has a gift for keeping me leveled, so to speak. I am impulsive; Ron is pensive. It's been this way between us since we first met. I can see how this difference may cause grief in some marriages, but for us, it created a balance.

While we drove, I chattered on about how beautiful these foals were, how much I couldn't wait until I saw them in person, how exciting it would be to raise and train a baby and how sweet a paint's disposition is. Ron nodded a lot and spoke little.

When we arrived, I was breathless, either from my incessant talking or overgrown excitement. We met Kim, her husband Chris and the Sealite gang. I felt like I'd found the Holy Grail, or like a sixteen-year-old who gets a brand-new car for her birthday. All of my senses were on overload as I tried to absorb each of the dozen or more paints all at once. Then I saw her. "Oh my God, Ron! Look at her!"

Ron followed my gaze. Off beside the run-in shed stood Sky, one of the black-and-white overo fillies I had seen on Kim's website. "Wow," was all Ron could manage, and I had to agree.

Large, brown eyes looked at us from her blazed face. The side closest to us sported a white patch that nearly covered her ribs, and on her neck was what could only be described as a bleeding heart. Her four white socks were of varying lengths, but best of all, she seemed to be very well balanced in her conformation—her graceful neck tied perfectly into a powerful shoulder, and from her back came a strong hip and rear, giving her the perfect equine engine.

As we stood looking at Sky, some of the youngsters became curious about the newcomers and warily approached us. Among them was Lacy, who promptly decided that she could fit in my back pocket. I gave her a pat and told her how pretty she was, all the while keeping an eye on Sky.

"She wants things on her own terms," I whispered to Ron as I dipped my head toward Sky. "I like that."

"You do?"

"Uh huh." Without seeming too obvious, I walked over to Sky. "Hey, sweetheart," I whispered as she smelled my hand. "How are you, baby girl? Over here all by yourself. You're not antisocial, are you?"

Sky's ears flicked back and forth like an air traffic controller's paddles as she assessed me, too. I scratched her withers, a favorite itchy spot of most horses, and saw her head lower and relax. I was hooked. Sky was independent and refused to beg for a scrap of attention from us mere humans. She was not easily spooked or skittish; she just approached new situations on her own terms. This was a familiar quality, as I too tended to set and adhere to my own terms in most situations. I wanted to see how she might do on her own.

We took Sky away from her herd mates so I could watch her move in a round pen. Her tail became a flag, and her nostrils became air horns as she floated around the pen, head held high. She trotted and cantered beautifully, and her eyes spoke volumes. They were animated but not wild, a thing I loved about her. Sky was so full of joy that it was obvious this filly loved life.

I talked with Kim about Sky's price, and I could tell that Ron was not, at this moment, loving life as much as Sky. He went off with Chris for a few minutes, then casually called over to me, "I'm going to check on the corgis." That was Ron's cue to me that he wanted to go, *now*, before I did something foolish like put a deposit on this horse.

It's fair to say that Ron would never say these things aloud, but living with him all these years, I've learned how to read his nonverbal clues. But this private message between us provoked me for some reason, even though the tiny voice of reason was knocking inside my head. Usually I'm good at ignoring that voice, but I overrode it and began to talk not just price with Kim and Chris but also transport, shot records, farrier care and the myriad details concerned with a new horse purchase. Ron stayed at the Jeep during this exchange, eyeing me warily. Eventually, I bid Kim and Chris farewell with the promise to be in touch.

Ron, predictably, didn't say a word as we started our drive home. "Tell me what you're thinking," I queried.

"What I'm thinking?" he asked. "About what?"

"The weather, Ron! What do you mean 'about what?' I mean about Sky!"

"Oh, she's nice, I guess. I don't know…"

"Nice?! She's gorgeous!" How could he not see this?

However, that pronouncement was met with more silence. Silence that lasted many more miles until I brought it up once again. "But she's special, Ron! And I know Kim and Chris would negotiate on her price."

In typical Sensible Ron fashion, my husband pointed out what I already knew in my heart but did not want to hear: "We can't afford a horse."

I couldn't really argue with this. The purchase price of a horse—any horse—is the easiest expense to meet. Maintaining an equine for the twenty-five years or more of its life is where the economic strain comes in. Ron was right, as he usually is in all economic matters. We could not afford a horse, period. I tempered this acceptance by adding silently, "Not now, anyway. I'll take the coward's way out and e-mail, rather than call, Kim tomorrow to tell her." These last words caught in my throat.

Later that evening, we stopped for dinner along the interstate. I don't know if it was the holiday decor of the restaurant or the Christmas section of the attached gift shop, but suddenly I was transported back in time. *It's Christmas morning. I race down the stairs and offer the brightly lit tree only a quick glance, for just past the tree is the picture window. It can't be! I shake my head and rub my eyes, certain that my mind is playing tricks on me. I look again, and it—she—is still standing there. Sky is standing in the front yard of my childhood home, her glistening black-and-white coat a stark contrast to the glimmering white Christmas snow.*

My husband's voice brought me back to reality.

"What? I'm sorry, what did you say?" I asked.

"I asked what you were thinking about. You've been really quiet, but you smiled just now," Ron said. That's when I realized that in nearly twenty years of marriage, I had never shared the story of The Dream Horse with him. Over dinner, I recounted the tale, with a bit of sadness in my voice that I just couldn't hide. Ron's normally brilliant blue eyes clouded over.

"I know exactly what you mean," he said with a sigh as he reached across the table for my hand. Like me, my husband grew up in a blue-collar family with never quite enough money. He, too, knew firsthand the feeling of The Dream, but his dream was a motorcycle on two wheels, not four hooves—the iron horse.

The rest of the drive home, we remained silent, arriving home just after dark. Exhausted and disappointed, I climbed into a hot shower and then managed to read a few chapters of a book. I fell asleep imagining my beautiful new filly cantering across the field to greet me. She offered me her soft, pink muzzle, and I wrapped my arms around her glistening neck and buried my face in her mane, breathing in her heady smell. I felt the level of contentment I'd been searching for, but it was only a dream.

★ ★ ★

"Are you going Christmas shopping with me on Saturday?" I asked Ron. It was December 18, and we had yet to do any big shopping for family and friends. With our work schedules, the coming Saturday was looking like our one and only hope of accomplishing any shopping together.

"Oh, um, well…" Ron stammered. "We can't go anywhere Saturday."

"What do you mean we can't go anywhere? We've got tons of shopping to do!"

"Well, I'm expecting a delivery, and we have to be here when it comes. You know how FedEx can be," he said.

I was furious with him for having waited until the last minute to buy my Christmas gift. Fine. I left him to his FedEx worries and did the shopping myself during the week. I was not at all gracious about this scenario.

I barely spoke to him that week, and when I did speak, it was only in short, clipped answers to something he said first. My Christmas spirit was obviously going to be absent in the Stahl home this year. I made sure this fact was not lost on Ron.

Saturday morning, I was in the den wrapping presents. I had a perfect view of the driveway via the picture window. I would certainly see the FedEx truck when it arrived.

My anger with Ron collided full force with my eagerness to catch a glimpse of the delivery. Eagerness was winning out. Where could he have been shopping? Did he go on his lunch break from work? That would limit the possibilities. Would the shipping box offer any clues? Would I know what it is from the box that it's in? Damn!

I wasn't paying attention and cut the wrapping paper too short. As I reached for a new roll of paper, Ron's thundering feet on the stairs made me jump. What startled me even more, though, was his voice. "He's here!" Ron shrieked, hitting a pitch I hadn't heard from him in all our twenty years together. I had no idea that Ron loved the FedEx guy this much.

"Come here, come here, come here!" Ron chattered. "You've gotta come here..." And he pulled me by the hand to stand in the doorway facing the driveway.

"Look!"

And then I did, but what I saw didn't register. White SUV. SUV? Pulling something. A horse trailer. A horse trailer? A horse trailer with "Sealite Paint Horses" written on the side!

I staggered backward, into Ron's arms, and he kissed me on the head as he draped a coat over my shoulders. "Let's go," he whispered in my ear, gently pushing me out the door.

As my brain spun circles trying to wrap itself around this image, the driver's window of the SUV rolled down, and the vehicle rolled to a stop. "Merry Christmas, Dee!" I heard the driver yell—wait, that's Chris!

I remember Chris getting out of the vehicle and giving me a hug. I remember holding my breath as he dropped down the window of the trailer. And I remember thinking, *She's home,* as her familiar white face popped out from behind the window. She looked at me, and her soft brown eyes reflected, "I remember you."

As I stroked her beautiful white face, I said something brilliant to Chris like, "You were supposed to be the FedEx guy!"

So how did Ron do it? How did he make my dream come true?

Apparently, the night we returned from Sealite, he called Kim and Chris and made the arrangements, all on the sly. My sad story of yearning and Christmas disappointment had moved him to action.

I stood wrapped in Ron's arms, watching Sky become acquainted with her new home. I turned and looked into Ron's eyes. My question was simple: "Why?"

"Because you wanted her from the beginning. I wanted to be the one who made your dreams come true."

Somewhere, in the deep, dark recesses of my memory, I felt the curtain drop down on an old yearning and a new kind of contentment fill every bit of those years of wanting and waiting. Then, I felt another curtain rise above a thousand new dreams as I settled my head against Ron's chest and looked into the eyes of my new paint dream.

Ron and I smiled, laughed, cried tears of joy and talked well past midnight about our new dreams and how we might make them come true for each other.

California Camper Christmas

Cheryl Riveness

---•◦❈◦•---

It was Christmas morning 1986. Thinking back to the day before, I recalled how everything had come together. It had been a pretty bad year, and Christmas promised to be more of the same. A fabulous holiday for the children was a luxury we couldn't afford. I had all but given up hope that we would be able to celebrate even in a small way. And then, my husband, a truck tire service technician, received an unanticipated service call. The driver was stranded and trying desperately to make it home in time to be with his own children on Christmas morning. He was short of money, but he had merchandise that he was willing to trade for services, enabling us to give the older girls, eleven and thirteen, exactly what they'd wanted: a VCR.

Two days before, we had driven sixty-five miles to pick up the one thing that our youngest had asked for (a Disney Fievel plush toy) before closing time. The drive and the toy had taken everything we had saved. I scoured pockets and the truck seat on the morning of Christmas Eve and found just over three dollars in change. Feeling optimistic, I headed for the nearest flea market, arriving just as the vendors were packing up.

I had tried repeatedly to get the kids to understand that there simply wasn't enough room for a tree in the dilapidated pickup camper that the five of us had been calling home for months now. But, I thought, maybe a string of lights and little candy canes would make the surroundings more festive. The camper was small, so luckily one string would do. As I was paying the vendor, something caught my eye, a glimpse of a very small, white artificial tree top being tossed from row to row by the breeze. Hastily wishing the old gentleman a merry Christmas, I waved goodbye and rushed after the treasure. My heart absolutely swelled with appreciation. Now I could grant their special wish, if only in a small way.

That evening, after we'd watched *Frosty the Snowman* and enjoyed popcorn and hot chocolate, I tucked the children in and listened to their prayers. They were simple: "Please help us find a home soon." I couldn't help thinking how Joseph and Mary must have been feeling the night of Jesus's birth; they too were homeless. At least we had shelter.

Once the girls' breathing was soft and measured, I retrieved the lights and the tree from inside the truck cab, and after quietly weaving the lights around the small branches, I asked my husband to place the tree in the corner above our youngest child's bed. After he managed to safely tuck it in, he ran the string down the length of the overhead cabinets and to the electrical outlet. "Well, here goes nothing," he mouthed, plugging the cord into the socket. We held our breath and waited. They came on, and they twinkled, with the smallest blue lights, their reflection glinting off the rusted chrome trim of the tiny "kitchen."

The night had been cold, the steady wind magnifying the

plummeting temperatures. Assorted leaves and debris still blew through the campground, and our large dog was crying to get inside. I was drained, mentally and emotionally. Crawling into our bunk, I pulled the curtain closed behind me; the gentle blue glow of the lights dancing on the ceiling lulled me into satisfied slumber.

Waking to hushed whispers, I heard Arianna's voice, quiet in the early light of dawn: "Santa brought us a tree! Look, Sissy, it's so pretty, and it's ours." Peeking through the curtains, I saw that our min pin dog was still nestled asleep in her arms, his breathing rhythmic. Her eyes were fixated on the little tree that had appeared while she slept.

I lowered myself from the overhead bunk onto the burnt orange cushion of the seat below. "Oh, Mommy, it's so beautiful," she whispered in amazement. "I didn't even *hear* him," she continued with the wide-eyed wonder that only four-year-olds possess. Santa had brought both of the things she had wanted so much. The little white tree top was absolutely resplendent, and her toy was a treasure that she still has thirty-some years later.

It would be several years before our Christmases became more like the ones the older girls remembered. Yet, when we speak of childhood memories, the magic of this special morning is among our favorites.

Christmas Love

Candy Chand

⟤⟐⟐⟐⟐⟤

This story shows up every holiday season in e-mail in-boxes around the world, frequently attributed to Anonymous. But it is not from an anonymous writer; it is a real-life experience from my friend Candy Chand. I had the privilege of publishing Candy's first story ever in my book *The Magic of Christmas Miracles*, and she hasn't stopped writing since. You will be as touched as the millions who have read this.

—Jennifer Basye Sander

Each December, I vowed to make Christmas a calm and peaceful experience. But once again, despite my plans, chaos prevailed. I had cut back on nonessential obligations: extensive card writing, endless baking, decorating and, yes, even the all-American pastime, overspending. Yet, still, I found myself exhausted, unable to appreciate the precious family moments and, of course, the true meaning of Christmas.

My son, Nicholas, was in kindergarten that year. It was an exciting season for a six-year-old filled with hopes, dreams and laughter. For weeks, he'd been memorizing songs for his school's winter pageant. I didn't have the heart to tell him I'd be working the night of the production.

Unwilling to miss his shining moment, I spoke with his teacher. She assured me that there'd be a dress rehearsal the morning of the presentation. All parents unable to attend that evening were welcome to come to the dress rehearsal. Fortunately, Nicholas seemed happy with the compromise.

So, just as I promised, on the morning of the dress rehearsal, I filed in ten minutes early, found a spot on the cafeteria floor and sat down. Around the room, I saw several other parents quietly scampering to their seats. As I waited, the students were led into the room. Each class, accompanied by their teacher, sat cross-legged on the floor. Then, each group, one by one, rose to perform their song.

Because the public school system had long stopped referring to the holiday as Christmas, I didn't expect anything other than fun, commercial entertainment: songs of reindeer, Santa Claus, snowflakes and good cheer. The melodies were fun, cute and lighthearted, but nowhere to be found was even the hint of an innocent babe, a manger or Christ's sacred gift of hope and joy. So, when my son's class rose to sing "Christmas Love," I was slightly taken aback by its bold title.

Nicholas was aglow, as were all of his classmates, who were adorned in fuzzy mittens, red sweaters and bright wool snowcaps. Those in the front row—center stage—held up large letters, one by one, to spell out the title of the song. As the class sang, "C is for Christmas," a child held up the letter C. Then, "H is for happy," and on and on, until they had presented the complete message, "Christmas Love."

The performance was going smoothly, until suddenly, we noticed her: a small, quiet girl in the front row who was holding the letter *M* upside down. She was entirely unaware that reversed, her letter *M* appeared to be a *W.* Fidgeting from side to side, she soon moved entirely away from her mark, adding a gap in the children's tidy lineup.

The audience of first through sixth graders snickered at the little one's mistake.

But in her innocence, she had no idea that they were laughing at her as she stood tall, proudly holding her "W."

One can only imagine the difficulty in calming an audience of young, giggling students. Although many teachers tried to shush the children, the laughter continued until the last letter was raised, and we all saw it together. A hush came over the audience, and eyes began to widen.

In that instant, we understood—the reason we were there, why we celebrated the holiday in the first place, why even in the chaos there was a purpose for our festivities. For when the last letter was held high, the message read loud and clear:

CHRIST WAS LOVE

And I believe He still is.

Unfinished Gifts

BJ Hollace

"I need to find the perfect gift. I need to find the perfect gift." The words circulated through my mind like the woodpecker that tapped on our chimney. Christmas was coming, and I needed it to be perfect this year.

Years had passed since my entire family had celebrated together around one Christmas tree. Those things that had kept us apart, including time and distance, were being put aside. It was time to heal old wounds. Forgiveness and healing were on my Christmas list this year.

The search began for the perfect gift for my mother. What does a perfect gift look like anyway? My mom's favorite treats are Brown & Haley's Mountain bars, so I quickly scribbled those onto the list. Hmmm, what else? The blank page stared back at me. Candy, even her favorite candy, was not going to be sufficient.

"What can we get for my mom?" I asked my husband, Bill. He shrugged his shoulders. Clearly, this assignment would require some soul-searching. Sometimes even husbands don't have all the answers.

As I went about my daily tasks, I thought and prayed and thought some more. Suddenly, in my mind, I could see the perfect present in wonderful detail. I knew exactly what would surprise and delight my mother, but the question was, Where was it? Living in a one-bedroom apartment, my filing system isn't what you would call perfect. It is adequate for those things that are filed, but as for the unfiled items stored in miscellaneous bins, well, it would be like finding a needle in a haystack.

Somewhere in the apartment was a gray envelope sent by my brother and sister-in-law about a year earlier. Inside were several photos and a note from my mom. I walked from room to room, eyeing stacks and piles. *Which one had I put it in?* After some digging, I found it. The first piece of the puzzle was in my hand. As I opened the envelope, I found the photos and note just as I remembered.

My great-grandmother Janke liked to knit. As a family tradition, she'd made baby bootees for her grandchildren and great-grandchildren. The photos showed an unfinished bootee with knitting needles still stuck in it, as if she'd put it aside for a few moments to go make a cup of tea.

My mom's request was that I write a short poem to go with this photo. I was touched and flattered that she'd asked, of course, but then reality set in. I didn't have a clue how to put words to this piece of my history. How can you honor someone who died when you were only two years old? I never really knew her, not like my mom knew her grandmother.

Memories of my own grandma and the many hours I spent with her over a cup of tea or laughing, baking and praying came easily to mind. Grandma is long gone. She was my mother's mother—she is a part of me.

I had the photo, now I needed some inspiration. Maybe if

I knew more about the actual woman, I could give her the tribute she deserved. Hmmm, I looked around my apartment again, checking all the logical places for the family history book. Ah, yes, here were the facts. Janke Heeringa was born on January 22, 1874, in Holland. In May 1891, seventeen-year-old Janke came to America by herself, joining her brother and sister who lived in Iowa. Immediately, she began doing household work in the area for American people even though she knew no English. She was married two years later in 1893 to my great-grandfather.

In October 1900, twenty-eight Hollanders from Iowa rented a train car and hired a porter to help them travel to Washington to start a new life. When Janke began the journey from Iowa, she was seven months pregnant and had three young children, all boys—two, four and six years old—to care for as well. Her fourth child was born in December 1900 after arriving in the Pacific Northwest.

Janke was described as a woman of determination. *Yes, you would have to be to survive that cross-country trip while pregnant,* I thought. *My mother and grandmother and even I could be described that way.* Must be a family trait.

When Janke died in 1961 at the age of eighty-seven, she left behind twenty-five grandchildren, fifty-six great-grand-children and one great-great-granddaughter. Great to have so many solid facts, but I was still without a shred of poetry.

The clock ticked on. This present didn't need to be finished until we arrived to visit family just after Christmas, but time was still short. The days flew by as I struggled to find the right words. How could a poem and picture convey the message of healing and forgiveness that I sought? Only God knew. I still didn't get it.

My husband and I talked again. "It's something that I need to do. The time is right, but I just don't know what to say."

"I know you can do it. I have faith in you."

"Thanks, sweetheart. It's more than faith I need. I need divine inspiration."

Finally, I was at peace. My struggle for understanding was over. Mentally and emotionally, I stood in her shoes, this woman who was part of me, whose blood ran through my veins. The answer was etched in my DNA. I just needed to write what was in my heart.

The frame was small, so the poem needed to be Goldilocks size—not too long and not too short, just right.

I needed to understand the subject matter, my great-grandmother, but also the audience, my mother. Mom had a special relationship with her grandmother. I understood that kind of grandmother-granddaughter relationship. For inspiration, I drew on the stories Mom shared of visiting Janke on Saturday afternoons after catechism and again on Sundays after church, sitting on her grandma's lap and slurping tea from the saucer. And if she was really good, dried apples were a special treat.

How could I bring these generations of women together? My great-grandmother and grandmother had passed on to their heavenly reward, leaving my mom navigating through life's changes, and me, who hoped to unite these generations with words and give them the honor they deserved.

I needed my poem to be a mixture of love, healing and wholeness that we seek to find in our families. It was a high calling, but I knew it was possible. Finally, the words came. The message was short, laden with emotion, and it painted the picture I saw in my mind—to honor Janke and this moment.

Holding the paper before me, I read it out loud in its final form and knew this was it.

With each stitch, she weaves a prayer,
for the tiny foot that will fit in there.
She stops for a moment and gazes outside;
the children are looking for a place to hide.
Her trembling hands slow her pace;
she knows that soon she'll see her Savior's face.
Now her knitting needles lay silent…

Yes, it was right. I believed it conveyed the message on my great-grandmother's heart in her final days. She knew the time had come to go to her husband, gone almost twenty years previously. Janke was ready, ready enough to leave this last bootee unfinished.

The photo and poem were carefully framed and secured in my carry-on bag as we flew across the state. The gift was precious and couldn't be trusted as checked baggage to be jostled around in the plane's belly. It wouldn't leave my sight until it was delivered to its intended destination.

We all gathered for Christmas at my parents' home, a place laden with memories. The Christmas tree was surrounded by mountains of gifts, and Mom's special package was tucked safely in a corner.

When it was Mom's turn, she opened several gifts before opening ours. Tearing away the paper, Mom realized quickly what it was, gasping as she removed the last scrap of wrapping. A piece of her grandma Janke was returned to her that day.

Four generations of women were united that night. We were four women who had known life's joys and sorrows. Women who were filled with determination to live their lives with all they had and to offer no less than the best to their families and their Creator. Women who know that miracles are found every day in unusual places, not just in perfection but also in the unfinished projects of our lives. There are miracles in the making that are often left for future generations to piece together until the circle is complete. My part was finished. I closed the circle of love that Janke, my great-grandmother, set in motion years ago while traveling from her birth country to a land she did not know, a land where she would find hope and love and, yes, miracles.

Dickens in the Dark

Jennifer Aldrich

———— •⟡• ————

It seemed like a good idea at the time. *"Come to the Great Dickens Christmas Fair with me,"* he had said. *"You will be able to dress in a beautiful costume."* And here I stood, in a plain, twill, button-down dress, watching the rain pounding the steel roof, the sound louder on the inside than outside. How did I get here?

Daniel, my husband of three months at that point, and I were spending our Christmas season working at the largest Dickensian festival in California. San Francisco's Cow Palace becomes London as Dickens saw it for four or five weekends each year.

Charles Dickens's characters are here: all the ones you would expect for this time of year (Mr. Scrooge and Tiny Tim) and others you may not expect to see at Christmas (Mr. Fagin and Bill Sikes), not to mention Mr. Charles Dickens himself. In addition to the Dickens characters, there are historical characters of the Victorian Era (Queen Victoria and Prince Albert) and even some fictional characters known to all at the time (Father Christmas, Sherlock Holmes and Mr. Punch).

Rounding out this eclectic collection of characters is the family of Charles Dickens himself. That's where we are: the Dickens's Family Parlour. Daniel is Charley Dickens, the eldest and most ne'er-do-well of Dickens's seven sons. I am Mrs. Cooper, the cook. I make a midday meal to feed the actors in our immediate cast of twelve.

It was the last day of the Fair for the season, and I had been inside the building since 8 a.m. preparing a special tea for singing performers, getting water hot before everyone else arrived. By 10 a.m., my castmates were dressing in our environmental area, the carpeted Parlour floor a sea of hoopskirts and crinolines. We all dress in costumes appropriate to the period, with great care given to historical accuracy. As I was playing a servant, I did not have the hoops under my skirts that the other ladies of my household were wearing. But like them, I was in a laced-up corset, long dress and button-up boots; my pin bib apron and hair tucked under a mop cap completed my less than glamorous look.

"I'm going to deliver teas now," I said to Mamie, the eldest Dickens daughter and our director. "I'll be back before opening."

"You okay, honey?" she asked concerned. "You look done."

"Stick a fork in me," I replied. "I'm just glad it's the last day of the season."

In truth, I was exhausted. There are some things which, even though you love to do them, can take a lot of effort. Working at the Dickens Fair was a lot of work, plus I had a full-time job on the weekdays. Also, it can be a very expensive hobby. This was the first year I worked at the Fair. I had only attended once before as a patron, watching Daniel perform in one of the stage shows.

I have always loved the fantasy of time travel and have been an avid reader of historical novels for years. I had such a great time as a patron that I decided to join in, jumping into the deep end feet first. I could be, if only for a short time, somewhere and someone else, to live the fantasy. I could have asked to do something simpler to start, but I have a hard time asking for help, especially when it involves doing something I say I like doing.

I walked out of the Parlour, near the entrance to the Fair, past the stalls and storefronts of the artisans who sell their wares of Christmas decorations, bonnets and wreaths, pewter goblets and jewelry. I headed into the breezeway, home of the London docks and the Paddy West School of Seamanship, which is in reality a band of very musical sailors who sing sea chanteys and nautical songs. I dropped off one air pot of tea, received a hug of thanks from one of the cabin "boys" (a lively woman with short hair) and headed down to Mad Sal's Dockside Alehouse at the other end of the bay to drop off the rest. Mad Sal's is where naughty music hall songs are performed and represents the seedy end of our London.

The rain was really coming down, booming and loud against the roof, the occasional thunderclap joining in for good measure. Heading backstage, I dropped off the last air pots to Weasel, our chief chucker in the Music Hall. Short in stature but big in heart, he can get you to sing along with a music hall ditty faster than you can say "Burlington Bertie from Bow."

"Oy! Weasel!" I said, in my best Cockney accent. "Where's Sal an' everybody?"

"Over by the door," he replied, gesturing with his thumb. "I'm stayin' in 'ere. Too bleedin' cold for me near the door."

"Too right," I said, nodding at the air pots. "I'll pick 'em up afore the last show."

I turned away from the stage and headed back to the Parlour along the sidewall of the Concourse. I saw Mad Sal, Dr. Boddy, Molly Twitch, Polly Amory and a few others sitting and watching the rain. I gave a quick wave and continued walking.

"Gee," I heard someone say, "you think all this rain might affect attendance?"

Suddenly, there was another loud thunderclap, and POP all the lights went out! The few exit lights in the building came on immediately after.

"That might," came the reply.

We will not be opening the Fair on time today, I realized. The entire hall felt nearly pitch-black at first, with the exception of the exit signs. We wouldn't be able to bring customers in until we could get the lights back on. I slowly made my way back to the Parlour, taking my time and stepping carefully, overhearing pieces of conversations as I went.

"Somebody forgot to pay the electric bill!"

At an ale stand: "I guess we have to drink all the champagne before it gets warm."

Someone talking to the dancing light of a cell phone screen: "What's that, Tink? The pirates have captured Wendy?"

I came back into the Paddy West area to see the whole group sitting on the stage, playing softly in the semidarkness. The side exit doors had been opened a crack to let in some light. I didn't want to move another step back into the darkness of the next bay, so I sat down on one of the benches facing the stage.

They started to play my favorite sea chanty, "Rolling Home." The beauty of the music, my fatigue, the dark and the rain all came together and washed over me. I started to cry. Then I started to think.

Do I really want to do this, year after year? "Rolling home, rolling home." *I am so wiped out, and it's such a huge commitment.* "Rolling home across the sea." *Is this something that Daniel and I should share?* "Rolling home to dear old England." *What if we have kids? Will we bring them, too?* "Rolling home, fair land to thee."

Our minutes in the dark stretched on past 11 a.m., our opening time. I returned to the Parlour at about 10:45. Daniel and I began to take the small, unlit candles off our Christmas tree, light them and set them in candelabras on the dining table. It gave a beautiful glow to our set, now a very realistic looking Victorian parlor.

We sat down at the settee, and I told him about my little breakdown in the Paddy West area. He held my hand and said, "Okay, today is our last day."

"Yeah," I said, "until next year."

"No," he said, "our last day ever. I don't want you to do anything that doesn't make you happy. And I definitely won't make you do something that is supposed to be just for fun when you hate it."

It didn't sound right to me the minute he said it. *I love doing this,* I thought. *I love creating the type of Christmas that probably never existed, but we all wish could have. I love the friends I've made here. They've become my family.*

"I love you," I said finally. "I love that you would be okay with my quitting. But I'm not going to. I found my people, where I belong. I may do things a little different next year to make it easier, but I won't give it up. There would be too many things I would miss and too much."

Daniel smiled at me in a way that told me he had known I would change my mind, cheeky bugger. Before we met, I wrote down all the things I wanted in a guy. One of them was "someone who would call me on my nonsense." Damn if I didn't find him.

A call went out to the cast members inside to gather together all the umbrellas in the building; the line of customers had extended past the building well into the parking lot for several yards. Charles Dickens and other cast members went out to hold the umbrellas and keep everyone as dry as possible. All the musicians available entertained them. The servers from Cuthbert's Tea Shoppe came out, too, dispensing hot tea.

Some people were escorted in small groups past the Parlour to the restrooms. Walking past, one woman gave a small gasp. "Oh!" she said, turning toward the Parlour and seeing our candlelit set, "You all look like a painting!"

By 11:30, I was providing the last of our tea supply to Cuthbert's when the lights came back on. We could hear the cheer from the crowd outside as plain as if they were standing next to us. As soon as it was safe to do so, the doors were opened to let the patrons into the Fair.

The abbreviated schedule didn't seem to diminish the experience of the day for anyone. The spirit of Christmas, it seemed, was present everywhere. Everyone was happy and smiling, patron and participant alike. The small kindnesses that our cast and crew gave to those outside was repaid tenfold back to us, in every heartfelt "Merry Christmas" and word of thanks. Patrons who had originally planned to spend only an hour or two at our fair told me they were going to stay all day, just to support us!

"Thank you for bringing the Dickens Fair outside!" one woman exclaimed.

That was my first year working at the Great Dickens Christmas Fair. Did I go back? Yes, and with a renewed enthusiasm. Last year, we brought our four-year-old for his first year as a participant. Daniel built a train for him out of cardboard boxes so he could be part of the Toy Parade. Bringing a baby or a small child to the Fair as a participant takes a considerable amount of careful planning, but it can be done. Those who are the most successful are those who ask for help. The Fair's community, like any large family, takes care of its own.

Will our son share our passion for this and join us even when he is older? It's hard to say at this point, but he will be raised knowing how much we love it and hearing stories of the Fairs of Christmas Past. And I am sure we will tell him about the day the Fair went dark.

Looking back, the best part of that day for me was seeing the quality of people in our Fair family. Some say we are crazy to spend our time, our money and our holiday season on this theatrical enterprise. But now I can't imagine a better way to spend my Decembers than with this group I am proud to work with and proud to know.

Finding Joy in the World

Elaine Ambrose

—•◦❍◦•—

December 1980 arrived in a gray cloud of disappointment as I became the involuntary star in my own soap opera, a hapless heroine who faced the camera at the end of each day and asked, "Why?" as the scene faded to black. Short of being tied to a railroad track in the path of an oncoming train, I found myself in an equally dire situation, wondering how my life turned into such a calamity of sorry events. I was unemployed and had a two-year-old daughter, a six-week-old son, an unemployed husband who left the state looking for work and a broken furnace with no money to fix it. To compound the issues, I lived in the same small Idaho town as my wealthy parents, and they refused to help. This scenario was more like *The Grapes of Wrath* than *The Sound of Music*.

After getting the children to bed, I would sit alone in my rocking chair and wonder what went wrong. I thought I had followed the correct path by getting a college degree before marriage and then working four years before having children. My plan was to stay home with two children for five years and then return to a satisfying, lucrative career. But, no, suddenly I was poor and didn't have money to feed the kids or buy them Christmas presents. I didn't even have enough money for a cheap bottle of wine. At least I was breast-feeding the baby, so that cut down on grocery bills. And my daughter thought macaroni and cheese was what everyone had every night for dinner. Sometimes I would add a wiggly gelatin concoction, and she would squeal with delight. Toddlers don't know or care if Mommy earned Phi Beta Kappa scholastic honors in college. They just want to squish Jell-O through their teeth.

The course of events that led to that December unfolded like a fateful temptation. I was twenty-six years old in 1978 and energetically working as an assistant director for the University of Utah in Salt Lake City. My husband had a professional job in an advertising agency, and we owned a modest but new home. After our daughter was born, we decided to move to my hometown of Wendell, Idaho, population 1,200, to help my father with his businesses. He owned about thirty thousand acres of land, one thousand head of cattle and more than fifty 18-wheel diesel trucks. He had earned his vast fortune on his own, and his philosophy of life was to work hard and die, a goal he achieved at the young age of sixty.

In hindsight, by moving back home, I was probably trying to establish the warm relationship with my father that I had always wanted. I should have known better. My father was not into relationships, and even though he was incredibly successful in business, life at home was painfully cold. His home, inspired by the designs of Frank Lloyd Wright, was his castle. The semicircular structure was built of rock and cement and perched on a hill overlooking rolling acres of crops. My father controlled the furnishings and artwork. Just inside the front door hung a huge metal shield adorned with sharp swords. An Indian buckskin shield and arrows were on another wall. In the corner, a fierce wooden warrior held a long spear, ever ready to strike. A metal breastplate hung over the fireplace, and four wooden, naked aborigine busts perched on the stereo cabinet. The floors were polished cement, and the bathrooms had purple toilets. I grew up thinking this decor was normal.

I remember the first time I entered my friend's home and gasped out loud at the sight of matching furniture, floral wallpaper, delicate vases full of fresh flowers and walls plastered with family photographs, pastoral scenes and framed Norman Rockwell prints. On the rare occasions that I was allowed to sleep over at a friend's house, I couldn't believe that the family woke up calmly and gathered together to have a pleasant breakfast. At my childhood home, my father would put on John Philip Sousa march records at 6:00 a.m., turn up the volume and go up and down the hallway knocking on our bedroom doors calling, "Hustle. Hustle. Get up! Time is money!" Then my brothers and I would hurry out of bed, pull on work clothes and get outside to do our assigned farm chores. As I moved sprinkler pipe or hoed beets or pulled weeds in the potato fields, I often reflected on my friends who were gathered at their breakfast tables, smiling over plates of pancakes and bacon. I knew at a young age that my home life was not normal.

After moving back to the village of Wendell, life went from an adventure to tolerable and then tumbled into a scene out of *On the Waterfront*. As I watched my career hopes fade away under the stressful burden of survival, I often thought of my single, childless friends who were blazing trails and breaking glass ceilings as women earned better professional jobs. Adopting my favorite Marlon Brando accent, I would raise my fists and declare, "I coulda been a contender! I coulda been somebody, instead of a bum, which is what I am."

There were momentary lapses in sanity when I wondered if I should have been more like my mother. I grew up watching her dutifully scurry around as she desperately tried to serve and obey. My father demanded a hot dinner on the table every night, even though the time he would come home could vary by as much as three hours. My mother would add milk to the gravy, cover the meat with tin foil (which she later washed and reused) and admonish her children to be patient. "Your father works so hard," she would say. "We will wait for him." I opted not to emulate most of her habits. She fit the role of her time, and I still admire her goodness.

My husband worked for my father, and we lived out in the country in one of my father's houses. One afternoon in August of 1980, they got into a verbal fight, and my dad fired my husband. I was pregnant with our second child. We were instructed to move, so we found a tiny house in town, and then my husband left to look for work because jobs weren't all that plentiful in Wendell. Our son was born in October, weighing in at a healthy eleven pounds. The next month, we scraped together enough money to buy a turkey breast for Thanksgiving. By December, our meager savings were gone, and we had no income.

I was determined to celebrate Christmas. We found a scraggly tree and decorated it with handmade ornaments. My daughter and I made cookies and sang songs. I copied photographs of the kids in their pajamas and made calendars as gifts. This was before personal computers, so I drew the calendar pages, stapled them to cardboard covered with fabric and glued red rickrack around the edges. It was all I had to give to those on my short gift list.

Just as my personal soap opera was about to be renewed for another season, my life started to change. One afternoon, about a week before Christmas, I received a call from one of my father's employees. He was "in the neighborhood" and heard that my furnace was broken. He fixed it for free and wished me a merry Christmas. I handed him a calendar, and he pretended to be overjoyed. The next day, the mother of a childhood friend arrived at my door with two of her chickens, plucked and packaged. She said they had extras to give away. Again, I humbly handed her a calendar. More little miracles occurred. A friend brought a box of baby clothes that her boy had outgrown and teased me about my infant son wearing his sister's hand-me-down, pink pajamas. Then, another friend of my mother's arrived with wrapped toys to put under the tree. The doorbell continued to ring, and I received casseroles, offers to babysit, more presents and a bouquet of fresh flowers. I ran out of calendars to give in return.

To this day, I weep every time I think of these simple but loving gestures. Christmas of 1980 was a pivotal time in my life, and I am grateful that I received the true gifts of the season. My precious daughter, so eager to be happy, was amazed at the wonderful sights around our tree. My infant son, a blessing of hope, smiled at me every morning and gave me the determination to switch off the melodrama in my mind. The day before Christmas, my husband was offered a job at an advertising agency in Boise, and we leaped from despair to profound joy. On Christmas Eve, I rocked both babies in my lap and sang them to sleep in heavenly peace. They never noticed my tears falling on their sweet cheeks.

Aspen's Last Trip

Kathleen Gallagher

·◆◈◆·

As I rounded the corner into the entrance of Boston's Logan Airport, my heart raced with excitement. Having spotted the Air Canada planes lining the arrival gates, I knew my bundle of joy had landed. "Morning, ma'am," the customs clearance agent greeted me. "We've all been wondering where this puppy was headed. She's been making some strange noises in that crate!" And sure enough, that little puppy was making quite the racket, the same noises that would eventually develop into her talent for talking and holding a squeaky toy in her mouth at the same time. "I think she's going to be a handful," the agent predicted.

I looked into the crate, and there she was—my first glimpse into what the next fourteen years together would bring. My new golden retriever, Aspen, had been flown from Alberta, Canada, to her new home with me. And what a life it would be.

"What a beautiful golden!" a restaurant patron once remarked, catching sight of Aspen outside a café window. Yes, that was my beautiful golden trotting by, having just chewed herself to freedom from the shady tree to which I'd tethered her leash. Aspen led the way in her life, that was certain.

She also loved all food at all times and could never get enough. "The day Aspen stops eating will be the day she is dying," I would sometimes joke to friends as I filled yet another dog bowl. But then there came that day when she didn't finish her meal, and what was once a funny comment became our reality. The vet diagnosed hemangiosarcoma, an aggressive, malignant cancer of the cells that form blood vessels.

Each moment spent with Aspen (yes, even when she was chewing her leash or plunging into a nearby body of water) was always a delight, but became even more so when she underwent surgery for the cancer in November. With Christmas coming, I piled us all into the car, packed to the hilt with not an ounce of space to spare, for our annual holiday road trip home to my parents' house in Maine. Aspen had been an integral part of our family Christmas traditions for the past fourteen years. Each season her stocking hung next to mine, and every year she eagerly tore open her treats and squeaky toys from Santa. Pictures of Aspen with Santa from each season adorned the mantle, and ornaments with the inscription *"Top Dog"* dangled from the tree.

But this Christmas trip was to be very different. It was clear as I set out that Aspen's will to live was ebbing. I hoped that making the trip back East to smell the fresh ocean air would do her good. As much as I tried to deny the odds, I knew in my heart that this would be Aspen's last Christmas. On this holiday trip, I was truly returning home for a special reason. It was time to return one of the greatest gifts in my life to the Giver.

Aspen's demise on the road seemed to happen overnight. Her spirit shifted so quickly from an energetic, inquisitive dog into a shadow of her former self and personality. At a Nebraska truck stop, I crawled into the back seat and held her in my arms, and together we breathed her last breath on that dark, cold winter's night. Carefully and gently, I wrapped her warm body into a soft, blue blanket. On that snowy December evening, I was left with her warm, limp body lying in my arms. Fourteen years of memories instantly melded together. It was a true Christmas miracle that I was fortunate enough to be with her as she lay dying in the back seat.

Aspen was gone. I sat frozen with heartsickness. As I held her, she radiated such a look of happiness and contentment. Her body and face resembled that of a puppy rather than a geriatric dog who had finally succumbed to a debilitating and painful cancer. What was I to do? Sobbing uncontrollably, my mind raced and my thoughts turned to panic. I was nowhere near my final destination of Maine.

What should I do with her dead body? What would someone think if I was found transporting a dead body across state lines? Was there even a vet clinic nearby? Compounding the problem of the situation was that it was only 3:19 a.m. I tried hard to think logically, *I'll wait it out until morning and locate an animal hospital to have her cremated.* I tried to picture that scene, shaking my head. That didn't feel right at all. What did? Home.

I will take her home for Christmas. I climbed back into the front seat and resumed the journey.

The day dawned gray and bleak. There were another cruel eighteen hundred miles ahead. Alone with my devastation, the miles at times felt unbearable. Tears left my eyes blurry, and it was sometimes hard to see the road ahead. My heart felt as frozen as the desolate and snow-covered landscape. A whirlwind of emotion enveloped me as I ventured onward alone. I wanted to turn around, and even more, I longed to go back, back to the beginning of her life.

The rest of the road trip home was somber and tremendously sad, but it offered me the opportunity to say goodbye to Aspen. It was comforting to turn and see her lying on the seat behind me. Each glance in the rearview mirror reflected back the happiness she had given me. As if accompanied by Aspen's spirit, much like a ghost from Christmas past, I embarked on a road trip thousands of miles down memory lane. My mind reverted back to her puppy-hood.... *Applause filled the room as we received our diploma from puppy kindergarten, which had not proved a huge success for us. Dutifully we had attended each weekly session, but most of the class was spent with Aspen contentedly sleeping in the middle of the training circle while the other puppies pranced around on command. Surprisingly, we managed to graduate due more to her being "cute" than any highly developed skill set; however, the trainer did claim that she had mastered the down position and was the best in the class! Oh, Aspen.*

Here among the crammed-in suitcases and carefully wrapped Christmas presents lay my most treasured and precious gift of all—my beloved golden retriever. Every once in a while, I was startled by stray road noises, certain that what I heard was her in the back seat making her special talking noises and sighs of contentment. It was as though she was talking to me once again, as she had done from that first day at the airport. Each perceived sound garnered a memory from within. *A handful?* I thought, remembering the assessment of the baggage clerk. With an unhesitant smile, I answered, *Yes!*

Each fuel stop afforded me another stolen moment to run my fingers through her silken fur. Her body had now turned cold and rigid. I carefully cradled her paws in my hands. Well-worn rough pads, they had carried her through in life.

At last, there it was, the "Welcome to Maine" road sign. Weary and grateful as I crossed the state line, I became mindfully aware that I had gained more than I had lost on this road trip. As I reviewed my memories, I knew this was the true meaning of the season. I stopped by the beach with Aspen one last time for her final swim in spirit. A spectacularly blue sky overhead and the sun glistening on the water helped carry the memories of her away.

Aspen truly did go home for Christmas. Only she returned home to stay—this time forever. Our journey home had been spent together, but the journey back was spent alone. The return trip from Maine felt doubly long, and even though the car was packed full, it felt extremely empty. Today, Aspen's spirit lives and travels in my heart wherever I go. And as I head back East for the holidays once again this season, she will be with me throughout the miles. As her ghost of Christmas Future showed me, someday when it comes time for my final journey home, I believe Aspen will be waiting to welcome my spirit home to stay. Until then, I will continue to rejoice in the present.

A Sears Catalog Christmas

Laura Martin

———•◦◊◦•———

It was a ritual as ritual as the Big Day itself. Before the wind and the storms and the snow and the ice and the freezing cold could encapsulate our tiny lumber town and seal it off from the only known route to civilization (Interstate 5), and on a given Saturday after dinner and seconds and dessert and baths (but before *The Love Boat* and *Fantasy Island),* my father would usher my little brother and me into the tiny, yellow kitchen with the nicotine-stained curtains adorned with dancing tomatoes and dishes from the day piled high and soaking in the sink. It was in this room that we were formally instructed to take a seat at the family dinner table, both of us kids armed with a writing tablet and pen. And in his two hands—behold! Our father bestowed upon us, right smack dab in the middle of the table in all its glossy cover glory, the most magical book in the history of magic books, full of wonder, anticipation, but more important, hope—the Holy Bible of Christmas everywhere—The Sears Wish Book, our family name for the thick Sears catalog. While mom stared at the TV in the living room and the dogs curled up tight on the brick hearth in front of the woodburning stove, my father took one long, lazy drag off the Marlboro dangling from the side of his mouth and—with the echo of his Air Force days behind him—laid out the rules.

"Here's the Sears Christmas Catalog. You kids sit here at the table. You each get ten choices. Write down what you want on the tablet. Here's a pen—you can't erase anything, so make every choice a good one and don't keep crossing stuff out and wasting paper. Write everything down in order of how bad you want it with #1 being what you want the worst. Write down the page number. If you forget the page number, Santa won't know where to find it. Don't write down clothes. Don't write down anything that takes a lot of batteries. Don't write down anything breakable. Don't write down anything heavy. Don't waste your choices on a bunch of expensive stuff. You can each pick out ONE THING that's $20, or you can pick out one BIG THING for $50 that you'll both take turns sharing and not fight over. Doug, don't write down a chemistry set—I don't want you blowing up the house. Don't write down anything that has any liquid in it or anything you need parental supervision to use or anything you're supposed to put bugs in. And Laura, you are NOT sneaking around in the middle of the night making chocolate cakes in your bedroom. Don't write down an Easy-Bake oven. You know, when your grandpa was a kid, his family used to use the pages of the Sears catalog as toilet paper, God's honest truth. Don't get your hopes up that you'll get anything you write down. This isn't a promise you'll get even one thing on your list. You kids have an hour. I'm setting the timer. Let your mom and me know if you're done early, and I don't want to hear any arguing between the two of you coming out of this kitchen."

Ignoring a good portion of these rules, we snuck in high-ticket items under the "To Share" part of our lists, thinking if we feigned a well-behaved, united front, we might just get something really cool. Elaborate walkie-talkie sets—denied. Big Wheel tricycle—denied. Rock tumbler kits—denied. My brother and I even tried the old switcheroo trick by requesting the chemistry set on my list and the Easy-Bake oven on my brother's, but that Santa was too smart a man. Denied.

But—oh!—the joy of opening up that big box containing Barbie's red-and-white VW camper van! Her Dreamhouse may have never come to fruition under our Christmas tree, but Barbie and her pals took many a wonderful adventure with my (extremely tolerant) cat in that van down the hallway, through the living room and across the kitchen linoleum. The blue toy typewriter with the catalog tagline "the perfect gift for little writers" was a dream come true for my wannabe newspaper reporter ten-year-old self, as was the highly coveted cassette tape recorder I carted around everywhere to record anything that anyone wanted to say.

As an adult, I grew to distance myself from the consumer side of Christmas as the importance of "things" became trite and even a bit silly. My yearly holiday list is now a suitcase-packing check-off list as my partner and I head out of town far, far away from family, friends and the conspicuous consumption of Christmas. Our destination—the central coast, where he and I trade stuff for memories and swap expectation for relaxation. (It's amazing how much we've grown to enjoy—and I mean REALLY enjoy—holiday music without the worry of a checking account shrinking out of control.)

I admit, however, that I really do like making lists, and admittedly, I've been known to use some of this holiday downtime to indulge in lists for the upcoming new year: home improvement lists, untried recipes and unread book lists, lists of lists that still need to be made, the writing down, the crossing out, the foregoing of pen for pencil and discovering the joys that a pink, nubby eraser can truly bring. Of course, I never call these resolutions, and I don't get my hopes up high enough to actually finish anything on these lists. I don't even take them too seriously either, remembering that as long as I always put what I want the worst at the very top, somehow everything else simply—and inevitably—falls right into place.

Christmas Without Snow

Rosi Hollinbeck

———◦◦✧◦◦———

Living in Minnesota has some drawbacks: the sweltering dog days of August filled with mosquitoes the size of Buicks, and Februarys that seem to freeze even time. But one of the true joys of being a Minnesotan is being there at Christmastime. It just seems so right. Minnesota is a Christmas kind of place. Cheeks and nose tips redden in crisp, cold air. Soft, fresh snow nearly always blankets the ground on Christmas mornings. Frost covers everything, turning trees and bushes into jeweled ice sculptures. The daytime sky is such a pure, hard blue that it hurts to look at it, and the sun casts purple shadows across the snow. The sweet smell of burning hardwood permeates the air through the long evenings.

It was 1961, and I was fifteen years old. I had never been away from home during that joyous time around Christmas. And this wasn't just any Christmas. This was to be the first Christmas for my first niece. Well, it was not technically her first Christmas. She had been born on Christmas Day one year earlier. Robin was a most special child, as special as her day of birth. She was as bright and beautiful and full of joy as

Christmas. I had looked forward to this, her first real Christmas, since the day she was born.

A friend who had a very complete woodworking shop had used his jigsaw to cut out the pieces so I could make a little maple rocking horse for her. I sanded every surface until it was smooth as a river rock and every edge was sanded round. There would be no rough spots or sharp edges on Robin's rocking horse. I painted it a deep, rich red and added features in midnight black. This would be a special gift for such a wonderful little girl. I had worked on it for weeks and couldn't wait to see her face on Christmas morning.

But that first Christmas for Robin would be stolen from me. My parents decided to take a winter vacation to Florida, and I had to go with them. I could stay with my sister, I argued. You will go with us, they insisted. The choir is doing a concert at the shopping center, I pleaded. They can do it without you, they answered. But this is where I want to be, I begged. You belong with us at Christmas, they said. Their minds were made up. Florida! No winter. No snow crunching under my boots. No mailman bringing packages to rattle from relatives in Chicago or a case of oranges from my uncle in California. No snow angels or toboggans flying down hills or snowball wars. But most important of all, no Robin on Christmas morning.

My parents had bought an old bread truck and outfitted it with beds and a camp kitchen. It was bulky, ugly and not at all comfortable. The heat didn't work well, and the only window was the windshield. Visiting distant cousins and dreary friends along the way, we showered in their homes and slept in our makeshift camper parked in their driveways and yards. Each day took us farther from where I wanted to be. Robin would be toddling around in new rubber boots, amazed at the sparkling lights under the eaves, red-nosed in the snow, sledding down the backyard hill in someone else's lap. We would spend Christmas in the Florida Everglades in a campground bordered by palm trees and surrounded, no doubt, by snakes and alligators and overly tan people in plaid Bermuda shorts and sandals. In my fifteen-year-old's mind, it couldn't be any worse.

I was mad. Madder than mad. And I acted like your typical angry teenager. I sat in the truck, read books and wrote dejected letters home. I couldn't write letters to Robin, though. She wouldn't know what they were. She would just know I wasn't there. I never looked out the windshield at any of the sights. I was determined not to enjoy one single minute of this miserable trip. I sulked at a medal-winning Olympic level.

Somehow we'd gotten behind schedule and found ourselves in a little town in southern Georgia on Christmas Eve. There were a few people about, but it seemed so foreign to me. Not only was it warm and there was no snow, but everyone there was African American. Minnesota didn't have a very diverse population in those days, and I had never met a black person before. I was in a place where nothing, not even the people, was in any way familiar.

It was late and we needed to find gas. Only one place in this tiny town was still open—a small store attached to a gas station on the south edge of town. A young African American man, not that much older than I was, pumped gas into the huge tank of the bread truck, nodding as my father chatted. Mom began making supper: bologna sandwiches on white bread with mustard. At home, we would have had a long table buried under mounds of Swedish meatballs, sliced ham, hot German potato salad, plates of pickled herring, sweet brown

bread, rice pudding and more. This year, we would have bologna sandwiches for Christmas dinner.

I thought my teeth would break from gritting them. I had
to get out of the truck, so I jumped down and strode into
the store. It was a small place with few items on the broad,
wooden shelves, but everything was tidy and clean. Three
tiny, chocolate-skinned children stared at me from behind
the counter, eyes wide with wonder at a white person in
their store. The smallest put his fingers in his mouth and hid
behind his mother's skirt, peeking up at me. His mother, a
young woman not much older than I was, spoke with a heavy
drawl. Her voice was as soft and sweet as caramel. "Merry
Christmas, honey. Can I help you find anything?" Her broad,
friendly smile beamed at me, and her kind eyes crinkled at
the corners.

I was too angry to be nice. "No. I don't want anything. I
just want to be away from *them*!" I wagged my head toward
my parents. It was as if something broke open inside me, and
I kept on talking. "I don't want to be here. I want to be home
for Christmas! I want to be with the rest of my family and
my friends. I should be in Minnesota. That's where I belong."
Tears sprang to my eyes, and I turned, fleeing back to the
truck. Fighting against the tears, I sat on my bed with arms
crossed hard over my chest, my trembling chin jutted out.

It seemed to take forever for that gas tank to fill, but finally Dad paid the young man for the gas, and I heard them
wish each other a merry Christmas. Dad climbed onto the
driver's seat and started the engine. A sharp rapping came at
his window. He rolled the door open, and a hand pushed a
Christmas box into his hands. They passed a few quiet words,
and Dad looked back at me. Then he said to the person out-

side the truck, "Thank you, and you have a merry Christmas, too," before closing the door and driving away.

Mom took a sandwich and Coke to Dad and, when she came back, handed me the box. "This is for you. The woman in the store brought it out."

I stared at it for a long time, touching the worn corners of a well-used Christmas box, picking at an old, yellowed piece of tape on one edge. Finally, I wiggled the red yarn tied around it and opened the box, taking care not to tear it, knowing instinctively that it should be saved. The sharp aroma of evergreen filled the truck. Inside lay a pine branch hung with a couple of handmade paper ornaments and draped with a short string of popcorn, the end of the branch crudely cut. A Baby Ruth candy bar lay in the box next to a folded piece of notebook paper.

"Those who you love are always in your heart, with you wherever you go. Think of them now and have a merry Christmas." Then I cried, really cried, with a gush of tears and deep, gulping sobs. Not for me, but for the chance I'd wasted to share a few words, a Christmas wish and a little time with a truly kind and generous woman, a woman who had no snow crunching under her feet or jeweled ice on her trees but knew the true meaning of Christmas far better than I.

Circle of Love

Valerie Reynoso Piotrowski

As we grow older, we come to realize that one of the genuine gifts of childhood is the magical way that a small child views even the simplest thing. The memory of opening our first pop-up book, finding the hidden toy in the Cracker Jack box or even riding a bike without training wheels—each of these events seems like magic at the time.

Much of the magic in my early years was provided by the gifts of my two glamorous aunts, Aunt Lupe and Aunt Mary. My mother, Vivian, was one of twelve children of a pear-farming family in the Sacramento River Delta. Her sisters lavished toys and attention on my sister and me; we were the appreciative beneficiaries of their undivided love and devotion.

Aunt Lupe was particularly exotic. She lived in Palm Springs, and to a seven-year-old like me, that seemed the very pinnacle of sophistication and elegance. Her frequent letters and postcards were exciting and colorful and told of fancy parties, perpetually sunny skies and swimsuit weather, and frequent sightings of famous movie stars. Like clockwork, the gifts from Palm Springs would arrive for our birthdays and at Christmas. Her carefully selected gifts brought joy and contentment to our young lives. Someone from far away loved and cherished us, and it made us feel tremendously special.

In the mid-1960s, Aunt Lupe truly outdid herself. Showing the sixth sense she seemed to have for our interests, that year she sent us each a beautiful satin-ivory jewelry box with hand-painted pink flowers and gold trim. When the box was opened, a delicate plastic ballerina spun around on one foot to the tune of "The Blue Danube" waltz.

But there was an even more wonderful surprise tucked inside the pink satin lining: a piece of costume jewelry, a Christmas pin that was the most perfect thing I had ever seen in my short life. It was in the shape of an old-fashioned Christmas tree, like a Currier & Ives Christmas card tree, framed by a snow-tinged window on a winter's night. Its enamel branches were laced with "snow," and semiprecious stones were scattered in abundance from top to bottom. The tip of the tree was crowned with a gold star with a crystal in the middle. To this day, I cannot think about that pin without feeling the love and security I felt as a young child and realizing how fortunate I was to have someone who thought that I was special enough to merit this sparkling treasure. It was pure magic.

Through the years and the Christmas seasons to come, my prized Christmas tree pin was an annual adornment. I pinned it to college blazers, to the red wool cape that I had sewn myself and to the first grown-up houndstooth jacket I purchased to celebrate my appointment to a political position. I so treasured the pin and the memories it contained of Christmases past that I neither checked my coat nor let it out of my sight during its holiday forays.

In 1988, I attended my boss's Christmas party in the company of the man I had been dating since our sophmore year in high school, Kevin. Naturally, I wore my Christmas pin. The combination of pink champagne and the frustration at our unresolved relationship brought the evening to an early and tearful close. I went home that night alone and unhappy.

As I sobbed alone in my house, I decided that if I immediately hung up my party dress and put away my holiday coat and purse, then perhaps I would have no physical memory of this night the following morning. It was as I was hanging up my black velvet duster that I noticed—the Christmas pin that had been with me for almost twenty years, for almost two-thirds of my life, was gone.

I searched my car. It wasn't there. Frantic, I called my boss and asked him to look around his house. No, came the reply ten minutes later, it was not to be found at his house. Despite my broken heart and the thirty-degree weather on that foggy night, I pulled a coat over my flannel nightgown and drove fifteen miles to my boss's house in my bunny slippers, armed with a flashlight and my prayers that the pin would be lying there on the sidewalk. I searched the surrounding neighborhood for forty-five minutes, but the pin was gone. And gone, too, were my cozy feelings of Christmas love.

The loss of the pin ushered in one of the darkest periods of my life. The breast cancer that had ravaged my beautiful mother for almost ten years was now winning its evil campaign to take her life, and through rivers of tears and counseling, I also realized that Kevin and I did not have the kind of future together that I both wanted and deserved. The prospect of those two losses occurring simultaneously in my life was unbearable. I found solace in myriad work projects, but I was scared to death. My father's grief at the approaching loss of his life partner, coupled with Kevin's emotional absence, left me alone to deal with my fears.

Christmas of 1989 would be the last one we would spend with my mom. Through a miracle of God, she was released from the hospital in time to attend Aunt Mary's traditional tamale dinner. I witnessed the joy in her eyes each moment she spent in the company of the family; I am truly grateful for my mom having had the strength to endure what would be her last Christmas season with us. She was storing up her own memories to reflect on during her quiet times in heaven.

My mother left this life just a few short months after that. Despite months of counseling before her death, nothing could have prepared me for the hopelessness I felt following her passing. There were entire days spent in my pajamas. I had lost half of my life base, and I did not know how to continue being the self-assured, ambitious young woman she had raised me to be.

But the darkness of winter passed, and spring finally arrived, and with it the annual invitation to visit the beach house of Aunt Mary and Uncle Roger. My childhood was filled with summer memories of white sand, starfish and walks with my parents on the beaches of Pajaro Dunes. The beach house was the last place I thought I could endure at this moment in my life. But Aunt Mary began to wear down my objections. She was grieving, too, she pointed out, and returning to the very spot where we had enjoyed so many good times would be therapeutic to us all.

And so I agreed to go. Surprisingly, the drive itself offered peace of mind, and as the odometer registered the passing miles, my sense of tranquility increased. Maybe Aunt Mary knew something that I didn't, something about facing our fears and healing.

At the beach house that year, Aunt Mary and I found common ground in the love and loss of my mom, her sister and best friend. We spent hours sitting on the beach, laughing and crying through our stories and recollections of summers past. On the last day of the trip, I awoke with a feeling of rejuvenation. It had been so long since I'd had any energy that I assumed this burst I was feeling was due to the ocean air. I had no idea then that I had passed one of the most important tests of grieving, six months after losing Mom. I had returned to the scene of happy family times and faced painful memories.

The drive back to Sacramento began peacefully. I was in no hurry to get back, as I felt so serene and didn't want to jeopardize this newfound calm. Impulsively, I stopped at a little town near Pajaro, where Main Street consisted of a block of antique shops. It was early morning, and some shops had not yet opened their doors.

The last antique shop on the right side of the street was open for business, though, and as I stepped in, I recognized the musty odor of old furniture and well-used books. Through the maze of Victorian lamps and curio cabinets filled with silver spoons and other standard antique fare, I spotted the jewelry case at the back of the store. Perhaps there was some small trinket there that I could take away to remind me of my newfound strength.

I have always believed that things happen for a reason, and what I saw then affirmed my belief. There, tucked in a corner on an old piece of velvet, was the twin to the Christmas tree pin I had lost one year before. I asked the shopkeeper to remove it from the display case and, with trembling hands, turned the little pin over. Yes, this was it, the very same company name inscribed on the back of the pin. In a miracle of rediscovery, I had found the one tangible thing I valued most, a treasure from my beloved past.

Although there was much work to be done emotionally for me and my family, I was now firmly on the way to healing. The boundlessness of the seashore, with waves breaking one after another for all eternity, and the Christmas pin that held within its branches so many feelings of warmth and love were again returned to me. In the years to come, I would face other losses and disappointments, but now I knew that I possessed the strength and support from my circle of family and friends that would protect me and sustain my recovery whenever I needed them. And my holiday symbol of love, my Christmas pin, would again accompany me into another year of life.

Mall Santa

David Scott Chamberlain
As told to Barbara Chamberlain

———— ◦◈◦ ————

My senior year in high school, my goal in life was to get closer to my perfect woman. Teddy Martin always seemed to be in a gaggle of girls. She would return my smiles, but one or another of her friends always seemed to be in the way of a real conversation. I am not ashamed to admit that one November day I eavesdropped and heard her talking to her friends about her Christmas job as an elf at the mall. Immediately, I decided to try there for some kind of holiday work. The last year of high school was expensive, I could use some extra money...and if I could be near blue-eyed, blonde-haired Theodora Martin, it would be a dream come true.

The human resources woman at the mall stared at me from behind her desk. "How tall are you?"

Okay, at 6'2" I was probably not elf material. "I could do stock work," I offered, hopeful. My dream seemed to be slipping away.

"We've already hired for most jobs, but there is someone we still need," she offered. "We need someone to give our

Santa breaks. It is only a total of three hours a day, but if you want that job…"

Three hours a day near Elf Teddy? And I would be paid? Frosting on my cake. A paycheck for handing out candy canes and saying, "Ho ho ho." I smiled and nodded in agreement. Santa was the job for me.

"Let's see how you look in the Santa suit," Mrs. HR said. Even more of a bonus, Teddy helped me with the suit. "Oh, Davey, you look great!" She helped adjust the beard. "Our Santa has a real white beard, but you look good. And you're taller than he is. How tall are you?"

My day, week and year were complete.

My assignment the first day was to observe. The line of kiddies seemed to be like that eternally full bowl of rice in a fable. They were there before Santa's appointed hour and groaned when Elf Teddy or one of the other elves put up the "Santa's Gone to the North Pole" sign at 8:30 p.m.

It is a well-known fact that candy canes turn into syrup in the hands of anyone under age eight. Why some mothers insisted on terrifying their children by dumping them on my lap in spite of wails from the offspring was a mystery. During my noontime assignments, I often thought that I might lose my hearing. It was worth it to hear Teddy say, "You are so good with the children."

One day, the full-time Santa didn't come back from lunch.

He was half an hour late when I told Teddy to put up the closed sign.

I could hear the snore from outside the door of the employee lounge. The form in the red suit was on the couch, his genuine round belly rising and falling with each snore. I shook his shoulder gently. He snorted, sat up and cried, "Bring on the kiddies!" and fell back onto the couch to begin the wall-rocking snore again. Santa had obviously had more than milk and cookies for lunch.

Just then, the woman who had hired me opened the door. "Where is Santa? The kids and moms are getting restless out there."

Santa bolted up and began an off-key rendition of "Jingle Bells."

"Oh, no," she groaned, understanding the situation immediately. "David, you are going to have to finish as Santa today."

And that was how I became the mall's youngest ever first-string Santa Claus. Anyone who thinks that being a Santa is an easy job should just try it. It's easier to be a football lineman, take it from me. But out of it, I got a paycheck, and yes, I got Teddy. She agreed to be my date for the senior prom, which was about the greatest Christmas present Santa ever brought me.

The Baby Flight

Paul Karrer

------ ◆◯◆ ------

I had never held such an unusual looking baby in my arms before. To tell the truth, I had never even seen an infant like this before. Now, here I was, responsible for delivering three tiny orphans to their adoptive parents on Christmas Eve.

Twenty-eight years old, a New England Yankee through and through, I taught English on Cheju Island, Republic of Korea. College students all over the country had been rioting and had succeeded in closing colleges. I was fed up and needed to go home, but I was short of money. One of my colleagues informed me of the "baby flights," whereby I could travel from Korea to the United States and back for a mere twenty-five percent of the normal fare. But there was a hitch. The traveler had to transport not one, not two, but three infants. That translated into at least three flight changes—Tokyo, Anchorage and New York, in my case. I would have to bring diapers, formula, pacifiers and much patience. The alternative was to pay the full fare.

I found myself boarding a plane with three infants, ages

three months, seven months and a year and a half. They came complete with runny noses and wet diapers.

When the plane finally took off, the poor kids let loose with a terrible howl. As the plane climbed, it began to vibrate violently. In unison, all three babies quieted. A few seconds later, the plane stopped shaking, and in unison, the babies resumed crying. The entire planeload of passengers burst into tension-relieving laughter. And that made my tiny charges instant celebrities.

But one thing had given me pause the entire time. The eighteen-month-old infant, quieter than the other two, had a massive head with disproportionately minute arms and fingers. Obviously, the poor thing was affected with dwarfism. My reaction surprised me. I was repulsed and began to worry whether the new parents on the other side of the Pacific realized what they were having delivered to them. I didn't look forward to the transfer, but I was too busy to give it much consideration.

Babies were hollering. The one on my lap was wet, and the milk formula was low. I rapidly learned how to clean a wet bottom, put on a new diaper and stick a pacifier in an open mouth.

Two American marines stopped in the aisle near me and stared down.

"You look like you could use a little help."

"I could. Three kids is a lot."

"Mind if we each take one for a few minutes?"

"No, I wouldn't mind at all." I happily passed a baby to each of them and watched the massive soldiers coo to the babies.

So, I sat there alone, holding the eighteen-month-old baby with the very large head. I noticed her long eyelashes. As I looked into her eyes, I couldn't help but see that they held a crisp, intelligent glow. Then, she smiled, and I was hooked. Funny how things like that can change you. From that point on, she radiated beauty, and she never left my arms.

In Tokyo, the plane had a stopover. The soldiers apologized for not being able to help anymore, as they had another flight. They each handed back a baby. I placed two babies in a twin stroller and carried the third in my arms. The four of us plunked down in a waiting area. I started to change the diapers of the two babies I had given to the soldiers, when a pile of single dollar bills fell from one of the baby's clothing. I quickly glanced at the departing soldiers. One of them gave the thumbs-up sign and blurted, "Little buggers gonna need all the help they can get. Merry Christmas."

Not many minutes later, an attractive Asian woman approached, stared at us and walked away. I rocked a baby as two fidgeted. The woman walked up again and stared.

"Are those babies yours?"

"No, I'm delivering them. They're Korean orphans."

"I thought so. Twenty-four years ago, I was one of those kids. I think we are on the same flight. May I please help you?"

She took the noisiest child of the three. During the flight, she'd show up and lend a hand, clean a bottom or soothe an unsettled little one. Finally, she took one infant, walked down the aisle, and I didn't see her until the plane landed.

By now, I had developed a strong bond with "my" baby. I even named her Tina. The more I thought about giving her to someone else, the more I worried about her prospective parents. I felt like a slave trader and a traitor all wrapped into one.

In New York, the plane landed. People rushed in, matched identification tags, and off they sped with their new children. But I still held Tina, and it seemed like nobody was coming on board for her. In the end, I trudged off the plane to a small crowd. Tina clung to me tightly and cried.

Then I spotted them, standing to the side of the exit. The man was no more than four feet tall, and his wife was even tinier. They walked toward me and reached up for Tina. As I passed Tina to them, she looked up at me and said, "Oma," to me, which means mom in Korean. At that point, I cried.

The next year, I paid the full fare. The baby flight was too expensive.

Childhood Magic

Jo Anne Boulger

———◦◦◇◦◦———

I grew up in southern California many years ago. After I married, my husband and I lived in several different states and had a child in each of our first four states. As I continued this pattern—four states, four babies—I worried about the fact that there were fifty states. Was I going for a world record? Fortunately, in the fifth state in which we lived, we broke the pattern. We left there after seven years without adding to our family.

During these times away from home, my father was involved with the construction of Disneyland. Because we lived in Washington state, we missed out on all the action, including the day before Disneyland was officially opened to the public, when my father, his family and all the other workers and their families were welcomed as guests of Disneyland. They were given a memorial plate, along with Mickey Mouse watches for the children and a day of free rides and all the meals they could eat.

So when we came home for a vacation, my father was anxious to share the excitement of Disneyland with his grandchildren. He was so proud of his part in the construction and eager to be our host and share his love of the park. We drove to Anaheim in anticipation of a world of excitement and magic.

My parents hadn't seen their grandchildren for some time, and I was eager for my children to be on their best behavior. Fingers crossed, we entered the park. The magic castle took our breath away, and we all stopped and took in our surroundings. The children were sidetracked by the characters from the many different nursery rhymes; right before our eyes, storybooks came alive. There was Sleeping Beauty, Mickey Mouse, Minnie Mouse and many others, all life-size.

Then it happened—along came the Big Bad Wolf chasing the Three Little Pigs, squealing like crazy. My five-year-old son, Quin, reacted immediately. He ran straight up to the Big Bad Wolf and punched him in the stomach. Sadly for the young man wearing the costume, a five-year-old's swinging fist lands quite a bit short, more in the groin area. It was a hard punch below the belt for the Big Bad Wolf.

The wolf keeled over and fell to his knees. Everyone around us looked on in shock, and my parents were aghast at their grandchild's outrageous behavior. My son shocked me, too—he was a very sweet boy, not in the least bit mean.

With a face red with embarrassment, I grabbed his arm. "What are you doing? Why did you hit the wolf?"

Quin looked up at me proudly. "To save the Three Little Pigs."

Oh, not a bully, but a hero in the making. My husband went to the aid of the fallen wolf while I reprimanded our son. This was really hard for me to do because I knew how kindhearted my son really was, yet I couldn't let it just pass as though nothing had happened. But I was proud of my son wanting to be a hero. It was at this time that I explained to him about the costume and the young man he had decked. The conversation did not sit well with him. On the way home, he started to ask more questions: If the Big Bad Wolf was just a kid in a costume, then what about all the other magic moments in his life? What about the Easter Bunny, the Tooth Fairy, even Santa Claus? I answered as best I could, dancing around the issue.

As we drove home, I sadly looked out the window at the passing scene. *What had I done to my son by taking away all the childhood magic?* Come Christmas, I knew I needed to do something to convince him of the magic in believing.

On Christmas Eve, I had all three children leave milk and cookies for Santa. That night, I made a note written with glue and sprinkled with red glitter signed with a big S for Santa. This worked wonders, and he was once again a believer. After all, only Santa could write with glittering red ink.

The following year, I worked extra hard for Easter, the Tooth Fairy and some Halloween goblins. I did my utmost to convince Quin of all the magic of the moment.

That next Christmas, we visited Santa Claus. Quin, now six years old, was eager to sit on Santa's lap. During his conversation with Santa, Quin's enthusiasm took him away again, and he put his hand on Santa's fake beard and gave it a big yank, gathering a handful of Santa's fluffy, white beard.

Oh, no, I thought, shocked by what he had done. *I guess he's on to the whole Santa thing. He really no longer believes.* It looked as though he were trying to prove something by yanking the beard, letting the rest of us know he would no longer fall for our make-believe stories. It made me sad to think that my young son had really lost the magic of childhood. At the same time, I was mortified by his actions. I stood frozen and red-faced, certain that all the other mothers were also shocked and worried that he was setting a very bad example for their children.

Luckily for Santa and me, the beard was well attached, and there was no harm done. I guess he had been through this before and used really good glue, so he just sat there with his face as red as his suit.

Quin ran up to me happily, a big smile on his face, holding a handful of Santa's beard.

"Look, Mom, I've got some of Santa's beard to hang on our Christmas tree for good luck."

I looked at Santa, and he gave me a wink, tapped the side of his nose with his finger and, with a big smile, waved us goodbye.

Silent Night

Liza Long

—◦◦◦◦◦—

We waited, our noses pressed into strangers' backs as if we were lost children in a crowded subway car. The air smelled of wet woolen coats, and the snow fell in silence, tickling our eyelashes and melting when it brushed our reddened, mittenless hands.

We were strangers to snow, a family of six children and two parents from southern California, waiting with thousands of other grumpy, chilled people at Temple Square in Salt Lake City, Utah, one Thanksgiving evening for the Christmas lights to come on. Already the winter shadows were deepening. We waited expectantly for something to happen.

No lights. "Don't worry, children," my father said, rubbing his hands together and blowing on them. "They'll come on as soon as it's dark. It will be worth the wait. You'll see." His breath blew out in a cloud, like a cartoon character. We nodded silently, squirming as unfamiliar elbows and knees jostled and poked us. Everyone around us was complaining now, a low, grumbling, wordless sound. Still there were no lights. And it was dark now.

The unpleasant rumbling grew louder. We caught snatches here and there, words that expressed sentiments very close to what we ourselves were feeling.

"I want to go home," one child, captured in his mother's arms, whined pitiably.

"You'd think they'd be more organized," grumbled a deep voice at my shoulder.

"Come on!" one young man yelled. "Turn on the stupid lights already!"

I looked at my white-faced brothers and sister, realizing that they felt as cold and miserable as I did. "Some Christmas lights," I said sarcastically under my breath.

And then, I heard the song. I looked up, surprised at first, then embarrassed, as my father began to sing. His rich, full baritone rang through the sudden hush that surrounded us, warming the cold winter with its golden sound. "Silent night," he sang, "holy night. All is calm, all is bright." As he sang that lovely tune, those simple words, the lights came on as if on command, a brilliant display of colors and beauty to welcome the Christmas season. A few more voices filled the air, then still more joined in harmony—first two parts, then three, then four, and soon I realized that everyone around us had joined my father's song.

I felt like one of the shepherds two thousand years ago, transfixed by heavenly choirs heralding a new birth and a new world. As we made our way around the beautiful grounds, Dad kept singing, and many of the strangers around us joined in as he moved effortlessly from one favorite Christmas carol to the next. People who had been cold and miserable moments before were warmed and transformed by the music. Suddenly, we were all friends, neighbors, fellow worshipers.

A few months later, Dad became ill. Three years later, after a long struggle with cancer, he passed away. His most powerful lessons live on, though. I have never forgotten the beauty of that "Silent Night" so many years ago, and the appreciation for the true spirit of Christmas that he shared with his family and strangers will always remain in my heart.

The Only Star

Harry Freiermuth

———•❖•———

During World War II, Christmas was crucial for keeping our spirits up. Our street's air raid warden would ring our doorbell if any light showed through our windows at night. For that reason, we used light-proof window shades or thick blankets to cover our windows to keep the slightest ray of light from escaping and telling the enemy planes where we were. We never knew if this Christmas might be our last. Already enemy submarines had been sighted near our coast. How soon would enemy planes reach our coastal cities and towns, just as they had bombed Pearl Harbor on December 7, 1941?

Wartime or not, we young people had to go to school. During my freshman year, 1942, at Watsonville Joint Union High School in Watsonville, California, I worked after school and Saturdays at Ford's Department Store on Main Street. I was Assistant Window Dresser First Class. The head window dresser, Miss Grahame, would brush her red hair from her grey-green eyes and say, "Harry, please go and bring the new adult female blonde mannequin to window 3." I would rush to the supply room to find the blonde with the big, blue, Bette Davis eyes that dared any woman to buy what she modeled. Then, I would put my strong right arm around her naked waist and carry her slowly to window 3 amid the whistles and catcalls of the male clerks. As a teenager, I tried my best to keep everything on a purely professional level, while inside my ego glowed and smiled triumphantly.

Christmas was our busiest time of the year. Besides outstanding clothes and eye-catching signs, our window was filled with beautiful Christmas trees with the newest sparkling glass ornaments in all colors and twinkling electric lights in all shapes and sizes—the great temptation to entice our customers to buy buy buy.

I looked at our finished windows and, in my mind's eye, compared these trees to my family's traditional little tree with its old-fashioned ornaments and electric light bulbs that were always burning out, causing us to spend what seemed like hours trying to find the burnt-out bulb.

On December 7, 1942, my mother's birthday, Dad took Mother, my younger brother, Gene, and me in his pickup truck to buy our family tree. In the tree lot on East Lake Avenue, we found a five-foot tree that would look like it was seven feet on top of our small coffee table.

Once home, Gene and I carried our tree inside and placed it on top of the coffee table in front of our front window covered with a thick blanket. The fragrant fir branches gave off their perfume, giving us all a taste of Christmas No. 5. I breathed deep to enjoy this tree's special gift to us. Mother brought the old cardboard box from her bedroom closet shelf and placed it on the carpet in front of our tree. We always offered to help her with this annual ritual. But she did not want anyone to see all of her treasures hidden in her special closet. Only later would I discover just what each one meant to her.

Gene and I began unwrapping the old tissue paper covering each ornament. When we discovered which ornament we had unwrapped, we squinted at our tree to see where it should find its traditional place. Then, we hung it on that branch, just where it should always be this year and every year.

Mother and Dad sat together on our chesterfield sofa, watching Gene and me decorate our tree. If we did not get an ornament in its exact right place, we heard about it fast. And just as fast, we made the correction. Our Christmas star was the first ornament to grace our new tree. This five-pointed star, four inches across from point to point, was a flat piece of aluminum. We wired it to the top of the tree where it lighted the way for the Three Wise Men to find the Christ Child.

The Christ Child was in a small paper manger, a heavy paper foldout held together by tape, and he was placed carefully at the bottom trunk of our tree. Jesus, Mary and Joseph rested peacefully on the manger straw surrounded by the shepherds and their sheep. The ox and the donkey poked their heads through a back window. On the two sides of the stable were the Three Wise Men. Two stood on the right side, and one knelt on the left side in adoration.

Gene placed the crayon-colored, paper Santa Claus halfway up the trunk of our tree. From that lofty position, Santa smiled to everyone and held his big bag of gifts for all. I attached the blue bird, a peacock with a worn-out feathery tail, by the clip under its feet to the branch about one-third of the way up the tree. It looked about ready to take off for a safer place to land. One by one, we unwrapped each ornament and returned it to its rightful place on this year's Christmas tree. Every year, the routine had been the same throughout my childhood.

Next to last, we unwrapped the strings of popcorn from their cardboard and strung each one very gracefully, beginning from the very top of the tree down to the bottom branches. Gene and I remembered popping this very popcorn many years ago in our old wire-mesh popcorn popper in the front room fireplace. We had to shake the popper to move the kernels around so they did not burn in the flames of the fire.

As soon as we had finished with the popcorn, Gene began stringing the electric lights down from the top of the tree around and around to the bottom. Then, we hung the tinsel icicles on the ends of each branch of our tree. Finally, we turned out all the lights and sat in the darkened room. With fingers crossed, I turned on the switch for our Christmas tree lights.

"Hooray!" The lights all lit up okay. No burnt-out bulbs so far.

This was a silent moment for our family. In the quiet tree light, our tree wished each of us a very merry Christmas. And without saying a word, we thanked our tree and wished it, and one another, a merry Christmas too.

That night in bed, before falling asleep, an unusual sparkling thought blossomed in the back of my freshman brain: *Why not change that old-fashioned Christmas tree with its worn-out ornaments for a tree full of the newest glistening ornaments from Ford's Department Store?*

The next day at work, I purchased the most expensive glass ornaments in my favorite colors, chartreuse and magenta, a fantastic improvement on the old traditional red and green for Christmas colors. I complemented that brainstorm with another brainstorm and bought yellow and purple twinkling electric lights in the shapes of bells and stars. I could not wait to change our old ornaments for these fabulous new ones. And catch the expressions of surprise and wonder on the faces of Mother, Dad and Gene.

I carried the big surprise home secretly in a big, plain paper bag and hid it in my bedroom closet. I waited for a time when everyone was out of the house. Then, secretly and unknowingly, I committed the Christmas crime of the century.

After supper, it was our custom to go, in the dark, into our living room. Mother and Dad would sit on the chesterfield sofa while Gene and I would lie flat on the floor and listen to our favorite radio program, *I Love a Mystery*. We delighted in the thrills and masterminds of Jack, Doc and Reggie, along with the spine-chilling screams of Mercedes McCambridge.

After all of that excitement and before anyone could turn on the lights, I lit my masterpiece. Total silence. No one said a word. The silence roared in my ears. Finally, Mother looked at my smiling face with her tender, light blue eyes and asked, "Harry, did you do this?"

"Yes," I admitted.

"WHY?" they all shouted together.

Mother, still with a soft and tender voice, said, "Harry, we know you must have had a good intention. But, our old, dilapidated Christmas tree ornaments hold memories that money cannot buy. I thought you already knew that.

"The aluminum star was designed and cut out by hand by your dear father for our first Christmas tree, after our marriage in 1925. It pointed the way for imaginary Wise Men to find the imaginary Christ Child at the foot of our first Christmas tree. The paper Santa Claus was hand drawn by your little brother, when he was in kindergarten. He was so proud of his work that we had to find a special place for it. We did, right on our family Christmas tree."

She looked at my father sitting next to her. "Each year, your father and I would buy a new ornament to remember something special in our lives. We bought the blue bird with the feathery tail the year you were born, 1927. And remember when you were sick in fourth grade? We could not have any parties in the house for a year because Dr. Giberson thought that you had TB and must have complete rest for a full year. That was the year we bought the musical ornament that plays 'Silent Night.'"

I hung my head. My moment of triumph had become a moment of shame. She smiled lovingly, "Yes, I could go on. But you can see how much our family Christmas tree means to us. I thought you knew that, too."

"Oh, yes," I cried with tears in my eyes. "Please, forgive me. Now I understand why these ornaments are family treasures."

"We forgive you and love you. Now take those ornaments off and put our old family ornaments back where they belong."

Dad died in 1968 after six years of battling Lou Gehrig's disease, and Mother tried to decorate our family Christmas tree alone that year. Gene and I were grown up and on our own. As soon as her wrinkled and trembling hands touched the aluminum star, she wept. After rewrapping the star in its wrinkled tissue paper, Mother placed it carefully in its place in the old cardboard box, closed the lid, placed the box back on the shelf of her bedroom closet and closed the door. That year, our family Christmas tree disappeared forever. But, in my heart, Dad's homemade star will always point toward the infant Jesus.

Virtual Christmas

Pat Hanson

———◦◦◦———

I prefer Halloween to Christmas. You have an excuse for putting on a mask, can dress up any way you'd like and just pretend. Soon after, when retailers start luring us with Christmas decorations, recorded mall music everywhere plays carols, television repeats all those sappy movies… All that jolliness can make me feel a little depressed. Some Christmases are more difficult than others, but one that could have been a catastrophe instead forever transformed how our family celebrates December 25.

It was 1996, the day before the office Christmas party, when my boss called me in to his office and gave me thirty days' notice. Since summer, I'd been the sole support of my teenage stepson and my husband, after his plumbing business tanked. Credit cards at their limit, stretched by one income, we'd done no Christmas shopping and hadn't even bought a tree. I didn't know how I would be able to get into the holiday cheer and forget the reality of my financial situation. Tears ran down my cheeks on the way home as the car radio reminded listeners that there were only six shopping days left, and the shrill voices of the Chipmunks sang, *"Christmas, Christmas time is here, time to sing, time for cheer."*

Somehow that week, out of the depths of my despair, I got an idea. We'd have a virtual Christmas. We'd each find and wrap pictures of five gifts we would have been thoughtful and generous enough to buy had there been money to put into circulation! And central to this plan was that one of the virtual gifts had to be intangible, like a quality within that you'd like the other to have.

Three days before Christmas, I hid the stockings. Instead of a big, traditional tree, we decorated our ficus tree with lights. We each looked through catalogs, magazines and our hearts to choose five presents for one another and place them under the tree. In addition to the gifts of a car, a driver's license, a baggy sweatshirt and pants and guitar lessons I'd give to my stepson was a fifth gift: "confidence in his own talent." I wrote that on a certificate for a course in entrepreneurship for teenagers so he could market the artistic skill so evident in his cartoons.

He really got into it. He gave me concert tickets to Sting and Gloria Estefan, a color printer for my computer and some Laurel Burch earrings, all wrapped in comics from the Sunday paper. His conceptual gift to me was a sign that read "No Speed Limit!" Besides a white Porsche, Larry gifted me with a vacation in Hawaii, a new PowerBook, a set of Cutco knives and a stud from the pages of Playgirl (for the few times our batteries are out of sync, he wrote). His conceptual gift to me was written on a 3" x 5" card: "I give you the magic sword to conquer your boogie man, permission to be gentle with yourself and license to proceed full steam ahead with the realization of your writing dreams!"

For my beloved, I wrapped up the picture of nose-hair

tweezers from a high-end gadget catalog. He got a car, too, a Dodge Viper like the one we saw the weekend we met, plus a leather jacket, more memory for his computer and a video camera so he could practice at his dream career: filmmaker. For his virtual gift, I inscribed a message on a magnifying glass to give him utter and absolute belief in himself and the unlimited power of his creativity. On Christmas morning, looking at his face as he stared out at the sunrise with tears in his eyes, I silently sent him that missing one percent of faith that would help us all actualize our dreams.

The virtual Christmas presents worked. It's amazing how a concept, once put in the mind, can manifest. One year later, we'd moved, and my stepson was registered for a course in art presentation at the local community college. My husband was finishing the college degree he'd stopped working on thirty-one years prior. His belief in himself prompted a midlife career shift to multimedia instructional technology. I'd successfully hoisted that sword to my writing fears, was studying screenwriting and had published some freelance nonfiction.

The three of us found a way to give and love without a worry about costs and returns. I offer it now many years later, with an economy in even deeper trouble than it was back then. I hope our idea helps your family feel the spirit embodied in the man, Jesus, whose birthday we sometimes forget in the rush to shop those few weeks at the end of every year.

We've practiced many a virtual Christmas since then. The bubble of actual gift giving seems to have been permanently burst for us. Perhaps it is time for more of us to let go of the commercialism that underlies this holiday season. I would virtually gift us a view of the human condition that goes beyond one's worth being determined by work, by your job. I'd bless us with divine insight as to how the preciousness of each moment must be cherished. I'd gift us all with the capacity to see the abundance around us everywhere. It is the power of positive intention that counts. Make your holidays this season virtual, and they can still be merry—and much more meaningful!

Hungry Reindeer

Cheryl Riveness

————◦⊰⊱◦————

"Rudolph ate the tree, Mommy! He did, really. Come see. You won't believe it!" The girls clamored around the bed and then jumped in, bouncing, squealing and talking excitedly as five- and seven-year-old girls will do. "Get up! Get up! Hurry!!" By this time, they had wrapped their hands around ours and were dragging us down the hall. We grown-ups played it for all it was worth.

"Girls, come on," their father implored. "What makes you think Rudolph ate our tree?"

"Santa left us a note, Daddy. Look!"

"Hey, babe, look at this." Ed mugged it up, holding out a familiar piece of paper. "It really is a letter from Santa Claus."

"Read it, Mommy, please!" The youngest one looked at me, her huge brown eyes framed by thick lashes. The long dark tresses of her older sister bounced in rhythm to the up and down shaking of her head. How could I not?

"Dear Mimi and Meri," I began. "Thank you so much for the reindeer food. Rudolph and Comet were very hungry, and your tree was just right. I liked the birthday cake, too. Love, Santa."

Presents were forgotten in the moment.

"Mommy, we'll be right back," they yelled as they bounded to the family room door.

"Hey, guys, what about your presents?" I asked, surprised that they were so distracted. "At least change your clothes before you go outside, then you can play until I get breakfast on the table."

They shot each other wide-eyed looks and shrugged their shoulders. "We'll be right back!" they shouted, running down the hall. They were half undressed before they even got to their room.

Five minutes later, they jumped on their red and yellow Huffy bikes and headed down the street. The sun was bright and the sky clear blue with only an occasional fluffy, white cloud. It had been an unusually warm southern California December, and the needles on our tree had turned to brittle tinder in record time. It was the exact kind of tree you hear about bursting into flames every year, and I was not happy about having it there in the living room. But how could I get rid of the Christmas tree before Christmas?

My mother and father were just beginning their snowbird years and had come to spend the holiday season with us. They were as concerned as we were about the potential fire hazard. Mom and I were beginning to get things ready for the morning when she looked at me and asked, "What if Rudolph got hungry tonight?"

Her hazel eyes twinkled in anticipation. Earlier, Dad had gone to the RV where they were staying, but my husband was still up. Grabbing a pruner usually reserved for the Meyer lemon tree, he began at the bottom. We formed a line and got a system going. Snip, pull, hand some cuttings to Mom. Walk it to the living room and hand it off to me to feed it into the fire. It was a relief to see it go. I understood a little better what a fiery inferno feels like and was grateful not to have to worry for another minute.

Once the trunk was fully laid bare, Ed took the strings of lights and wrapped them around it several times. It had begun its life with us as a beautiful fir. Now it was a six-foot knobby stick with illumination.

We had taken artificial snow and left a light dusting from the fireplace to the tree. Using Dad's boots, I managed a few (apparently) believable footprints to add to the illusion. I stuck the note through one of the middle stubs. It looked like something out of a comic strip. We'd have to wait until morning to see if it was believable.

"Hi, Grandpa. Merry Christmas!" The girls clamored past their grandfather and jumped on their bikes, screaming in delight all the while.

Dad managed to keep the coffee in his cup as he whirled around. "What's going on around here?" He grinned. Laughing, we were filling him in when he raised his cup toward the family window. "Take a look at that."

Turning around, I knew we'd been successful in bringing a small piece of holiday magic into the girls' lives. There were at least a dozen kids of various sizes, all crowded up to the window, hands pressed to the glass, eyes focused on the unbelievable.

Mistletoe Memories

Jeanne Gilpatrick

———◆>❍<◆———

During the holidays, when conversation among friends and coworkers turns to Christmas and favorite memories, I am always reminded, with a rush of emotion, of my grandson's bittersweet birth.

December of 1994, ten days before Christmas, I pulled up in front of the Florence Crittenton Home for Girls and stared dully at a string of bright-colored, blinking Christmas lights that framed a front window. The lights were entirely out of sync with my heavy mood. The carols, sparkling decor and good cheer of the holidays seemed like a performance put on for somebody else; I was in the cheap seats and too far away to catch much of the show. I was anything but merry. I set my hand brake and steeled myself against the tears that were one cross look away from spilling.

Once inside, there was nowhere to talk to my daughter, Tara, privately. Her roommate, Rochelle, heavily pregnant, sprawled across the bed on her side of their narrow room and talked on the phone, while her runny-nosed toddler clutched at my pant legs and searched my face for affection. A dozen babies throughout the building cried all at once, and their tired, teenage mothers shouted to one another over the din. Despair seemed to echo through the cold hallways. And so, despite crisp December temperatures, Tara and I headed across the street to sit in my car. I was bundled in a thick jacket and chilled; she was rosy cheeked and toasty in a sleeveless cotton smock and stretchy pants. If she had been older, in a committed relationship or even if this pregnancy had been an accident, I might have teased her about "the little heater" growing inside her. But, it hadn't been an accident. There had been no protection. She had wanted a baby and had ignored my attempts at reason, my pleading and tears. She had refused books outlining the tragic statistics of teen motherhood. At sixteen, she had believed the baby's thirty-year-old, no-account father when he told her he would help her. Abortion? "Out of the question!" she had retorted. Adoption? "How could I?" It was her body. It was her baby, and she wanted it.

And so, too late, perhaps, I had laid down the law: "If you insist on keeping this baby, you cannot live with me." She later confessed that she had thought I would change my mind. But, even as I grew to love the little boy developing inside her, I had stood firm. When she was six months along, I announced that there was a place for her at Florence Crittenton.

I can't remember my heart ever aching more than it did the day I left her there. I prayed that I was doing the right thing. For weeks, I lay awake nights hoping that she would watch the other young mothers' struggles and decide to give her son up for adoption.

But at nine months and two weeks along, as we sat in my car tying sprigs of mistletoe with curly, red ribbon, she remained determined.

She shifted her bulging belly, lifted her chin and threw back her shoulders to give her lungs more room. "Me and Rochelle are going to sell mistletoe on Market Street tomorrow. Rochelle's going to bring her baby. We should get a lot of business, huh? People will look at us and say, 'Poor things,' and give us their money." Her laugh was cut short by one of those "practice" contractions that are common in late pregnancy. She winced and laid her hand on the shelf of her belly as she waited for it to pass. "Whew. I'm getting a lot of those."

"Maybe you're in early labor?"

"Naw."

"Just tuning up, I guess," I said. My heart fluttered momentarily with anticipation of the birth. But the fears that had haunted me since she disclosed her pregnancy were not far away: *She's just a baby herself, single, uneducated. How can she give this child the life he deserves? Only two years earlier, she and her brother climbed trees like children to collect mistletoe to sell in front of our local grocery store.* My chest tightened again, as if in the grip of a giant fist. I had long before given up being angry with her and had committed to making the best of the situation.

"Have you been doing the relaxation exercises?" I asked.

"Sort of." She looked away suddenly, and a heavy silence hung between us. "Rochelle is going to coach me," she blurted at last. My face must have registered this wound. "You said you would be sad and cry, Mom," she explained. "I don't want anybody crying at my baby's birth."

"I said that a long time ago."

"Well, would you?"

"I can't promise that I wouldn't. I love him already. I've told you that. But, it still feels tragic to me." We'd been over it too many times for me to say more. My eyes stung and threatened to spill over. I drew a long breath and gathered my composure. "If you change your mind, you know where to find me." We laughed, and the air was light for just a moment.

"I hope he'll be cute," she said as she zipped a piece of ribbon across the scissors' sharp blade. "I just couldn't stand it if I had an ugly baby." Her words landed like heavy stones, making me weary.

Early the next morning, the phone's jingle wrested me from a dream. "This is Mark calling from Florence Crittenton. Tara went into labor this morning, and she's on her way to the hospital."

"Does she want me there?" I asked, my heart racing.

"I don't know. You were just one of the people on her list. We call everybody on the list."

I hung up and dialed the hospital. "Just one of the people on the list" echoed in my head until someone answered.

"My daughter has just been admitted. She's in labor," I heard myself say. It all seemed surreal. Despite the preparation, the therapy, the support group, it still seemed impossible that my baby girl was about to give birth.

"I'll ring her room."

"Hi, Mom. I'm in labor," she chirped. "Are you coming?"

When I arrived, I was alarmed at the commotion in the room. A television hanging from the ceiling was tuned to MTV, full volume, and flashed chaotic images; the phone was ringing; Tara's friend Belinda sat on the hospital bed holding a stuffed, musical bear in a red-and-white Santa's hat. The bear's red nose flashed off and on while it played "Jingle Bells," and Tara and Rochelle stood in the middle of the room convulsed with laughter.

"She peed on the floor," Rochelle screamed.

"I couldn't help it. I was trying to get to the toilet, and it just came too fast," Tara howled, wiping a tear with the back of her hand. She finally composed herself and answered the phone. Her father. He and his wife, Cheryl, would be there soon. The phone rang again. Tara's friend Natalie this time. Tara promised to let her know as soon as the baby was born.

Belinda seemed determined to keep the "Jingle Bear" wound up in between snapping photos of the nurse, the room and Tara's tremendous belly. "Here, hold the bear and smile, Big Mama. Now, you get in the picture, Rochelle. Smile. Everybody smile!"

Within an hour, though, the contractions had become longer and more intense. Tara turned off the television and asked Belinda to stop winding up the bear. The party was over. She climbed onto the bed and sank into the pillows.

"Want me to rub your back, Big Mama? Want me to massage your feet? Are you hungry or thirsty or anything? You want anything?" Belinda asked, bouncing about the bed.

Tara fluttered one hand like a goodbye gesture, her signal that a contraction was coming, and told Belinda breathlessly, "I want you to go out of the room. I'm sorry. I just want my mom and Rochelle."

Insulted and hurt, Belinda left not only the room but the hospital, too.

"She doesn't understand 'cause she's never had a baby," Rochelle said, gently dabbing at Tara's brow with a damp washcloth.

With the room finally quiet, Tara fell into a predictable rhythm. First, the fluttering hand, a conscious effort to relax, then long deep breaths followed by short pants as she reached the contraction's summit. Once over the top, she sighed, closed her eyes and rested. Rochelle and I, silent and patient, waited on requests for ice chips, juice, a pillow adjustment, a back massage.

Then, suddenly, Cheryl exploded into the room with Tara's father, Brad, hanging uncertainly in the doorway. Her very presence was like screeching chalk. She hugged and kissed, consoled and laid presents on Tara right through a contraction.

Like a marathoner reaching for the strength to cross a finish line, Tara struggled to muster a smile. "Thanks, thanks," she said, setting the presents unopened on her bedside table. Tara's father excused himself while Cheryl made herself at home in a rocking chair and began to chatter. Tara's eyes implored me as her belly began to tighten again. As this contraction gathered strength, it alarmed her. Her eyes grew wide, and she let out a moan before it was over. Her eyes begged me. "Mom, I don't want everybody seeing me in pain," she whispered. "Please tell Cheryl to go." I did. Then she turned to her friend. "I'm sorry, Rochelle. I only want my mom here now."

When the nurse determined that Tara was dilated to six centimeters, she suggested that a warm bath might be comforting.

I watched her, lying on her side, naked in the bath with her knees pulled up under her great belly, and I marveled at how she had once floated like this inside of me.

Her eyes were closed now, rolled back deep. Tiny beads of perspiration glistened on her forehead. Her breathing was quiet and shallow as she rested between contractions. She opened her eyes and tightened her grasp on my hand. Our eyes locked, and we breathed together, long, deep breaths. Her grip grew stronger and more urgent as she climbed the contraction's arc. We panted. Reached the top. And her hand relaxed in mine as she slid down the other side. Watching her, breathing with her, feeling her contractions through the squeeze of her hand, I was transported along with her into a timeless, spaceless dimension. The fixtures in the room were fluid. The floor, the walls, the ceiling breathed with us, throbbed along with our pulses. There was no one in the world now but us—two women working together to give birth to a baby.

"Mom," Tara whispered. I leaned close. "This is so hard."

"I know," I said. "I know."

Nine centimeters. The nurse went out to find the midwife. The contractions were intense and close together now. "Why does this have to hurt so much?" Tara implored.

"You're almost there, Tara," the midwife cooed as she entered the room and pulled on exam gloves. "Ten centimeters! You can push as soon as you feel the urge." Instinctively, Tara hoisted herself from her back onto her hands and knees and beared down. Three long grunts, and the crown of his dark, wet head was visible. My heart danced. "Push hard!" the midwife commanded. Tara screamed and pushed out his shoulders.

"Oh, my God!" I said.

One last, great push, and he was out.

I was breathless as I watched the midwife place him on his mother's deflated belly, riveted by this tiny, perfect person, his umbilical cord still throbbing. "My God," I heard myself say again and again. His eyes blinked slowly and reflected the kind of wisdom I have seen in the eyes of very old people who seem at peace, ready anytime to go to their God. For just an instant, I was certain that he had come to us from God, and my heart, suddenly filled with hope, seemed too big for my body.

My eyes and heart followed him as the nurse took him to

a metal table to be weighed, measured and tested. His mouth turned down at the corners as she jabbed and jostled him, and his chin began to tremble violently. Suddenly, he let out a wail that resonated through every cell of me, and I yearned to snatch him from the nurse and comfort him. I wanted to wrap him in something warm, rock him and hold him close to my heart. He was so tiny in her hands, naked and vulnerable. His life depends entirely on us, I thought, and my chin began to tremble, too. "My God, forgive us," I said to myself, and I turned my back to my daughter so she wouldn't see my tears.

Nine days later, a tiny Santa in a shiny red suit trimmed in fluffy white at the collar and cuffs lay sleeping on a soft blanket beneath my Christmas tree.

My daughter is 34 years old now, and my grandson is 17. She has raised him mostly on her own, with financial help from me and various agencies. It has not been easy, nor ideal, and they have their struggles. Every Christmas season, though, the sight of mistletoe, just like hearing a familiar song, brings back a crystal clear memory of my grandson's birth, and I am reminded of the amazing gift that he is.

Mr. Christmas

Ruth Andrew

——•◦✕◦•——

After my marriage of twenty-three years ended and we divvied up the family ornaments, I hated the thought of putting up a Christmas tree.

Divorced, living in an apartment alone in Spokane, Washington, with an all-consuming marketing job, Christmas had become a lonely time for me. I wondered what other divorced women did for the holidays, after their families had moved on with their own lives. Of course, there were the usual Christmas lunches, office parties and gift exchanges, the hurry and scurry of Christmas cards and last-minute fudge making. For the first time ever, I bought Christmas cookies at the grocery store. The only thing that saved even a little bit of holiday spirit for me was going to church for the lighting of the Advent candles and the Christmas hymns. There was no joy left in giving gifts to friends, baking Christmas cookies and decorating the family tree.

A nice, red poinsettia on the dining room table was the most I could get into the spirit of the holiday. I still enjoyed the Christmas cards, but I also found that many of our married friends no longer kept in touch. I didn't understand this. I could still enjoy their holiday letters and photos, even if I no longer wore a wedding ring. How could this happen? We'd always been good friends. I felt left out and alone.

Each year leading up to Christmas, I dreaded the holidays with a vengeance. It would start in October, around Halloween, and dominate Thanksgiving for me. By December, I always felt like Scrooge. One particular Christmas was worse than the others. My son, Phil, a college student, met and fell in love with Diane, the beautiful young woman he would later marry, and spent Christmas with her family in Mt. Vernon, Washington. This same Christmas, my daughter, Allison, was in France for her junior year in high school as a World Experience exchange student. I was alone for the holidays.

And then, during this most lonely of all Christmas seasons, I met Mr. Christmas himself. He smiled at me whenever we passed each other in the building where we both worked. One chilly morning, he stopped by my desk, handed me a cup of coffee and invited me to lunch that afternoon. His name was Dennis, and we married on November 25 of the following year. Then, our holiday problems began. Dennis loved Christmas, wanted a big Christmas tree and wanted it early. I hated the thought and insisted that a poinsettia on the dining room table was enough. By this time, I reasoned, we were empty nesters. We did not need a Christmas tree, and the poinsettia would do. But he insisted on a tree. The first year, I actually won the battle, and instead of a tree, we hung a cedar swag over the family room entertainment center.

After a few days, I began to notice ornaments adorning the swag, and they looked eerily familiar. Then, more ornaments appeared on the swag. Each day, after coming home from work, I'd check the swag, convinced that it held more ornaments than the day before. After a week, every ornament stored downstairs in boxes found their way to our Christmas tree swag, as Dennis called it. When I'd adjusted to this, I walked into our family room one evening to find him stringing twinkling lights around the swag.

From then on, for the next twenty-something years, it was the same issue: have a tree or not have a tree. He always won. At least I nixed a real tree with needles falling all over the carpet. Dennis bought a reasonable-size artificial tree. He put it up, and he took it down. You'd think I'd have gotten over it in time, but years later I still wanted no part of a Christmas tree. And besides, I reasoned, it only affected me once a year.

Last year in November, just before Thanksgiving, I e-mailed my good friend Gail, whom I'd known for years, and bemoaned that Dennis was talking about Christmas and I was dreading it all over again. I described the sad evening my children's father and I sat in the downstairs of our family home to divide up our Christmas ornaments, before the divorce was actually final. He got the Raggedy Andy ornament. I got the Raggedy Ann. He got the furry lion ornament. I took Mrs. Claus. And so it went until our twenty-three years of collected family ornaments were divided, including ornaments from Gail and her husband when they were in Germany with the Air Force.

And now, all these years later, our family still didn't gather to decorate the tree. Each December, it seemed like we weren't a family anymore, and I could hardly look at our ornaments without a deep sadness sweeping over me. Sitting in my home office that afternoon, sipping a glass of Merlot, I read Gail's return e-mail. She scolded me soundly. "It's time you get over this," she wrote. "Why would you let your ex-husband steal your Christmas joy? Dennis loves Christmas, and he loves a tree. He must feel horrible every year when you act like this."

I thanked her for her wisdom and knew she'd spoken from the heart. I felt consumed by guilt, realizing I'd deprived Dennis of his own Christmas joy the way I thought my ex-husband had stolen mine. In reality, I'd done it to myself. This had gone on long enough!

That evening, as Dennis and I ate dinner, I asked him quietly if he would mind getting out the tree for Christmas. He was stunned.

"Really?" he asked. "You mean it?"

"Yes."

"Even before Thanksgiving?"

"Yes. Absolutely. Tonight!"

I gave him a kiss and explained my change of heart. "Gail told me this afternoon that I should not let my ex-husband steal all of my Christmas joy any longer and that I had been unfair to you all these years, when you love it so much. I've decided she's right. Now I want to enjoy every minute of Christmas with you."

"Great!" he exclaimed.

I smiled. "From now on, I'd like to put our tree up in late November, before our anniversary on the 25th. We can call it our anniversary tree, if you like."

He kissed me, then hurried downstairs and returned with our tree, already decorated with the ornaments and lights from the previous year. Getting me to put ornaments on it the last year was such an issue for me that he left it decorated and threw a sheet over it in the downstairs storage closet. He told me he never wanted to go through that hassle again, and neither did I, for that matter. It turned out to be a blessing. In a mere ten minutes, our beautiful anniversary tree was ablaze in the living room with twinkling lights, ornaments and love.

This tree held my family ornaments, and I felt only joy remembering the ones my son and daughter had given me, treasures from long ago. Phil and Diane had given me a beautiful White House Christmas ornament from when they were first married and living in Maryland, as well as sweet ornaments from their children, my darling granddaughters, Jamie and Tate. I found five red-and-white candy canes that Allison had made when she was only five years old in kindergarten, when she was the same age as her small son, Asher, himself in kindergarten last December. I found the bread dough sheep from Phil's Cub Scout days, which he'd always insisted he didn't make, but his name was still printed on the back. And I found the white star Allison had made in preschool, with the pink ball fringe in the middle.

Standing in my living room surrounded by ornaments from my children when they were small, I understood how much I'd missed our family Christmas tree. We were still a family. That was the important thing. I felt like rolling up my sleeves and baking a big batch of Christmas cookies.

The more I looked at our tree, the more I realized how many ornaments my husband had collected from family and friends over our years together. A moose looked at me from beneath a branch on the tree. I found a small computer, several kayaks, a Santa in a canoe and many others that spoke to my husband's job in manufacturing and also his love of kayaks, canoes and the outdoors.

Later that evening, Dennis and I sat on the living room sofa with the lights out in the room except for those twinkling on the tree. I marveled at the beauty of our tree before us, the love it represented, and wondered how I'd ever allowed myself to be too sad to want a Christmas tree, especially when my husband loved one so much.

I sat there long after Dennis had kissed me goodnight and gone to bed. When I finally turned out the tree lights, I found myself quietly singing and humming a bit of "Santa Baby" as I headed off to bed myself, eager to get up early the next morning to turn on the tree lights for breakfast. I wanted to be up early and bake those Christmas cookies, even if it was before Thanksgiving. I smiled to myself, knowing my lemon sugar cookie recipe was from Gail, when we were both new brides so many years earlier.

This year, I was the one who reminded Dennis in late November that it was time to get out the Christmas tree, even before the Thanksgiving turkey was to go into the oven. And that's the way it is at our house now, thanks to a very good friend with a whole lot of wisdom, and a husband who always understood.

Is This A Good Time?

Ruth Campbell Bremer

———◆⋈◆———

Cradling a sleeping baby in one arm, I was trying to throw together an afternoon snack without tripping on the dogs when my phone rang. It was my husband, Alex. "Is it okay if I invite a couple guys over for dinner?" he asked.

I hesitated, scanning the messy kitchen and cluttered countertops. This was our first year hosting Christmas, and I had this idea that it should be picture-perfect, complete with handmade decorations and a big holiday feast. My attempt at personalized Christmas stockings had resulted in a glitter paint disaster, and I'd run out of time to do anything else crafty. The living room furniture had been awkwardly rearranged to accommodate our hand-me-down artificial tree, decorated with unbreakable ornaments near the bottom.

Picture-perfect it was not. After more than a year of renovating our house, it was still a gallery of unfinished projects. A section of cabinets remained unpainted, face plates were missing from light switches and outlets, and the fixtures were mismatched and outdated. The refrigerator was decorated with fingerprints and magnetic letters, and various objects were stacked on top in a most unattractive fashion. In one corner, a large potted plant was dying a slow death.

"Sure," I told Alex, trying to sound enthusiastic. "The more the merrier." My parents had just arrived, and to be honest, it didn't feel like an especially good time to have additional company. Still, I couldn't bring myself to say no. After all, it was the day before Christmas Eve, and these poor guys were stuck in Denver when they were supposed to be at home enjoying the holiday break with their families.

A few days earlier, a blizzard had dumped two feet of snow on the area, closing the airport for forty-five hours and causing power outages, road closures and shortages at local grocery stores. People were gradually digging out and getting back to work, but there were piles of snow everywhere, driving was still a little sketchy and the airport had a backlog of flights trying to get out of town.

For some reason, Alex's company had chosen the week before Christmas to bring in a group of salespeople from around the country for training. Everyone else had managed to secure a flight home already. These two guys, however, were stuck in town for one more night. Although they each had a nice room at the Hyatt and an expense account to cover dinner, Alex thought they might prefer to hang out with a family instead of spending the evening alone.

Just as I got off the phone, my two-month-old daughter woke up and started screaming in my ear. No, it definitely was not a good time to have people over. Fortunately, my mom was there to help. She started peeling potatoes and planning the dinner menu while I fed the baby. Then, we got to work clearing off the dining room table. Even in my slightly panicked state, I felt excitement bubbling up at the thought of gathering a crowd around our table. This was my opportunity to host a big Christmas dinner. So what if it wouldn't be anywhere near perfect?

For years, Alex and I had lived in small houses and condos. With space tight and our budget even tighter, we ate dinner off whatever hand-me-down or cheap, prefabricated table we could squeeze into the available dining area. Then we were finally able to buy our own home: a 1960s two-story with scuffed-up hardwood and drafty, single-pane windows. One of our favorite features was the dining room. Taking up a quarter of the main floor, it was big enough to hold a real dining table. And for the first time, we could afford to buy one.

When we brought home the large, sturdy, solid wood table, I could already picture us enjoying it in the decades to come. Oh, the plans I had for that dining table. It would be the centerpiece for holidays, family gatherings, celebrations and impromptu dinners with friends. We would start eating dinner as a family every night, complete with meaningful, stimulating conversation. I could host play dates and bunco night, throw intimate dinner parties and large rowdy gatherings. Having a real dining room with a real dining table was going to transform our very lives.

Then, reality interfered. Once the table and chairs were set up in the dining room, we managed maybe two or three chaotic family dinners before proceeding to gradually cover the table with stuff. Since the dining room was located immediately to the right of the front door and directly on the path to the kitchen, one half of the table became a landing pad for junk mail, canned food, arts and crafts projects, assorted papers and all kinds of homeless items. The other end was where we ate (rarely all together), and it usually held a few dirty dishes from the latest meal.

Somehow, the festive gatherings I'd always imagined taking place around the table still hadn't materialized. Between keeping up with two little boys, a draining pregnancy followed by the utter exhaustion of caring for a newborn, I never seemed to have the time or energy to complete even the simplest home improvement projects. I was always in a foggy-headed survival mode, with toys scattered everywhere, dirty dishes in the sink and the boys making messes faster than I could clean them up. It was just never a good time to have people over.

Well, I guess this is just going to have to be a good time, I thought as Mom and I cleared the papers and junk off the table. I would never have planned a big dinner on this particular night. But then again, maybe I never would have planned it at all. When was I ever going to decide it was a good time? When the house was completely fixed up and sparkling clean? When we had nothing on the schedule and nothing stressful going on in our lives? It hit me that it would never truly be a good time. But ultimately, what that meant was, any time could be a good time.

As the sun set and the temperature dropped outside, our house came alive with holiday music, noise and voices. My brother Jeff lived in Denver at the time, and he came over with his girlfriend, Danielle. Alex arrived a bit later with the two visiting salesmen, Lamar and DJ. They were in high spirits after a narrow escape from the snow-covered office parking lot and a slow drive home on slick roads.

Sure enough, it was a good time. No, it was a *great* time. As darkness fell outside and the bitter cold settled in for the night, our home was transformed into a safe haven of light and warmth. When I glanced into the living room, the string of lights on the Christmas tree seemed to glow a little brighter. Mom had dinner going, and the delicious aromas filled the house. Alex opened a bottle of wine. Danielle held the baby while Jeff wrestled with my two-year-old son. Dad and Lamar chatted about the snowstorm, and DJ was locked in a deep discussion with my four-year-old about the existence of Santa Claus and Pluto's recent demotion to dwarf planet.

When the food was ready, we pulled more chairs around the table, poured some more wine and sat down to enjoy our humble feast in the company of new friends. Everyone shared stories, jokes and laughter. Lamar and DJ were successful financial wholesalers with generous expense accounts. They were used to the best of the best, regularly taking clients out to trendy restaurants and drinking expensive wine. They could have eaten steak or lobster that night, yet they both seemed genuinely grateful to spend the evening sitting down to a home-cooked meal with us instead.

Because of the sleep deprivation that accompanies a new baby, I don't remember a whole lot from that period in my life, but I will never forget that evening. I can't recall what we ate or what kind of wine we drank with our holiday meal. What I remember is the warmth, the laughter and the bonding taking place around that big table. I was overcome with joy at having the opportunity to finally use the table exactly the way I'd always wanted. But I also realized something deeper. It wasn't the table. I could have been experiencing this all along, around any table, in any kind of living space. That night, nobody noticed or cared if there were face plates on the light switches, dust in the corners or abstract art on the stockings. I was experiencing perfection in spite of the messy, imperfect setting.

For me, the warm glow continued through the holiday season. It was wonderful having my family there, reveling in the kids' excitement and snuggling with the new baby. I don't remember any of the presents I gave or received that Christmas. I only remember one perfect gift that came in the form of a blizzard: the realization that there will never really be a good time. My life will never be tidy and organized, and my house will never look like a scene from a Pottery Barn catalog. A good time to get together with friends, family or complete strangers is right now.

In the years since, we've moved to other houses in other cities, and life has not slowed down one bit. I still haven't managed to get everything in order or keep my house clean for more than two minutes. Not once have we hosted a picture-perfect Christmas. Now I just count myself lucky if nobody comes down with the flu during the holiday break. I've come to terms with the fact that laundry and dishes are never really done. Now, with three big kids and all their activities and projects, our house is still messy, our schedule is busier than ever, and most of our friends seem to be in a time crunch, too.

Sometimes I still find myself thinking it's not a good time to invite people over. But when I look at our big, sturdy dining table (which is typically covered in crayons, construction paper, Lego bricks and dirty dishes), I'm reminded of the Christmas gift I received on that snowy night in Denver, and I know the truth.

First Family Christmas

Jack Skillicorn

———•◦✕◦•———

It was sixty days before Christmas, and all were apart. I had just re-enlisted in the Air Force and was stationed in Massachusetts. I was engaged to a wonderful woman, Sandy, who came complete with a small daughter, Jeanette. My family-to-be was at home in California. Since Christmas was fast approaching and our telephone calls were getting longer and more expensive, I knew it was time for me to head west. With a wedding, I would make my family-to-be officially my family, and the three of us would head back east to start our new home together.

I found us a place to live. I got permission to head back for a few days, and soon we were in the happy midst of a small family wedding ceremony. We were joined by my mother, the bride's five-year-old daughter, her mother and father and the minister at the Los Altos United Methodist Church.

After the wedding, my wife and I, along with our daughter and my mother, checked in to a marvelous hotel. With its gardens, fountains and statuary, it was a magnificent wonder in the eyes of a five-year-old. Even more wonderful to a five-year-old was the announcement I made at the dinner table.

"Jeanette, this is a very special occasion. Our first dinner together as a family. You can order anything you want from the menu. Anything at all."

She studied the menu carefully. "Anything?"

"Yes, that's right. Anything you want."

She sat up and put the menu on the table next to her fork. "All right, I want cheesecake."

"Cheesecake? Is that all?" Her mother and I exchanged quick smiles.

"I want my cheesecake first, that's what I want." Well, she had us there, anything she wanted meant just that. Our waitress was upset by the idea. She had never seen it done before, so it must not be healthy, and she told us so, in no uncertain terms. Years later, whenever we bring up that first meal together, Jeanette does not remember anything else she had, but she sure remembers the day she got to eat her dessert first.

The next morning after breakfast, we said farewell to my mother and our cross-country adventure began.

For our trip, we had purchased a brand-new 1962 Nash Rambler station wagon. We had carefully planned our trip to be a relaxed drive on Highway 80, approximately 3,200 miles. The plan was to drive six hours each day, not including whatever stops we made. While we drove east, our furniture and other items, including our daughter's Christmas gifts, were being transported by a moving van. We knew we were cutting it close, but the van was scheduled to arrive two days before Christmas.

What a feeling. Christmas in the air, the magnificent Sierra Nevada mountains as a backdrop to our first day of driving across the country. A couple of small bears playing at the side of the road gave Jeanette a thrill almost as big as the cheese-cake, as did the discovery of free Howard Johnson children's coloring books. Every morning at breakfast, we sought out a Howard Johnson restaurant, and she would carefully fill in the same pictures she'd done the day before.

Over the following days, we stopped in many states, cities and villages, seeing many interesting places and sights. But in between our stops, we played games, like who could recognize the most license plates from different states or the alphabet game, where you find letters on signs along the road. To keep Jeanette in the proper holiday frame of mind, we sang whatever Christmas songs came to mind, such as "Away in a Manger" and "Santa Claus Is Coming to Town." Our voices might not have been professional, but to me the sound of our three voices struggling to hit the notes and remember the words was better than anything on the radio dial.

We had lucked out with the weather, and it was beautifully clear for the first few days. Getting toward Illinois, we began to notice dark clouds overhead. I turned on the radio. According to the reports, it was a big storm indeed, and it sounded like it would be moving in lock step with us as we headed back east.

"Do you think this is going to delay our moving van?" my wife asked quietly, not wanting Jeanette to hear.

"I don't know," I said, glancing up at the sky. "I hope not. Everything we have is in that van, including her presents. I would hate for her to wake up Christmas morning in a new town, in a new house, and find nothing under the tree."

Finally, there we were, and I was pulling the Nash into our own driveway. I borrowed some furniture from the squadron where I worked, to use until our furniture arrived and we moved in.

"We need a tree," my wife said, looking at the mismatched furniture scattered around the living room. "The ornaments are all in the moving boxes. We should have brought a few in the car with us. Well, we can make them this year." And make them we did, the three of us. We bought cranberries, popped popcorn, and Jeanette and I sat on the floor, stringing beautiful red-and-white garlands for our tree. We wrapped our colorful, homemade garland around and through the evergreen branches of our tree. Now, really in the Christmas spirit, we decided the tree needed something more. We found some apples, ribbon and cardboard and made our own hanging ornaments. Shiny stars dangled among the branches, and a larger, glorious star was at the top of the tree. It may not have been the fanciest tree in the neighborhood, but it was OUR tree.

Therefore, for us, it was the best tree anywhere.

The van had been scheduled to arrive on December 22, but where was it? My wife and I whispered about it, and she made more than one call to the company headquarters to hear their apologetic reports of a truck in the midst of severe weather. We hope Jeanette wouldn't notice our concern. But she did.

"Santa, will you be able to find my new house on Christmas Eve? We just moved here," we heard her explain to a Santa in a local shopping mall.

He smiled and reassured her, bless his heart. "Of course, dear. I can find everyone on Christmas Eve."

Could he really? On December 24, the moving van was already two days late from the last promised arrival day. We were sitting around the tree, anxiously waiting to see the moving van come rumbling up our street, when the phone rang.

"It's our driver," my wife whispered, covering the phone

with her hand. "He's asking if he can stop at his sister's house for Christmas Eve!" I sighed and shook my head. "Can you please try to make it," she asked him. "All of our presents are in that truck." She listened quietly to his response. "He'll do the best he can," she told me, hanging up the phone.

Jeanette went to bed early that night, dreaming of Santa's visit. Her parents, however, were too nervous to do anything other than pace in front of the window, pulling the curtain back regularly and holding their breath every time headlights turned onto the street. Finally, at ten o'clock on Christmas Eve, weeks after we had loaded our cardboard boxes into a moving van, a pair of headlights pulled into our driveway.

Jeanette crept down the stairs in the morning. Arms around each other's waists, we watched as she caught her first glimpse of the living room.

"He did it! Santa did it!" she shouted as she sat among the many packages by the Christmas tree. "He found our new house!" She hugged an enormous stuffed puppy to her chest—it was almost bigger than she was. Yes, Santa finally came, spreading gifts under the tree, filling her Christmas stocking and giving this brand-new family a holiday to remember.

Lipstick Christmas

Ingrid E. Lundquist

Sue and I met in 1975, and every December we provide each other with moral support and the nod of approval when selecting Christmas gifts for our sisters, brothers, parents, boyfriends and husbands. This year, she arrived at my office wearing broken-in jeans, a denim shirt and a burnt-orange rain jacket that had seen several wet winters. Tall and thin, Sue looked like she was making a denim-casual fashion statement. I, however, was average height with extra pounds. I was dressed in similar denim, but my look was of someone who grabbed the first clothes she could find, newly warm from the dryer.

We'd both become comfortable with dressing casually, unlike our dating years when we slipped our callous-free feet into red, ankle-strapped stilettos, pulled on short saucy outfits, kept a full palette of nail colors in our refrigerator vegetable bins and wore lacy underwear. In our younger days, we always painted our lips.

"Forget your lipstick?" she asked, looking at my pale face.

"Yeah," I said, with the enthusiasm of opening a utility bill.

"I guess," I added, as if my response required more than just acknowledgment. Maybe with the passing of time, we had forgotten or perhaps just didn't care anymore about being stylish.

Our lives had certainly changed since we'd met back in college, but there was one constant: our mutual lack of holiday spirit. Instead of looking forward to the retail-promised jingle bell cheer, Sue and I both dreaded the holiday season. This was just another dreary, rainy Thursday in December. On our gift lists, we both had a family member who requested a leaf blower. The year was 1999, fondly remembered as the leaf blower Christmas.

Sue and I were our fathers' sons. We owned power tools and knew every aisle in every hardware store in town. There was a leaf blower sale at a hardware store close to my office. We went there, and it was an easy three-minute purchase, so we wasted another ten minutes groveling through the bargain bins to stock up on tape measures, screwdrivers and night lights.

In the parking lot, we inhaled the memory-laden smell of steamed hot dogs. "When you were a kid, did your dad take you to the hardware store on Saturday mornings?" she asked.

"We usually went to Sears," I said grinning. "They had fresh popcorn with real butter by the paint section."

On the drive back to my office, I noticed empty parking spaces in front of a local bar. "Let's stop and see if it's still the same," I said, pulling into a space and not waiting for Sue to reply.

The Palomino Room was an old-time hangout, aptly named for attracting male patrons primarily over the age of sixty-five. We had both just turned fifty-two. The place hadn't changed with the times. There was still the dark wainscot paneling and blue fleur-de-lis wallpaper with an occasional stain of men's hair cream. "Hey, look," I said, pointing to the starched, white table linens. "I bet those apricot-colored napkins have been folded a million times into swans."

Today's diners were holiday shoppers or older children with their elderly parents, who gummed soft white rolls and chicken rice soup. Some were savoring the signature dessert, chocolate mousse with a generous dollop of whipped cream, served in a glass, soda fountain–style ice cream dish.

The bar area was empty. The cracked red leather on the stools seemed more inviting than the corner alcove. It was always dark here, a place where secrets are kept. Dark and close like a cave. This was the place married men took their girlfriends.

The bar was quite a distance from the main door. We mounted two stools and settled in. We had a good vantage point from which to survey the crowd. The bar menu featured New England clam chowder served with soda crackers—a perfect winter accompaniment. Soup it was.

"Can I get a white roll and butter?" Sue asked the bartender.

"Tabasco sauce for me," I noted.

Over bowls of thick, creamy soup, we were content, eating, talking about Christmas plans and sketching holiday table decor ideas on paper cocktail napkins.

The rain pelted the sidewalk, splashing up against the swinging door, but the sky occasionally pushed through a ribbon of afternoon light. The door swung open and closed several times without incident. Then, a temporary blinding wedge of light shot across the empty cocktail tables in front of the bar. A man and woman snaked their way to the bar and sat down. *Hmmm, wonder what the story was there…*

"They're not married," I whispered to Sue.

"At least not to each other," she whispered back.

He wore a well-tailored, indigo banker's suit with a Santa tie, and she looked like an elongated, pink cotton ball in a straight skirt and matching fuzzy sweater. The intimate bar area now felt inhabited, and everyone was talking so loudly about nothing that eavesdropping was impossible.

Another streak of light ushered in two more silhouettes. This time, the hinged door swung shut slowly, leaving a sunlit haze and making it difficult to see. I studied the incomplete outlines as my mind melded a hodgepodge image, forming a recognizable shape I could only define as male.

"They look like lumberjacks," I said to Sue.

"After a hard day's work," she replied.

Okay, we were wearing faded and casual denim, but these guys looked downright scruffy. They wore wet jackets, maybe plaid or fatigue style, and both had shaggy beards. From their rugged appearance, I grimaced as I instinctively knew they smelled of something unpleasant. I was glad the nicely dressed man and fuzzy woman served as a shield between us and them.

The men's movement through the door was at first swift but came to an abrupt stop. I looked closer at the back-lit men, trying to determine whether we were in danger. "Are they going to hold up the restaurant and take us hostage," I asked beneath my breath, "or kidnap us, tape our mouths and drag us off to their shabby, pungent pickup truck?"

My eyes focused on the figures while thoughts raced through my mind as if preparing to give the police a description for a lineup. The taller one had familiar eyes—no, he had familiar something else. It was his size that was familiar. I noticed he must have been 6'4" or 6'5" as he ducked under the doorjamb. Sue was looking at the other man. He was shorter, probably about 6'. He didn't catch my attention at all.

"The tall one is staring at me," I either said, or thought I said, as I tried not to stare. He'd walk a pace or two forward, then stop and stare, then walk another pace forward, and stop and stare. I was uncomfortable and shifted my attention to my soup.

I guess the shorter one was looking at Sue. Her stiff body language indicated she was scared, too. "Ingrid...don't those guys look familiar?" she asked.

I glanced at the shorter one and responded bluntly, "No." I was really afraid and forced my eyes back to the chowder, all the while trying to imagine how I would react if they pulled a gun and wondering if I had anything of value in my purse to offer them in trade for my life.

I sneaked another peek at the taller one as he continued to walk closer. I focused. I focused harder. I literally felt my head tilt as if to question whether I was really seeing what I thought I was seeing. My memory collided with the man before me. Now I was staring into his stare, eyeball to eyeball. I became anxious. My face flushed more quickly than it had since junior prom, when my date touched my nylon stocking–encased thigh. My heart thumped like a train on old tracks, picking up speed down a snowy mountain.

Our eyes made direct, close contact. "Look familiar?" I yelped, leaping into his now outstretched arms. "Sue, it's your ex-husband!" Sue couldn't hear me, crushed as she was in a warm embrace with my ex-boyfriend.

Don and Herb. Some thirty years before, Sue had been married to Don, and I had been head over heels in love with Herb. Both moved out of town shortly after college but returned each Christmas to visit families. That day, they were buying last-minute gifts for their wives and kids. For the afternoon, it felt like old times. We were happy, the four of us, laughing, hugging and reminiscing.

Since then, Sue and I make it a point to go Christmas shopping wearing proper clothes and makeup. You just never know who might turn up in your life.

When we recall the excitement on the faces of our loved ones when they opened the leaf blowers, we're primed to meet the ghosts of Christmas past. But nearing 40 years now, it's become evident that our annual treks during the holidays are not about shopping at all. No? No, it is actually about the bond we've formed by adding yet another unbelievable story to yet another year of friendship. It's our holiday tradition.

Enough Time for Christmas

Julaina Kleist-Corwin

———◦⊙⊰⊙◦———

Every year, I groan when I think about sorting through all the Christmas decorations, the time it takes to decorate, and then a few weeks later, to pack it up again. What makes it all worthwhile is a crumpled and now yellowed piece of newsprint, a story that my son, Adrian, wrote for a newspaper contest. I keep it in the storage box to reread each season. A few years after he wrote it, he passed away from an accident.

I don't have any specific memories of Christmas because they have blurred together over the years. I don't see Christmas as a celebration of a religious leader's birthday mainly because I'm not a religious person. I see it as a time of happiness and good feelings. A time when relatives come over, a time of giving things, pine needles and presents. I can remember things that happened on Christmas, but I can't accurately remember when they happened, if it was last year or the year before or the year before that.

I remember my father buying a tall tree and trying to make it stand up straight in the stupid and poorly designed stand. I remember him stringing the tree lights and wondering if we needed an extra set. We always needed another set.

I remember hanging the ornaments, the gold and blue shining ones, the old, fragile ones that came from my great-grandmother. The dorky ones I made out of paper plates and Shrinky Dinks in second grade, the reindeer from clothespins and the heavy ones made from plaster molds that could only be hung on the low, thick branches. The gaudy tinsel strings that are always spread around the house for lack of a better place to put them. Now my dad hangs the ornaments about a week before Christmas. We don't seem to have much time anymore.

I remember Grandma toting presents and her hugs and kisses. I remember the presents, the bow and arrow, the space men and Legos, the shirts and socks, the plastic Creepy Crawlers set, the bag of doohickeys and thingamajigs, the model sets, the electric trains and toy cars, the abundant supply of aftershave for Dad and Grandpa and the never-enough See's chocolates.

I remember the box of presents from the relatives in Wisconsin. The undersized box would burst and spew unknown gifts. My mother would always open them before Christmas. She said she was just checking to see if she bought the same thing so she could take it back in time to get something different. I knew she just wanted to see her presents early.

I remember the Christmases in the mountains at the rented cabin. We would lug the suitcases, presents, skis, car chains and the miniature, plastic tree, complete with lights and ornaments that Grandma brought. We don't go up to the cabin anymore. We just don't seem to have the time.

But the thing I remember the most is the lights. The glowing tree lights in the windows of the houses down the street, the flashing lights tracing the edges of the roofs. The giant tree of lights on the top of the Concord Park and Shop sign. I made a habit the last couple Christmas seasons to look out the front window right before I go to bed. With the house lights off, I can see the lights from the other houses far down the street. I see the lights glowing and flashing their message of Christmas.

As I grow older, I seem to lose the time to enjoy Christmas like I used to. I just hope I always have enough time to recall my Christmas memories.

Who knew that he wouldn't have enough time for more Christmas memories, not enough time to enjoy future holidays? I hear Adrian's voice clearly when I read his story, I see the scenes he describes. I feel the childhood memories as if they were yesterday, bringing him close to me again.

Foggy Day

Louise Reardon

———◦❊◦———

It was not the best of Christmas seasons that year, 1944. As I rode down through California's Central Valley on the train on December 23, I had plenty of time to think about my husband, Ed, in the Air Force, loading bombs onto planes at the Battle of the Bulge. Although he had been diligent about writing two or three times a week, it had been weeks since I'd last heard from him. I dreaded the news that might be slowly winding its way toward me.

The usually dependable Southern Pacific train was anything but dependable during wartime. As the hours wore on, I realized that although the schedule called for the train to arrive in Tulare at 11:00 p.m., we were not going to arrive at 11:00 or 12:00 or even at 1:00 a.m. Finally, at 3:00 in the morning, the train pulled into the station. The depot had long since closed for the night, and I looked anxiously around for signs that someone had come to meet me. As a schoolteacher living up north in Sacramento, I made this train trip home quite regularly, and my folks always came to the station to pick me up. But that morning, there was no sign of them.

"Louise!" I heard someone calling my name from the parking lot. Peering out into the thick tule fog peculiar to the valley, I could make out a lone car. To my surprise, I saw that it was not my parents emerging from the fog but two old pals from high school who had been sitting there in the cold and dark for hours waiting for my train to arrive. They were tired and worn out, not only from the long wait but also from the yearly ritual that orange growers undergo in cold weather to keep their trees from freezing—lighting smudge pots in the orchards to create a low, heavy smoke to keep the warmth close to the ground. Growers' children would sometimes drag into school in the morning with rings under their eyes from smudging all night and black streaks on their faces from the oily smoke.

I was overjoyed to see them, but I wondered where my parents were. As we drove through the countryside toward my hometown of Strathmore, they filled me in on my family's news: My grandmother had broken her hip and was in the hospital. My sister Barbara, due to give birth to her first child, was in the same hospital with what appeared to be serious complications with her baby. An X-ray showed a breech baby with an abnormally large head. The doctor feared the worst. My father had been close to a breakdown and was lying in bed with worry.

I added this distressing information to the worry I already had about my husband. I thanked my friends for the ride and went into the house to see what I could do to help. I found my sister's best friend close to hysterics. Like mine, her husband was also at the Battle of the Bulge. He was a doctor stationed at Nancy, and she had not heard from him in weeks either. But the immediate problem at hand was to track down Barbara's husband, Giz, to tell him the latest development with his wife's pregnancy. The two of us turned our attention from worrying about our own husbands to worrying about Barbara's. He was a B-24 pilot scheduled to head out to fight in the Pacific, and we found that he was currently only three hundred miles to the north of us, on an air base in San Francisco. His commanding officer told us that he was on alert status and ready to be shipped out to the Pacific at any time. He would not be able to attend the birth.

December 24 passed slowly. We went back and forth to the hospital all day long, listening all the while to the terrifying news on the radio about the fight raging in Europe. As the day wore on, we were told that the doctors did not want to delay Barbara's delivery any longer and that they planned to do a cesarean. Good news arrived when another set of doctors at the other end of the hospital told us that Grandmother was doing much better. And then suddenly, standing before us, bleary-eyed, his uniform rumpled, was Barbara's husband.

In a foolhardy, split-second decision, Giz had decided to go AWOL the minute he'd heard of his wife's condition. If a baby was about to be born, he was determined to be there, despite how the Air Force felt about it. Hitchhiking on Highway 99, he'd caught ride after ride from sympathetic drivers all too willing to stop and help a serviceman. After a dozen or so rides, he arrived in town and made his way to the hospital. Barbara was overjoyed to hear that her husband was at hand, and the beautiful, perfectly normal baby boy was born without incident.

We spent a joyous night that Christmas Eve. My father got out of bed in great spirits to begin the holiday celebrations. With our Christmas looking brighter, we turned our attention to the next problem: getting Giz back to San Francisco before the Air Force noticed he was gone. Gas was a precious commodity during the war, and none of us had enough gas coupons to last the long drive up through the valley to San Francisco. Hitchhiking slowly back on Christmas Day was his only option.

I drove Giz out to the road to begin his journey back that morning. As I made my way through the orange groves along the country road toward the main highway, the gray tule fog was so thick that I could hardly see the front end of my own car. *Oh, Lord,* I thought to myself, *how will Giz ever be able to pick up a ride in this fog? In his beige uniform, no one would be able to see him standing by the side of the road.*

But when I let him out of the car, a battered, black farm truck stopped almost immediately. Sizing up the driver as one of the local farmers out to make an early morning delivery, I felt even more discouraged. "Giz will never make it to San Francisco at this rate. I bet that fellow is just going up the road to the next ranch."

It turned out that the local farmer wasn't headed for his ranch. He was on his way up to San Francisco on business, with enough gas coupons in his wallet to take him the whole way. The farmer dropped Giz off a few blocks from the barracks. Giz slipped in with a few other fellows on their way back from Christmas services, and no one was ever the wiser about his absence from the field to attend his son's birth.

The letters from our husbands started arriving from France later that week.

Sandpaper Christmas

R. Bob Magart

The Christmas of my third grade, the winter of 1962, I tiptoed from my attic bed and descended the cold, squeaky staircase to steal another look at our magnificent tree. I treaded gingerly on each step because I was being bad. I'd been sent to bed, and I would be disciplined if I was caught. Our stairs led into the kitchen. Mom would be seated at her chair by the table, and by turning her head sharply, she would discover my entry.

I nudged the door open with my nose and peeked through the crack to see if the coast was clear. Mother was seated with her back partially to me, and instantly I knew that she was crying. Shame quickened in my every joint. I wanted to run to her, to hug her and drive away the tears.

I could do no such thing. For one thing, I sensed her tears were her silent cross, and I would be violating some ancient rule. For another, I wasn't supposed to be up, and such bold action would terminate my mission. So, I stealthily pushed the door forward just enough for my slight body to slip through the crack. Without making a sound, I descended the last two steps to the kitchen floor. Silently, I turned the handle and pushed the door closed.

Again, I glanced to Mother, fearful I had been discovered. No, her back was still to me. I turned to the living room arch, where a glow beckoned from the tree lights. In a flash, I was standing before the giant tree that filled from floor to ceiling almost one whole side of our living room. Around each light, the green boughs of the grand fir glistened bright and reflected off colored ornaments—red, green, blue, orange and white. Tinsel danced in reflection.

That afternoon, my mother, brother, sister and I had carefully placed the glass ornaments so they ascended in size, with the very large, glass ones on the bottom, one clear, one red, one blue, some so delicate I remembered being scolded "not to touch." We placed distinctly hardier ornaments at the fronts of boughs, where if they were bumped, they were strong and would more likely survive the fall. Near the top, Mother and my brother had attached to the very tips of the delicate branches a dozen or more tiny, gold balls, as small as the tips of my fingers. Gold was also the color of the garland that spiraled the length of the giant tree, like a road up a mountain. At the very top stood our little angel, adorned in a white robe bordered in gold, her hands in prayerful attention, and her eyes closed in concentration.

My plan now complete, I knew not what more to do. I decided to stay a few moments more, and an impish plan appeared. Next to the kitchen archway, standing on eight large legs, Mom's sideboard filled the better part of the wall. Previously playing with a cousin my age as pretend pirates or Indians, we had climbed between these cylinders. Conspiring and smart, we avoided other villains. A perfect cubbyhole was created at the end of the giant cupboard. Open space, the size of a small boy, remained before the intersect of the adjoining wall.

I slipped into this space, drew my knees up against my chest and lay my head against one of the large legs of the sideboard. In this towering world, I gazed at the magnificent tree. I was only dimly aware of the rest of the room: Mom and Dad's bedroom door, the skirted potbelly stove that sent light from small windows in its door and then, before me and through the tree branches, the front door from where Dad would soon be making his entrance.

I fell asleep, although it must have been only minutes. A cold breeze splashed me awake, and Dad was in, brushing snow from his coat and stomping his feet. He hung his green-and-black plaid coat on the hook by the stove. My hiding spot did not fail me as Dad slipped by into the kitchen. I knew to stay put. Then, I heard him discover Mother still crying.

While Dad consoled Mother, coaxing her to talk, I learned Mother's secret. She was crying because they didn't have presents for us kids. In consoling her, Father cried, too. And a warmth of joy wrapped around me because now I saw they were united. I resisted a giant urge to rush to them. With Dad, though, Mom's voice quieted. In those moments, I had learned my first inkling that there was no Santa Claus, only parents.

All was right. What was I to worry of presents when my mom and dad loved each other? It had never occurred to me that we were poor. I had never gone hungry, never gone without clothing, shelter or security. I was too young for such concerns. Father reminded Mom that the turkey for Christmas dinner was purchased and thawing on the back porch. He further reported that the rungs on the sled had been welded. *Sled,* I thought, *a sled?* He had fitted the boards tight and covered it in a single coat of paint. Tomorrow, Christmas Eve, he would coat it again and hide it under the tree that night. It would be a gift for all three of us children.

A sled, a sled. My entire frame delighted in excitement. What was I to care for another present? A sled would be great. Wrapped in the joy of Christmas coming, I was beside myself. And with this certainty, I gazed even more appreciatively on our Christmas tree. Presently, I drowsed into sleep again. When I awoke, shivering cold, the room was dark, and the tree lights were off. Mom and Dad had gone off to bed, and I was free for my escape upstairs.

The next morning, I woke before the others. Through the windows at both ends of the attic, dim, winter light shadowed the room in breathy coldness. My brother and sister were sound asleep across the way. But I, I was awake! Excitement and purpose thrilled me. I had a job to do; I would make a picture as a present for Mother. My sister would help me wrap it, and it would tell Mother of my undeniable love.

So many, many years later, the remainder of the day until evening is lost to my memory. We were seated at the table for dinner when our father came in, and with him was a hatless man I guessed was about fifty years old. He carried nothing. Dad announced that he was staying with us, that he would take my brother's bed, my brother would take mine, and I would sleep on the floor in my parents' bedroom. To this arrangement, Mother immediately assented. Our father simply made the announcement, our mother put another place at the table, and my brother and sister moved over on the bench to make way.

Dad had been filling the Dodge with fuel when he had discovered the man. The man was hitchhiking from Kalispell to Missoula, and some rancher had brought him to Hot Springs with the mistaken belief that he was bringing the man closer to his destination. This was true, but it had also brought him clearly off the beaten path. The man had stood by the stove at Pehmcke's Station waiting for a ride since noon. No one was stirring. It was snowing, cold, and people were settled in for the birth of the Child. It would be nearly a thirty-mile walk to a main road, and then it was entirely possible that no one would be traveling. The man's hopes of reaching Missoula that night were drawing on impossible. Mrs. Pehmcke was closing the station and putting the man out. The man had nowhere to go but out into the cold and snow. Thus, it happened that the man joined us for Christmas.

Evening drew together. Mother made a bed for me out of blankets snug between the wall and her side of the bed. Dishes were washed, dried. We settled down. I slept soundly.

I woke to my brother and sister chattering from the living room. I burst from the bedroom. Father and Mother were seated in front of the sideboard on chairs they had brought from the kitchen. To my left, just this side of the stove, sat the stranger, also on a kitchen chair. Next, I looked to the tree, and beneath it sat my brother and sister, who hurried me to join them so presents could be opened. But, beneath the tree also sat not only a wonderful green sled but also present upon present, wrapped in colorful paper, some in newspaper comics.

I was beside myself in disbelief. Where had all these presents come from? I was dumbfounded and looked to Mother, but in the same second, I understood clearly that Santa had come. I am certain that I did not give it a second thought. Christmas had come.

My brother handed me my first present. It was wrapped in colorful comic strip newspaper and tied with ribbon. I opened it and found sandpaper. I looked with some disbelief to my parents who were laughing; it was intended for my father. Each present was addressed to the wrong person.

Whether it was by intuition or conspiracy, my aunt Cleo from far away Spokane, Washington, had the day before mailed us the box of presents. She and her children had gathered together an unusual assortment of presents and wrapped them, but they had addressed each to an unlikely person.

Besides the sandpaper and sled, most of that Christmas morning is lost to me, but I clearly remember one more detail of importance. It is a miniature portrait in my mind of Dad and Mom seated at the sideboard. Dad is seated to the left of Mother, his left leg crossing his right at the knee, his cup of coffee still in his right hand and his left arm hugging Mother, and Mother is laughing.

Seldom is a memory so easily recalled. It does happen, however, and most of us have early memories in which a single theme emerges brilliantly. It isn't the box of presents coming unexpectedly, although I have referred to the whole event as "my sandpaper Christmas." It isn't Father bringing home the strange man, although that remains a tender reminder of responsibility to do what we can do for those facing an emergency.

No, it happened the evening before when Dad introduced a stranger to our Christmas Eve meal, and Mother placed another plate at our table. In that act, she gave over to hospitality that which still rings across the American West.

The ease with which she agreed with Father had to have put the man at greater ease to accept. We children were provided a silent lesson of giving which no number of present giving could equal. Now that I am much older, with children of my own, I appreciate all the more Mother's acceptance of

Father's judgment. It was the generosity characteristic then not to be questioned. Questioning Father would have exposed doubt not just of him but also about the goodness of all mankind. It would have hampered the Christmas spirit. Now, I know she was merely being polite to a stranger. It isn't any more complicated than that. Mom and Dad gave the man a Christmas he would not easily forget.

To Hope and Pray

Candy Chand

My mother was, to me, the greatest example of love, kindness, tenderness and self-sacrifice. She was the truest teacher of fairness that I have ever known, and not a day goes by that I do not miss her in my life.

I grew up in a home my parents bought just before I was born. My childhood was filled with tiny moments of caring and love—hot cocoa and cookies on a rainy afternoon, warm smiles and a pat on the back whenever I needed one. And when I grew up and moved to a house to start my own life, I didn't go far—just a few miles away. I hoped that I would be able to share my parents' love with my own children and give them the same feeling of safety and security that I'd grown up with.

But as I drove through the rain one December afternoon in 1989, all of that security seemed to be dissolving, washing away with every raindrop that fell. My mother was dying of lung cancer.

Christmas was my mother's favorite time of the year. Oh, she'd sometimes complain about the hectic season she was having, but our family tree was always carefully decorated with her prized ornaments, and I knew she took great pride in having such a special tree.

Please, God, I prayed as I drove through the rain that day, *please let my mother live through one more Christmas.* I pulled into a crowded shopping mall parking lot. *I'm not ready to let her go, and I need her here with me.* My heart was not up to shopping for presents that day, but I selected a gift or two for my husband and daughter. I knew I shouldn't let my own feelings of impending loss spoil the holiday for my young family.

In the center of an aisle stood a large display of Christmas ornaments. I thought an ornament might be a cheerful gift for my mother, something that would reconnect her with her love for Christmas and give her some hope. Once again, my thoughts took the form of prayers, and I prayed that the gift of a simple ornament would give her the hope to see this blessed day one more time. One ornament on the display stood out in particular. I was drawn to a beautiful satin and pearl-encrusted heart. I removed it from the display and walked over to the cash register, pleased with my choice. As I laid it on the counter, I turned it over. And there, outlined in seed pearls on the back of the ornament, was the word "hope."

I stared at the ornament in disbelief. This was surely a sign that my mother, too, would receive hope from my gift and was meant to survive long enough to share one more Christmas with us.

I rushed to her house with the ornament, so eager to give it to her and tell her the story that I didn't even stop to wrap it. Clutching the plastic bag to my chest, I breathlessly told her my story. I told her what hope meant to me. She smiled quietly as she listened to my tangled tale, and then she carefully hung the glimmering ornament on the big Christmas tree that stood in the corner of the living room.

But her hope was not the same as mine. As Christmas grew closer, my mother began to tell me that her desire was to die before Christmas came. She feared being ill over the holiday and forever filling our future holidays with sorrow. I assured her that all my father, my daughter and I wanted was for her to be with us for one last Christmas, sick or well. But she was insistent. "I hope to die before Christmas."

And she did. On December 7 of that year, my mother passed away, ending her long struggle against cancer. I buried the satin and pearl ornament with her. She left me, her only daughter, not only saddened but also confused.

Hadn't my prayers helped me find the "hope" ornament as a sign that she would survive, through a Christmas miracle? As the months after her death passed, I slowly began to realize that in the end, God in His wisdom had answered my mother's prayer, not mine.

The Gift of the Magi

April Kutger

—◦❊◦—

The lawn was the color of straw. The rented house was a bland, mustard-colored ranch style on a curved street plotted out with other ranch houses with straw-colored lawns thanks to water use restrictions. A dry fall. The rolling hills that should have been turning green remained a fire danger. Less than a hundred dollars in the bank and Christmas just around the corner. Nothing new.

I was a single mother who worked in a city across a bridge, taking the train early in the morning, coming back after the winter darkness had fallen. My children were used to a few toys and *always* a book from Santa Claus, although they really knew I was the jolly old fellow. I counted on their grandmother and a few friends and coworkers to fill in the gaps.

But my mother had died only two months before. I was still grieving, crying unexpectedly, telling stories about her and listening to my children's memories, leafing through albums with pictures of her. Holding me on my christening day, putting me on the bus on my first day of school, standing beside me in my cap and gown, helping me put on my veil before my wedding, holding each of my children on their christening days.

Children are always bright-eyed on Christmas morning no matter what they get, even if it's cheap, plastic water guns and flimsy, balsa wood airplanes from a charity. One friend had bought the boys Evel Knievel action figures *with* motor-cycles. A small thing, but I knew Joby and Benjie would love them. Every boy under the age of twelve loved Evel Knievel. I planned to get a baby doll for Tana. She of the pursed-lip smile and shy eyes was a little old for baby dolls, but who cares; she liked playing mother. Maybe because she hardly had one herself.

I walked up the hill from the train station. A few blocks of solitude before the onslaught of noisy children and din-ner to fix. I walked slowly, head down. I knew the route by heart. Where all the cracks in the sidewalk were. How many paces until the curb. Which houses had barking dogs behind chain-link fences. I was wearing my plum wool suit and black pumps, very professional. But anyone who passed me on that evening would have thought I had gone a little crazy. I was muttering to myself. Actually, I was praying for a miracle. What kind of miracle, I didn't know. I wouldn't be getting a Christmas bonus, and I didn't expect to win any contests—hadn't entered any. No very-late-arriving tax returns. But I believed in miracles. After all, it was Christmas. My kids were shining children. God had to want to bless them.

I opened the mailbox before I went in and found the regu-lar miscellany, including offers for car insurance and Christ-mas sale advertisements. A few Christmas cards. And a slim, business-sized envelope with handwriting I recognized. Someone I hadn't heard from for more than a year—my dad. We were estranged. We'd been estranged off and on for most of my life. Knowing him, it could have been a tirade of criticism. What kind of life was I living? Why didn't I go back to school? What kind of person was I? And again, why didn't I make my ex-husband support his children? Maybe if I knew where he was! The car he had given me sat unused in my driveway. A twenty-year-old gold monstrosity that feasted on gasoline and needed an alternator. Great present, Dad. I knew I'd never hear the end of that sacrificial generosity. I'd open that envelope last. Maybe I wouldn't open it at all.

Children overflowing. Hugs and stories to tell. "Wanda threw a rock at me."

"I won the math quiz."

"Mr. Wilson needs you to sign this." And hungry eyes. I needed a glass of wine. I needed to get out of my work clothes, especially the panty hose that left welts around my waistline and always worked their way down below my hips. God, I hated them. I washed the "lady" makeup off, ending with a splash of cold water and the whinny of a pony. I put on my nightgown, the big flannel one faded to a pink so pale that you might have thought it was white. One elbow was liberated; the fabric was so exhausted that it had just worn through. But it was comfortable, and there was certainly no man to see me looking like a frump.

On to the business of the evening. Leftover chili. No prep needed. Cornbread. Only twenty-five minutes to mix and bake. My wine. From one of the 1.5-liter bottles that cost less than five dollars. A girl has to find solace where she may. Check the homework. Make sure Joby finished all of his. Sometimes he lies. Showers. The boys shared. Had to save water. Not because there was a shortage, we just had to save on everything. Then a half hour of television. My parents had never let my sisters and me watch TV on school nights, but I needed the peace and quiet of diverted minds.

I sat on my bed and opened the mail. Bills I couldn't afford to pay until my next paycheck. A Christmas card from a friend I hadn't seen for at least ten years. It was a beautiful photograph of a perfect family dressed in matching red sweaters sitting in front of a fire, a perfectly decorated Christmas tree next to them. Was it staged? No. I knew it was their home. Why couldn't they send a card without a picture? A card from my sister with Bible text quoted. Her own message: "May you have a blessed Christmas." The "you" was underlined twice, the "blessed" three times. I guess she really meant it.

Finally, the letter from Dad. I already knew what it would be written on. Five-by-seven-inch notepaper with a crest and the exorbitant title he had carried in his final government job. Jeez. He still wore a concealed weapon under his old flight suit on the days I visited him. Talk about men who can't give up their jobs.

Dad's second wife had forced him to retire. When the war ended, she had to leave Thailand where she had lived a life of luxury, holding court for ambassadors and consulates in tuxedos and dress whites and their wives in handmade silk shantung gowns that cost a dollar. Life back in the United States on some military installation would not suit her. She'd been there and done that. For five years in the late fifties, they'd lived in officers quarters on McConnell Air Force Base in godforsaken Kansas while Dad kept the country prepared to bomb Russia.

So, what was it this time? Same paper. But, oh my God, a check! His note said, "Merry Christmas. Love, Dad." Jeez Louise. When was the last time my dad gave me money? At least ten years ago, and that was like pulling teeth. If I hadn't been close to eviction, I never would have asked him.

The check was for $500. My heart leapt. I flew into the living room. "Guess what? We got money for Christmas!"

Christmas morning wasn't overflowing. I paid off some bills with part of the money, left a hundred in my checking account. But we were as happy as newborn kittens. Tana didn't get a baby doll—she got a coveted Sasha doll with three outfits. I dressed Sasha in her pajamas and terry-cloth robe and slippers and laid her in bed next to Tana so she would see her when she woke up. "I got a Sasha doll, Mom!" I think Tana believed in Santa Claus for a minute. The boys got a football, real team football shirts and metal, cylinder storage bins with their favorite teams' symbols on them. Joby's was the Miami Dolphins, Benjie's the San Diego Chargers. Of course, each child received a book. Traditions must be carried on, or they aren't really traditions.

I had given five dollars each to Tana, Joby and Benjie to buy presents for one another. The nearby toy store had tubs in which each small toy was a dollar or less. Whistles. Plastic rings with giant rubies and diamonds. Lifelike black, plastic spiders. Yo-yos. Joby gave Tana a tiny, pink baby, the kind they put in Mardi Gras cakes; Benjie gave her a doll hairbrush. He couldn't have known the Sasha doll had long, brown hair. Tana could braid her doll's hair to match her own tangled mess. Joby received fake blood and a cricket that I knew would drive me crazy. Benjie got a compass the size of a quarter with an arrow that never stood still and a striped, wooden top. Not the greatest haul, but the givers were proud, and the receivers were truly excited and grateful.

But the best gifts on that Christmas morning were the ones I received.

My friend Ozzie had sold Tana a garage-sale wooden chair for exactly two dollars and fifty-six cents, her change after buying presents for her brothers. She knew I needed one for my sewing table, and Ozzie helped her paint it with bright yellow lacquer. Tana was up before me on Christmas morning. Aren't all kids? She retrieved the canary chair from our neglected garage and placed it next to our popcorn-and-cranberry-strung tree. Across the chair's spindled back was a big red-and-green plaid bow that Ozzie had supplied along with the chair and paint. There were rolling-on-the-floor hugs and plenty of tears.

A few weeks before Christmas, Joby had asked me what I wanted. I said, "Oh, you don't have to give me a present."

"No, Mom, what do you really want?"

"Maybe a new spatula." Thinking bigger, I said, "Or an alternator for the car."

"Not something you need, Mom. If you could have anything, what would you ask for?"

There *was* something I really wanted. On the low side of the price range between a spatula and an alternator. "I'd like a clock radio." I wanted to be able to wake up to music instead of a blasted buzzer.

That was the end of the conversation.

On Christmas morning, Joby handed me a haphazardly wrapped box large enough to hold a cowboy hat. I held it to my ear and gently shook it. Something knocked around inside.

"Don't shake it, Mom," he cried.

Dark-eyed Joby was bouncing with delight before I even opened the box. Inside was his own clock radio. Scuffed up a little, some fingerprints, a smudge that looked like tar, but I knew it worked. My mother had given it to him the year before. I started to blubber. For my mother and for my little O'Henry son.

But that wasn't the end of it.

Seven-and-a-half-year-old Benjie handed me a card in a white envelope with "Mom" written on the front. "This is my present for you, Mom." He stepped back and smiled tentatively. I noticed that his ringleted head was badly in need of a haircut.

I pulled out a blue Hallmark sympathy card with a picture of a dove.

On the front, the flourishing script read, "We are thinking of you with deepest sympathy. Those we love are with the Lord and He has promised to be with us. If they are with Him and He is with us…they cannot be far away."

Inside: "Though our words of understanding are inadequate and few, our hearts are filled with loving thoughts and sympathy for you."

Then Benjie's penciled closing:
"Love Benjie
and Merry C—
hrismas."

Now my Christmas dinners are made for seventeen; my children and their spouses have given me nine wild grandsons and a princess of a granddaughter. Telling the story of the year of the chair, the clock radio and the card of sympathy has become a Christmas tradition, along with a book for everyone on Christmas morning. The Christmas miracle I had prayed for as I walked home from the train in that dry, winter twilight did not come in the form of a $500 check from my father. My Christmas miracle was found in the kind and generous hearts of my shining children who knew that Christmas was not about what they received but about what they gave.

Homeless Santa

Jennifer Basye Sander

———•◦✕◦•———

A crummy 1988 was winding down as my roommate, Margaret, and I set out for an afternoon snack on Christmas Eve. I'd just returned to California after a dark three months of hiding in the Swedish woods in my own private Ingmar Bergman film after a star-crossed romance. My arrival home had been as dramatic as my sudden departure some months before. I was booked on a Pan Am flight from London to San Francisco. Having been away from home for so long, I told myself that if I missed the flight, I would take the next available one to the United States, Pan Am 103. I made my flight with just minutes to spare. Passengers for the San Francisco flight were checking in at a counter directly across from the New York flight, and I absentmindedly joined the New York line. When I noticed my mistake, I joked about it with the folks near me in that line and made my way across the room to the other flight counter.

As my parents drove me home from the airport over slow-moving California freeways, they told me about the midair explosion of Flight 103 over Lockerbie, Scotland. "But I saw those people," I said. "How can they all be dead?" My dreams that night were haunted by the image of the Scottish countryside strewn with carefully packed Christmas gifts, steamed puddings from Harrods and little piles of the Christmas candy that an airport Santa had handed to everyone waiting in the security line.

When I woke on Christmas Eve morning, yes, I was back home, but it was a strange sensation. I felt tentative, oddly disconnected from what was going on around me. I'd come home after an absence of months, but I didn't feel like I'd come home in one piece.

Craving the taste of authentic Mexican food after so much Swedish butter and cream, Margaret and I chose to head for a ramshackle burrito house in a dicey part of town. Near the train tracks and several homeless shelters, it was not the part of town you'd expect to find two middle-class girls on Christmas Eve. We ordered our burritos and sat outside in the sun to wait for our order. The streets around us were deserted; office workers and commuters had gone home to get an early start on the holiday.

Margaret nudged my arm. "Oh, great," she said. "Looks like we're about to get hit up for money." A disheveled man was making his way toward us across the parking lot, his progress slowed both by his age and by the oversized, green sack he carried on his back. His hair was long and snowy white, his thick beard spread over the top of his tattered jacket. Margaret and I clucked our tongues and shook our heads and began to search our pockets for loose change to disperse him quickly and get on with our meal.

Slowly and quietly, he made his way across the blacktop until he was standing in front of us. He stopped, and without saying a word, he rolled his heavy bag off his shoulder and set it on the ground. Untying the top, he reached in and began to rummage through the contents of his bag. Margaret and I watched quietly as he found what he was seeking and removed his hand. He held a shiny, red apple. With great dignity, he held it out to Margaret. She accepted his gift.

He reached into his duffel bag a second time and this time pulled out a candy bar and offered it to me. "No," I said. "We can't take your food. You need it!" She and I both held our gifts back out to him. "We can't take your food."

The man smiled shyly and shook his head. "I can't eat it," he said sadly. "My teeth are no good. Merry Christmas."

He would not accept the money we tried to give him that afternoon; he just kept quietly shaking his head and smiling as we tried to press dollar bills into his hand. Finally, he agreed to the purchase of a cup of coffee. He took the steaming foam cup and, shouldering his bag once again, continued on his way.

I have told this story many times since it happened, and every time I shake my head. I think about the quiet man with the big, white beard and the bag of presents who gave two privileged girls part of the only food he had. It would have been so easy for us to get up and move inside of the café that day, avoiding someone who looked scary. I am so thankful that we stayed where we were, sitting on the porch fence, open to what life could teach us. The burrito house has long since been torn down, but every time I drive past the spot, I give silent thanks to the man with the generous heart. He reminds me that we should all give openly and often to everyone we meet, every chance we get, 365 days of the year.

★ ★ ★ ★ ★

A Kiss
Under the
Mistletoe

Introduction

Jennifer Basye Sander

---•◦✕◦•---

A kiss under the mistletoe? Who doesn't want that? We all long for it, a quick kiss and a tight hug in a hallway, or a longer, lingering kiss in a darkened living room... Hmm, it must be December, and Christmas must be coming.

Yes, Christmas is a wonderful time of year, a time when the whole world seems to be decorated with pretty lights and people smile for no reason and do kind things for strangers and exchange really great gifts. But Christmas may also be a time of great strain for married couples—fights over how much was spent at the mall, whose turn it is to mix the eggnog and "What happened to the directions for assembling this bicycle?" It may also be a time of great strain for couples who are dating—lots of time to worry about what type of gift might be appropriate for someone you've only known a few months, questions about whether she should invite him home to meet her parents and whose apartment should have a tree. Oh dear.

Instead, why not focus on the amazing opportunities for accepting love at this time of year? I have gathered up twenty-six stories of love, romance and connections at Christmas from writers around the country. Some are funny, some are sweet and some are heartbreaking, but all of them show that if our hearts are open to giving and receiving love during this special season, incredible things can happen. From a snowy impromptu game of Frisbee in the center of a holiday light display to a woman's trepidation as she arrives home on Christmas Eve with crates of rescued shelter dogs, these stories will help get you in the mood for love in your own life. Blind dates, well-chosen gifts and even a crumpled holiday card can make our hearts sing at a time when our world is festively lit and celebration surrounds us. Look around you— love is there, yours for the asking…

May all your dreams come true and all your romantic wishes be granted.

Merry Christmas!

Two to Tango

Teri Wilson

———•◦✕◦•———

A breathless four months into our dating relationship and before we were married, my future husband and I gave each other the same Valentine's Day card. I opened mine first, and when I saw the familiar Shakespeare verse on the front of the card, my heart raced.

"What is it?" he asked, narrowing his gaze at the giddy smile on my face.

I didn't bother answering. I just pushed his red envelope toward him. "Open yours."

He broke the seal and his hands froze. He looked back up at me. "We gave each other the same card."

"I know. Crazy, right?" I smiled.

We both smiled.

I don't remember exactly what we said or did next. The details are a bit fuzzy after nearly two decades. But I don't think either of us ascribed any huge, earth-shattering meaning to it. We were in love…so in love that we'd chosen the same special card. We were giddy with the effervescent newness of each other, and now we had a glaringly obvious example of what a perfect fit we were. End of story.

Until it happened again.

The following Valentine's Day, my husband opened his card first. This time, he stared at it for a long, quiet moment before he looked up.

When his gaze met mine, he was clearly shell-shocked. "You're not going to believe this."

"No," I said, reaching for my card.

No way. We lived in the seventh-largest city in the United States. We hadn't even bought our cards at the same store. What were the odds of this happening two years in a row?

Yet when I opened the pink envelope, there I found a card identical to the one I'd chosen for him. Again. Something special was happening. I could feel it. I gazed down at Bouguereau's romantic painting of Cupid and Psyche on the front of the card, and found it more beautiful than I ever had before. I felt as though, like Psyche, I had butterfly wings, and could float straight up into the clouds.

Less than three weeks later, my husband proposed. After I'd said yes and wiped happy tears from my eyes, he told me that he'd known we belonged together the moment he opened that second card. He thought God was trying to tell him something, so he wasted no time before slipping a glittering diamond on my finger.

For years afterward, I held my breath every time I opened a card from my husband. Fifteen Valentine's Days, fifteen Christmases and fifteen wedding anniversaries came and went, but we never again gave each other duplicate cards.

I tried not to think too much about it. Obviously, it couldn't keep happening year after year. That would be impossible.

And at least we were still giving each other cards. I knew plenty of married couples our age who'd ceased giving each other cards and gifts altogether. We still did these things.

Granted, after fifteen-plus years it becomes rather difficult to surprise someone. Typically, I chose gifts for my husband that I knew he wanted—things he'd mentioned in passing, or pointed out in catalogs. Until the Christmas I decided to really go out on a limb.

"I'm thinking of getting my husband something kind of crazy for Christmas," I said to my friend, Bess, as we stood in line at the movie theater one chilly December evening.

She glanced up from her popcorn. "Oh, really? What?"

"Tango lessons." I bounced on my toes and waited for her reaction. I was sure she'd be awed.

She wasn't.

There was an awkward pause. Then finally, "Tango lessons?"

"Yes. It will be romantic, don't you think?" I nodded, willing her to agree with me.

"Sure." She snickered into her popcorn.

She didn't sound so sure. In fact, she didn't sound sure at all. And my own certainty began to slip away.

I mentioned the tango lessons to two more of my friends, each of whom had the same reaction. By the third uncomfortable pause, I'd really started to doubt myself.

"Do you think he'll be surprised?" I said into the phone.

My oldest friend, Christy, was on the other end. She'd known my husband even longer than she'd known me, so I figured this was my last chance for someone to tell me what a brilliant idea I'd had. "Oh, I think he'll definitely be surprised."

"In a good way?"

"*My* husband would be mortified. But I don't know…yours might actually like it. Has he ever mentioned wanting to learn how to tango?"

I swallowed. "Sort of."

Once.

He'd mentioned it once.

We'd been watching *Dancing with the Stars,* because that's what people who've been married for fifteen years do on Monday nights. It was tango night, which was always one of our favorites. My husband sat on the sofa with a bowl of peanuts in his lap, while I curled up in my chair with one of our dogs.

"That looks really fun." I sighed dreamily at the television, where Derek Hough and his partner were getting their scores from the judges. Perfect tens across the board.

My husband cracked open a peanut and popped it in his mouth. "I read an article once that said ballroom dance lessons will make you fall in love with your spouse all over again."

I slid my gaze toward him, wondering where this thought had come from. Was he just making conversation? Or did he think we needed to fall in love all over again? And, if so, was this the sort of thing we just casually discussed now over peanuts and reality television?

Two years had passed since this short conversation, but I still didn't share it with Christy. "He mentioned something about it once. A long time ago."

"Then he'll probably be into it." She didn't sound altogether convincing.

With only four days left until Christmas, I drove to the ballroom dance school I'd found on the internet. I had to stop myself from taking a detour to Best Buy along the way to buy something safer. What man wouldn't be happy with something like a big-screen television? But we already had a giant television. We didn't, however, know how to tango.

The door to the ballroom dance studio opened to a huge, mirrored room with smooth, wood floors. Music filled the air—a cha-cha, if my *Dancing with the Stars* education had taught me anything. There was a tall Christmas tree in the window beside a matching his-and-hers set of rhinestone-bedecked ballroom dance costumes. I tried to imagine my husband in the room, wearing even a few sequins. I failed.

"May I help you?" The man sitting at the desk at the back of the enormous room smiled at me.

I thought about fleeing. Then a couple appeared in the center of the room and started to dance. I wondered if they were married, or if they were engaged and were learning how to dance for their upcoming wedding. Oddly enough, I couldn't tell. When was the last time someone mistook my husband and me for an engaged couple? Had anyone *ever* made that mistake?

As I watched the dancers, a certain wistfulness came over me. I was reminded of my husband's comment.

Ballroom dance lessons will make you fall in love with your spouse all over again.

Seeing the elegant, happy couple glide across the smooth, wood floor, I became a believer.

I wrote a check for a package of four private lessons. It was a sizable check. Not big-screen TV sizable, but close. And the lessons had to be used by March, so if my husband wasn't thrilled with his gift, it looked as if I would be learning how to tango all by myself.

I wrapped the gift certificate in a box, to make it look like any other gift. It sat innocently under the tree until Christmas Eve, and I was sure my husband thought it was something completely ordinary, like a tie or a pair of socks. If my hands shook when I handed him the box, he didn't seem to notice.

He peeled away the wrapping paper, lifted the lid and found the plain white envelope beneath the layers of tissue paper.

My heart hammered as he lifted the seal. He slid the gift certificate from the envelope and stared at it without uttering a word.

"Dance lessons," I said to fill the excruciating quiet. "I thought we could learn to tango. Doesn't that sound fun?"

"It does." He cleared his throat.

My heart sank. He hadn't reacted with horror, as some of my friends had predicted, but he didn't seem exactly thrilled, either. He was pensive. Quiet. Too quiet.

"Here, open yours." He handed me a perfectly wrapped box tied with a silver ribbon.

Disappointment coursed through me as I untied the bow. I'd wanted this Christmas to be special. Different. Romantic.

I opened my gift. Inside was a plain white envelope. As I lifted it out of the box, my heart fluttered in a familiar way I hadn't experienced in a long, long time. I searched my husband's gaze.

"Open it," he whispered.

I did. "Dance lessons? You gave me dance lessons, too?"

He took me in his arms. "I guess it really does take two to tango."

In the soft glow of the lights from the Christmas tree, I kissed my husband. As our lips met, I imagined the two of us dancing on that smooth, wood floor to the dangerous, sultry beat of a tango. And I sent up a silent prayer of thanks that even after all the years, God was still trying to tell us something.

The Dress

Sheryl J. Bize Boutte

———••◦✕◦••———

By the mid-1960s my parents had four school-aged daughters to support and a fifth change-of-life daughter on the way. Birthday and Christmas gifts were often new clothes to supplement outgrown or worn-out school clothes, although we would also get the begged-for doll, bike or skates. Sometimes we got something special: something homemade, handed down or handed over that always gave a unique and precious feel to the celebration.

It was in this tradition on Christmas Day in 1966, while the lights on the aluminum tree changed from blue to green to red and back again, that my mother gave me the gift. Referring to me by my "old soul" nickname, she said, "This is especially for you, Grandma," as she handed me a gold-ribboned box.

Inside was a simple frock; a multicolored, multiflowered shirtwaist dress with a wide belt and a full skirt. It was clearly a gently worn hand-me-down from one of my mother's wealthy acquaintances, but I rushed up to my room immediately to try it on. The bottom of the hem hit just below my knobby knees and fit my still-growing fifteen-year-old body perfectly. It was a spring dress, of course, but I could not wait to wear it to school when the holidays were over.

That next Monday I dressed with a new sense of pride and, in my mind, womanly elegance. My fingers were already turning the front doorknob when my mother's voice called out, "Girl, don't you know it's *January?* You are going to catch pneumonia in that thin little dress!" But I was halfway down the street and around the corner on my way to school before she could finish her warning. My inaugural wearing of this dress would also be the day a seventeen-year-old boy would look out his window from the third house on the right and see me for the first time.

I wore The Dress much too often, but I had never had anything like it. It had the power to make my teenage self feel like a big, grown-up lady, and it quickly became the favorite in my sparse wardrobe. It also made that neighbor boy wait for me to pass his house each day and then fall into step behind me. He walked behind me, stealthily and silently, for the five blocks to school for the rest of the school year. A bookworm and a loner, I was totally inside my own head as I made my way, and I never once thought to look back.

Months later the forces emanating from The Dress would give that boy the courage to ring my doorbell.

"Hi, I'm Anthony from down the street. Does the girl with the flowery dress live here?" he asked the sister who answered the door. Rolling her eyes, she said, "You must be looking for Sheryl. She is always wearing that old-timey dress."

From that day forward, Anthony, the boy who had been my silent and unseen companion, became my boyfriend and, soon after that, my fiancé.

On a beautiful spring day in 1971, we married in the living room of my family home with only our parents, my grandmother and a few friends in attendance. I did not wear The Dress, choosing instead an elegant nonflowery peach chiffon and silk, the perfect complement to my new husband's ruffled peach shirt and coordinating bow tie. Our reception consisted of postwedding photos taken in my parent's park-like backyard, while our few guests dined on crustless tuna and chicken salad sandwiches cut into little squares accompanied by Mumm's extra-dry champagne.

The years passed as we settled into married life, our college graduations, career building and then child rearing. Anthony and I were so destined to be together that people came to refer to us as "Sheryl and Anthony" or "Anthony and Sheryl," as though they could not bring themselves to separate our names. Friends would say, "If you see one you see the other" and actually seemed proud to know a couple that had been high school sweethearts. Our love for each other remained strong and true, but after a time, The Dress that had brought us together became so faded that the flowers were barely visible, and so threadbare that it was no longer wearable. Tearfully, I threw it away.

A thoughtful gift-giver, Anthony would often come home on my birthday, our anniversary or Christmas with a ribbon-tied box containing an exquisite dress, suit or shoes from a small boutique he claimed as his territory for his gifts to me. Once he presented me with a beautiful white suit, and when I asked what the occasion was, he replied, "Because it's Tuesday." He always chose the correct size and only stopped the practice when his boutique of choice went out of business.

But of all the wonderful clothes he bought for me, he never found anything as special as The Dress had been.

Then one rainy December day, while flipping through a Christmas catalog, I saw it. A multiflowered shirtwaist dress with a white background, a full skirt and a wide belt. Could it be? I ordered it immediately. When it arrived I was a bit disappointed to find that the fabric had an unworn stiffness, the flowers were not as vibrant and the belt was a skinnier version of its beloved predecessor. But after so many years of The Dress drought, I decided this dress and I would make a pact to stay together, even though we both knew the relationship would never be ideal.

Anthony loved me in this dress, even though I knew it for the poseur it was. And because he loved it, I wore it to work and out to dinner. I wore it to the movies and to the supermarket. I wore it with a shawl in the spring and with boots and a jacket in the winter. I continued to wear it after our daughter was born in 1977, and I was surprised yet happy that, after I punched an extra hole in the belt for just a bit more room, it continued to fit. I wore it through my daughter's early school years and into her entry to junior high. After she told me how much she liked it, I wore it even more. Still, through all that, this dress could not convince me that it was The One.

Since I could never get enough of how happy it made my family, over time the dress and I had settled into an easy truce. I came to accept the fact that it could not help me to recapture the feelings I had had when I wore the anointed original. And it seemed to know that, although it was not The Dress, my family's reactions would make it a most treasured piece.

After nineteen years of wear, I put the dress on one day and discovered I could no longer easily button it. Could I loosen the belt, perhaps? No, I had run out of room for more belt holes. Not wanting to give in to the truth, I buttoned the dress and fastened the belt anyway, breaking a fingernail to the quick as I did so. The dress countered my determination with sharp and intense rib pain that took away my ability to breathe. We stood at loggerheads in the mirror for a few seconds before I gave in and feverishly began to free myself from its grip. My disappearing waistline and the dress had finally conspired to betray me. With mixed emotions, I knew we would have to part ways.

As loved ones became new angels and babies were born, so too my Christmases came and went. They were always special and filled with the joy of being with family and friends. Christmas Day would always find my famous Creole gumbo bubbling on the stove and my homemade cinnamon rolls in the oven.

Christmas Day 2010 Anthony presented me with a large golden box wrapped with a golden bow. Weeks earlier we'd decided that because we felt so blessed, we would forgo gift buying that year. I was both surprised and somewhat annoyed that he had broken the pact and, with pursed lips, I launched into a protest, "But I thought we weren't going to…" Smiling that same smile he'd worn on my parents' front porch so many years ago, Anthony waved off my objections and said, "Just open it!" I peeled off wrapping paper printed with the words "Zell's Vintage" and opened the box.

Inside was a simple frock.

A multicolored, multiflowered shirtwaist dress with a wide belt and a full skirt.

With moist eyes and a choke in his voice, Anthony whispered, "No matter how many years pass, you will always be the girl I followed to school." Anthony and Sheryl and Sheryl and Anthony were still here, and The Dress was once again back for Christmas.

Two Trees

Chels Knorr

———◦⟨✕⟩◦———

My husband, Tyler, and I have two different ideas about the nostalgia of Christmas trees. He remembers Douglas fir. I remember polyvinyl chloride. His were carefully chosen. Mine was 90 percent off at Target's after-Christmas sale. He remembers the aroma of pine. I remember the smell of dust from the attic. This means that my first real Christmas tree–shopping experience was in the Home Depot Garden Center when I was twenty-five and a newlywed, and still trying to figure out how I, we, wanted to do this "Christmas thing" as a new family.

I have listened to my husband tell many stories about Christmas as he tries to show me why having a real Christmas tree is so important. He tells me about being bundled up in the bed of the pickup truck with his sister. He tells me about visiting five or six lots to find the perfect tree. He tells me about complimentary candy canes, and his father, spinning the trees around like ballerinas for his mother to examine. He tells me about returning to the first lot trying to find the almost-perfect tree they had passed on a few hours before, when their standards were higher.

From my understanding, shopping for a real Christmas tree is a lot like shopping for IKEA furniture—buying it is only half the process.

Tyler and I carry our first Christmas tree inside and put it into the cleanest room in our house, despite the mess of dirt and sap and needles. He tells me about his father holding the tree, and the impatient conversations between his parents trying to get the tree to stand up straight, about his dad crawling to tighten the eyebolt screws against the trunk, only to have the tree move and having to start the whole process all over again. He tells me about carols that turned to cussing after untangling, stringing and restringing the lights. These quibbles don't taint Tyler's memories of Christmas, though. They don't lessen his buoyant nostalgia.

At my house we left the lights wrapped around the tree from year to year just to avoid this process. Having an artificial tree all my life was a remedy for more than just my dad's allergies. It was a remedy for conflict. There was no cold. No indecision. No mess. And with the lights already wrapped, no fighting. Conflict, I believe, would have strained my family's Christmas memories, so we created our own version of nostalgia. The American family stereotype of Tyler's experience is so sharply contrasted to my, also very American, experience. Mine didn't involve getting a new tree every year. There was no process of starting over.

So here I am, the second Christmas as a married woman, and we're Christmas tree shopping at Home Depot in the cold. I'm told this isn't the way tree shopping should be. We're not bundled up, this is our first and only lot, and there are no candy canes. But it feels real to me. The place is covered in pine needles and it smells like Christmas. We haul the tree home and bicker about whether it is standing up straight and which way to face it so the bald spots don't show. We wrap and rewrap the lights. We try to evenly space ornaments and smooth the wrinkles in the felt tree skirt.

I am seeing there is something refreshing about tree shopping every December, year after year. Real trees are forgiving. We start from the beginning, with clean carpet and pungent pine. We do not have to reexamine the mistakes of last year's light wrapping. We do not have to breathe the dust of past errors. Each year we get a blank slate.

We don't have kids yet, so I'm not sure how this Christmas thing will work once we do. I do know we will continue to have a real Christmas tree—a new one each year. We will unfold our own traditions. There will be bundling, and scouting and leveling and decorating. We will argue about whether it's straight and about bald spots. But we'll never argue about the process of starting over.

Velveteen Boyfriend

Marsha Porter

———◆◆◆◆———

At nearly sixteen, I was in love with an older man. Richard, with his long, dark-brown hair and soulful brown eyes, was nearly seventeen. He was the strong, silent type, and I was a talkaholic. I loved to share every detail of my day at my all-girls high school during our nightly phone calls. He said little, offering an occasional "Yeah" or "Sure." For all I knew, he could have been walking away from the phone to watch a ball game and only returning to offer an intermittent affirmation.

It was at my first high school dance, more than a year before, that we met. After that, we were an item and, though he lived on the other side of town, we managed to see each other every week.

My sophomore year, I focused many of our one-sided conversations on the English teacher I adored, Sister Margery. We were reading *The Catcher in the Rye* and the theme was being real. I jumped on Holden's antiphony bandwagon and began ferreting out any phonies in my school or the world at large. Naturally, I shared my observations with my beloved, and even a grunt from his end of the line encouraged me to continue with details and examples galore.

If Holden's descriptions of his boarding-school classmates wasn't an advanced course in phoniness detection, then his New York odyssey made the distinction between fake and real even more clear.

I was convinced that Sister Margery, who seemed to see into the hearts of her teenage students, was a mystical mind reader. The discussions she led made us squirm, question and grow simultaneously. It was the children's novel *The Velveteen Rabbit* by Margery Williams, though, that hit the idea of being real right out of the ballpark for me. I told Richard that my teacher brought a book full of pictures to class. It looked like it was for kids, but I assured him that it contained very adult themes.

I was so impressed by Margery Williams's classic that I couldn't stop talking about it. I even wondered if my inspirational teacher was the same Margery who'd written it. When I found out she could not have been born when it was originally published in 1922, I was sure that her chosen nun name, Margery, was a tribute to my now-favorite author.

I began to quote, paraphrase and adapt Williams's ideas in my nightly talkathons with, or perhaps *to,* Richard. I used these ideas to convey my growing love to him. The very idea that someone on the other end of the line was allowing me to share my every thought, from the inane to the insightful, was irresistible. Today I'd compare it to the crush one develops for a counselor or psychiatrist.

I'd say, "The book says 'When a child loves you for a long, long time, not just to play with, but *really* loves you, then you become real.' That's just like us! We've been together forever (nearly a lifetime: fifteen months), and we do so much more than play (translation: make out). I mean we're on the phone every night and, when we're together, we take long walks, watch movies, hang out with friends and dance. Ergo, our love has to be real!"

Richard would usually offer a one-syllable response that I took as complete agreement. He certainly never argued with me about any of my elaborate comparisons, and I loved that about him.

Next I moved on to the hurt in a relationship. Just as the Skin Horse had explained to the Velveteen Rabbit that becoming real hurts sometimes, we had experienced our share of pain. I didn't appreciate it when his mother insisted that he take the daughter of her friend to a dance, and he didn't like it when the star discus thrower invited me to his junior prom. I was convinced that dealing with pain had strengthened our love, making it more real.

The tear of the Velveteen Rabbit when he was about to be destroyed in the bonfire punctuated my point. Having this true emotion led to the rabbit's freedom and made him real to everyone. Likewise, our relationship became real to everyone when they saw us work through problems and become ever closer.

My *Velveteen Rabbit* obsession was one of many phases I went through that year, and I was not sure that Richard was especially moved by it. I was wrong; apparently, he had been listening rather closely.

On Christmas Eve, he brought me a big white box tied with a shiny gold ribbon. Inside lay a beautifully illustrated copy of *The Velveteen Rabbit* and a stuffed brown bunny with pink satin-lined ears. I hugged Richard, realizing he was actually a very good listener who understood that the book meant so much to me. Our hug led to a kiss, but he surprised me by being the first to pull away.

"You missed something."

Confused, I looked inside the now empty box. "What?"

He pulled one of the floppy bunny ears toward me. I realized that the tip had been squeezed together to hold something. Leaning in to get a closer look, I gasped. There was a delicate gold ring with a heart cut out in the center. Within the heart was a tiny diamond. It was a promise ring—all the rage at the time. Carefully pulling it from its pink satin lining, he placed it on my finger saying, "You were right about us...our love is real."

Perfect Present

Charles Kuhn

———◦❦◦———

The significance of my purchase that day didn't register on me at first.

I had spent more time than usual asking questions, trying to understand the explanations thrown back at me. Mutely, I nodded to the descriptions of pixel density, lens size, battery life, brightness and opaqueness as if fascinated by every detail. Truth be told, I wasn't.

Only one thing interested me. The price. "What was the price?" I fumed inside as the saleswoman droned on and on. I know that we men get a bad rap for not being sentimental gift givers, but in this case I really had a good reason.

Could I afford it? That was the question that I needed the answer to. Two weeks left before Christmas, and I had a set budget for this. The money had been squirreled away specifically for a gift for my wife. I knew if I didn't use it soon, the funds would be used for any one of a hundred other expenses waiting in line this time of year.

I had already taken care of the main gifts for the kids, but what about wrapping paper, stocking stuffers, pet toys that would be ripped apart in hours, if not minutes? Who knew how much those would cost? That's why these funds were reserved, emblazoned with bold black letters in my mind, for Melissa's gift. My wife, Melissa. I hadn't asked her what she wanted for Christmas. That was always a risky proposition, but one well worth taking this year.

My wife. It was still hard to believe. This was our first Christmas as a married couple; we'd just been married earlier that year. No big deal, except I was in my early fifties and she…well, suffice it to say that she was younger than me by a few years. We had both gotten out of failed long-term relationships and had met online through a political activism website which, considering that we lived in different states, made our long-term relationship even more special to both of us. It scared me sometimes, to stop and think about the odds, the long shot of our ever connecting. What would my life be without her?

The idea for her gift had come to me through long conversations with her about her likes and dislikes, previous hobbies, childhood experiences, secret ambitions and the usual silly, but memorable conversations spent in getting to know each other. Long ago she had enjoyed photography and, after a lot of encouragement and persistent badgering, had shared some of her best photos with me. She was clearly talented. I was confident in her abilities and wanted her to again pursue something that obviously meant so much to her.

Persisting in my queries, I'd learned that she had given up photography because in her last relationship she had come into constant criticism. She was told the shot was from the wrong angle. Or the light wasn't right. That the picture would turn out horribly. Tired of being criticized, she simply gave up. She finally sold her camera and, it seemed to me, she lost part of herself.

I listened as she told me the story. I heard the pain, the lost moments and the desire to take pictures again. I knew right then that I could change that part of her life and help restore her creative spark.

The next day, I went online to research digital cameras. It was new, it was exciting and it quickly became my Christmas mission. I watched holiday flyers, keeping a stringent eye out for sales and descriptions of cameras that met my requirements. On a Wednesday, I spotted the perfect camera for her. The next two days, I dropped casual comments about our need to go Christmas shopping that weekend.

We made it to the mall on Sunday. We separated inside, each heading off in our own direction, she on foot, me in my wheelchair.

This was another special ingredient of our relationship. After our first few e-mails I had explained to Melissa that I had multiple sclerosis, although I worried that this would spell the end of what seemed like the glimmerings of a love relationship. It never stopped her or scared her away. At our first date, I walked into the restaurant for lunch using a cane and promptly knocked over a strategically placed ornamental tree. We laughed, shrugged our shoulders and enjoyed the remainder of our first date, full of stories and laughter.

Now, three years later, my MS had progressed. My cane was traded in for a wheelchair, and our amusement and comfort had turned to enduring love.

Of course, by the time I wheeled myself up to the camera counter that Sunday afternoon, the camera I had targeted was already sold out. That brought me to the endless discussion I found myself in with the long-winded clerk. In the end, my budget could still handle the new selection, and I left that day feeling proud of my purchase and certain my bride would be happy.

Christmas morning rolled around, and I had managed to keep my secret. My wife unwrapped her gift and fell silent. She cautiously opened the box and extracted her new camera, never saying a word. Attaching the strap, she placed it around her neck. After fidgeting with the camera for a few moments, Melissa leaned in to me, placed her arms around my shoulders and pulled me to her face until our foreheads touched. She whispered, "Thank you. You have no idea what this means. You've just given me back a piece of myself I thought I'd lost forever."

In the days ahead, Melissa pursued her revitalized passion with zest. She photographed migrating snow geese in northern California, soaring hawks in the Central Valley, incredible blooming flowers in our neighborhood, scenic old-growth oak trees in the local park, towering pines in snowstorms in the Sierras and so many more loves in her life. Her photo gallery grew on a daily basis, as did her belief in herself. There was a mutual growth of our bond together, knowing we could help each other heal and rediscover faith and trust. It was a gift of renewal to last a lifetime.

Chains of Love

Jennifer Bern Basye

———◦◦◦✕◦◦◦———

Oh, I can see your face now, Dear Reader. Blushing a bit and thinking to yourself, "Oh no, is this one of *those* stories? The kind I keep hearing everyone else whisper about…?" Rest easy, my dears. There are no mysterious billionaires with helicopters and handcuffs in this tale, and I am far from a young college coed just learning about the world. No, far from it…

As a girl, my happiest moments were those when I'd snuggle under the covers in my small room at the top of the stairs ("It's the maid's room, you know," I would tell my friends on the school playground, hoping to conjure up a sad *Little Princess* sort of life in their minds), listening to the sound of the rain on the roof. My father would play the piano at night and the sound would drift up to the second floor. He'd play Beethoven, Bach and sometimes a little Brubeck if he was feeling jazzy after a long day at the office. And then, done playing, I could hear him turn the heavy lock on the front door on his way to join my mother for the night. Mmm, I would sigh to myself, that is what my life will be like when

I am grown. I will have a big house and a grand piano and children asleep upstairs, and they will know how much I love them and protect them when they hear the sound of a door lock turning for the night.

Well…does life ever turn out the way we think it will? In some ways my life does look an awful lot like my parents' life: I live in the same town; my friends are the children of their friends; Beethoven, Bach and Brubeck still comprise my personal sound track. But in many ways my life is far different. My parents smile and laugh and enjoy each other's company; theirs is a model marriage in all respects. And while my own marriage resulted in two delightful boys and a sixty-year-old ski cabin in Tahoe, it did not last a full two decades. Which brings us up to the present, and my sudden need to be over the mountain and through the trees a few days before Christmas.

"Okay," I told my sister, Anne, on the phone, "I can still come to the Father-Daughter Christmas lunch at Dad's club, but I will have to leave right after they clear the plates. The heater is out in Tahoe, and I have renters coming for the next two weeks. The Christmas and New Year's renters offset the mortgage payments in a big way, so if I don't get an electrician in there, I'm in trouble." Anne and I have been going to the holiday lunch with our father since we were little girls in velvet dresses and patent-leather shoes. She'd come down from the Pacific Northwest especially to be there this year, so at least I wouldn't be leaving our eighty-five-year-old dad sitting alone at the table.

The weather forecast looked…well, it looked bad. And it sounded bad when I called the recorded highway conditions line to see what they had to say about what was going on in the Sierras. Winter storm warning. That is never really the moment that you want to head up a narrow road in the forest by yourself, even if you are a woman with a four-wheel-drive Jeep.

"Have you checked the weather yet?" David, my boyfriend, asked me on the phone. "What is it supposed to be?" I was quiet. I knew exactly what the weather held, and I also had a good idea what he would say when I told him. David is a worrier. In the time we'd been a couple, I'd listened to him worry about his three grown sons, about his garden, about his Suduko score, about his roof, about his...you get the idea. He worries.

"Oh... I think it will snow," I finally offered up, closing the window on my computer that predicted a heavy storm a few hours away. "But, hey, the Jeep is four-wheel drive. So I should be just fine." Maybe I downplayed the severity of the forecast a bit, but I needed to be in South Lake Tahoe, and having him tell me I shouldn't go was literally not something I could afford to hear.

I dressed carefully for the luncheon, choosing a warm, knitted wool dress and tights (a great underlayer if I ended up getting stuck on the summit for the night), a silk scarf (I could use it to wave for help if the Jeep went into a snow-bank), low-heeled boots (because no one should drive in the Sierras in stilettos) and a cashmere throw (something to snuggle under if that whole spending-the-night-in-the-car thing came to pass). My timing was tight enough that I planned to jump in the car and head straight from the club parking lot to the freeway. It is usually a quick two-hour drive to Tahoe, but with a storm warning, who knew. I figured I'd have at least four hours of daylight in which to make it safely to my little red house in the woods.

"Call me before you leave," he said, in his low and even voice. How I love the sound of his voice, so calm, even when he's worried. He is a large man, my David. It's not hard to squint and see the young college football player he once was. We met years ago in a bookstore, when I thought the big blond man was just pretending to be interested in books so he could flirt with me. He wasn't flirting with me, and he wasn't pretending to be interested in books. Now, becoming a couple so many years later, it looked as if we might have the rest of our lives to sit side by side and read together.

I fidgeted through the luncheon, delighted to be with my father and sister but distracted by my concerns about the weather. Finally, the music program reached a pause where I thought I could slip out without attracting too much notice. In my family, you don't walk out while someone is playing the piano. "Thanks for the lunch, Dad. See you, Anne," I whispered. "Be safe," she whispered back.

"Okay, I'm headed up now," I told David on my cell phone as I snapped my seat belt on and adjusted my scarf. No reason to look frumpy on the road.

"I know you're in a hurry, babe," he replied, "but please stop off the freeway near my office. I have something for you. Meet me at the gas station just off the exit. I'll be in my car."

He has something for me? I smiled as I put the Jeep in gear and pulled out of the parking lot toward the freeway entrance. It was still a week before Christmas—what could he be giving me this early? I let my mind wander as I drove, imagining all manner of bejeweled finery. Maybe he wanted me to wear something special to his office party. Maybe he'd seen me turn back to that magazine ad for diamond studs last night. Maybe a new watch to help me stay on time for dinner? Or maybe…as I pulled up, I saw him standing next to his car, right where he said he'd be. Hmm, empty hands, not a gift bag in sight. What could this be about, then, I wondered as

I pulled in next to him and parked. David made a quick gesture with his hand, telling me to roll down my window. I did.

"Here, I went out at lunch and got you this," he said, reaching into his car and pulling out a black canvas gym bag. Didn't look much like a jewelry bag to me, unless it was one heck of a large strand of pearls. He set it gently on my lap as I sat behind the wheel. "Go on, open it," he urged.

Raising my eyebrows at him, I slowly unzipped the bag to reveal...tire chains. Chains. Big chains for a four-wheel-drive Jeep, the kind that will get a girl through any kind of weather system. He smiled sheepishly, then said, "Yes, I know your car is fine, but I just wanted to make sure you were prepared for anything. I hear there's a storm coming in."

"Oh, David. Thank you. Thank you so much." I leaned toward him for a kiss. Here was the man I'd imagined all those years ago, the man who would prowl the house at night to make sure everyone and everything was safe and sound. The heavy lock on my heart clicked shut, with David safely inside.

Short and Sweet

Judy Stevens

—◆◇◆—

The holidays were a twinkle away as I did my best to recover from surgery. My days were filled with range-of-motion exercises, pain medication and naps. I needed something fun, something to think about other than myself. It had been two months since my surgery, and everyone was tired of my being sick and in pain, myself included. The chemo had compromised my immune system, so I spent a lot of time at home. But at that point, I just had to get out. Go somewhere, do something, other than dealing with my newly diagnosed cancer.

In mid-December, Ron, my husband of just two years, my teenage daughter and I took our nine-month-old infant to the church Christmas party to see Santa. We were so excited to put the baby in Santa's lap for that special first time. Walking around the gym–turned–Christmas wonderland, I relished the feel of her solid little body in my arms. She was so adorable in her little maroon-and-pink dress with the butterflies on the hem. Her beautiful blue eyes were as amazed as a nine-month-old could be.

"Do you think Isa will sit on his lap or cry?" I wondered out loud as we stood waiting our turn. She was at that age when babies put everything into their mouths. That age when they reach out to pull on hair. Grabbing at my hair as it swung into her face, she pulled, and out it came. I looked down. Her tiny hand was full of my hair.

I handed her to her father and, feeling sick to my stomach, I stumbled a little on the hard gym floor and found a seat on the bleachers. "This has to stop," I said to myself as I sat there trying to compose myself. "The chemo has kicked in, and my hair is all gonna fall out."

My head hurt. Not just on the inside, but the very roots of each hair screamed whenever anything touched my head, and this tiny baby tug was no exception. My head was also flooded with worry—*Will I be alive to see Isa turn one? And my older kids—they just lost their dad two years ago. They can't lose me, too.* Sitting there in the gym on that hard gray metal chair, my stomach churned.

"Honey, are you all right?" my husband asked as he took a seat beside me. I could only stare at him, barely hearing as the Christmas carols and happy faces swirled around me.

At last it was our turn with Santa, and the minute we were done I knew I needed to go. Driving home with the baby safe in the back seat and my husband at the wheel, I said out loud, "Oh please, God, just one more Christmas. I can't have a bald family photo."

My husband just looked at me. "Yep," he said, a note of firmness in his voice. I stared out the window into the gloomy December day. Yep, please.

The month passed day by day, and as Christmas approached I hurt more and more. The chemo was working its way through my system. Bit by bit my hair fell out, leaving odd areas still covered. Christmas cards arrived, many with hand-written personal notes, saying, "I am so sorry to hear...", "We were so upset when your mom told us..." and the "I know what will make you feel better, if you just..." I knew they meant well, but it was all too much. Tossing another card into the woven basket next to the tree, I thought, "Can't anyone just wish us a merry Christmas with our new baby?"

The next week was a blur. A wintry blur of feeling icky but still trying to enjoy the holiday and making the best of the time we had together as a family. Both teens were off school for two weeks but were saddled with caring for me and the baby. With busy teens we didn't get much family time any-way, and they were resentful, angry at me for getting sick. My daughter complained to everyone while my son stood silently in the wings. I knew this was extra-scary for them; they couldn't lose another parent. Sometimes when you are ill, it just hurts the people you love too much to look at you.

Christmas Eve I did my best to look good. I tried my hair one way, I tried it another, but it was just not cooperating. "I hate this," I muttered to myself. "I have to do something drastic." In frustration I chopped my long hair short as best I could, which, since I could really only use one arm, turned out not to be very good. Choppy and uneven. My daughter's expression of shock and dismay said far more than her simple, "Oh wow, Mom."

My husband came home from work and, although it was clear that he noticed what I'd done, kindly said nothing. Christmas Day arrived and we were up early as usual. The smell of a special holiday breakfast turned my stomach, but everyone else enjoyed it. As the time approached to go to my mom's for dinner and the family photo, I grew increasingly frustrated at how horrible and lifeless I looked. My color gone, my hair a weird choppy cut and the huge black circles under my eyes left me in tears.

"I hate being sick! I hate my hair!" I railed against the turn of events as I tossed party clothes around the bedroom when I should have been getting ready for the family dinner. My husband walked into the bedroom, and I exploded again about how horrible my hair looked. "Well," he said, "why don't I cut it like mine? We could be twins, like those couples who wear the same T-shirts," he joked, trying to get me to laugh off my rage. His head is shaved clean. But his solution only elicited more tears and frustration from me. "Why don't you take a quick nap before we leave," he suggested. "Maybe that will help you feel better."

I lay down gingerly beside the baby, and my head stung as it hit the pillow. When I woke, Isa had her hand in my hair and was kissing my head. She sat up, covered with the short hairs from my head. "This is it," I thought, "the end has come. Merry Christmas to me."

I managed to get through the dinner at my mom's, but when we got home that night, I pulled my husband aside. "Cut it off, cut it off now!" I demanded. My hair, my long beautiful hair, had been such a source of pride my entire life, but I just did not care anymore. It hurt too much and, even cut short, it was falling out everywhere.

"You're joking, right?" he asked. "You don't really want me to shave your head?"

Tears filled my eyes as I nodded. "Yes. Take it all. Shave it clean."

Ron reached for his electric razor. "Wait," I said. "Isa needs to watch. She might not know who I am if she suddenly sees me without hair."

"Good point." We sat her on the floor as if it were just another moment of baby play. He chuckled and joked with me as he shaved, "So, shall we try a Mohawk first? Or I could do fun designs like the athletes do?" His jovial attitude brightened my sour mood, and the baby laughed and giggled at the sight of her parents' silly talk.

I sat in that bathroom watching in the mirror as my new husband shaved every single hair off my head. Gone was the cute skinny paralegal he had married two short years ago. In her place was a cancer patient, sick and weak. Ron didn't seem to notice. "See, we are twins after all," he teased. "People wouldn't be able to tell us apart." I smiled. "Also, think how much we will save now that you won't be buying fancy hair products." I smiled again. "And," he continued, holding my chin in his hand and gazing at me with his blue-gray eyes, "hair or no hair, you are beautiful." Who would have ever thought that the most romantic thing a husband could do for his wife would be to ever-so-gently shave her painful head for Christmas?

Five years have passed since that Christmas. Isa is six years old. I am healthy. Once again I have a full head of hair, but it is lovely to know that Ron would love me even if I didn't.

Christmas Blind Date

Suzanne Lilly

I'm late. Again. Why can't I ever be on time? My internal guilt chided me as I pressed my foot harder on the gas pedal. It was a sunny Saturday, two weeks before Christmas, but from the Arizona heat wave, it felt more like early summer. Watery mirages shimmered above the blacktop as I sped down the rural road to my sister Diana's house. I wished I was skiing in a parka instead of wearing shorts and a cotton top.

I'd overslept this morning, in part to recover from a Friday night blind date gone doubly wrong. After that holiday nightmare, staying single forever looked like my best choice.

I pulled onto the dirt road, trailing a fishtail of dust behind me. My niece and nephew ran out of the house to greet me when I arrived.

"What did you bring us?" Grange peeked in the back seat of my old Chevy.

"It's a surprise." I gave him a hug. "You'll find out soon enough, in exactly two weeks."

Emma stood back, shaking her head. "He always tries to

sneak peeks at the presents under the tree. He's going to get caught and get in trouble someday."

I put my arm around her shoulders and gave her a squeeze. "That will be the year he gets plenty of coal in his stocking, won't it?"

She laughed. "He deserves coal this year."

"I do not!" He pulled the gift-wrapped boxes out of the car. "Look at me now. I'm helping her carry all the presents into the house."

Emma snorted and rolled her eyes, trying to act more mature than her brother. "We have a surprise for you, too." She linked her arm in mine.

"I can't wait to find out what it is."

My sister stepped onto the porch, wearing a flour-covered apron and wiping her hands on a dish towel. "If you weren't late, I'd go into shock. I started the baking without you."

"Hi, Sis. Love you, too." I kissed her on the cheek, catching a whiff of cinnamon and ginger. "I have to stay true to form, you know. Never less than thirty minutes late."

She shook her head, a perfect replica of the head shake Emma had just given Grange. "Come on inside. My cookies are almost ready to come out of the oven."

I stepped inside the front door, and right away noticed the man sitting on the couch. How could I miss him? His tall frame and confident, relaxed posture made him look as if he'd just stepped out of a calendar photo. My brother-in-law was nowhere in sight.

"Where's Chad?" I asked Diana.

"Working. He got called in this morning. Being a volunteer firefighter means he's out saving the world more than he's here." She smiled her mischievous smile, always a cover for one of her schemes. "This is Brandon. He's a friend of Chad's."

Brandon's smile lit up his blue eyes. He held up a hand to greet me. *No ring on his finger. Too bad I'm done with blind dates.*

I nodded in return and gave him a half smile. "Pleasure to meet you." Taking Diana by the elbow, I led her toward the kitchen. "Let's go check on those cookies."

As soon as we rounded the corner, I put my hands on my hips.

She spread her hands wide. "What? I told Brandon he didn't have to wait for Chad, but he insisted on staying."

"Diana, I had the worst blind date in the history of the universe last night, and now I walk into your house, and there's some strange guy sitting on your couch. You could have warned me."

She reached in the drawer and pulled out a rolling pin. "He's not strange. He's actually kind of cute, don't you think?"

"How long have you known him?"

"He got stationed here at the Air Force base a few weeks ago. Chad met him at work, and they found out they have a lot in common. He's very nice."

I washed my hands and grabbed the rolling pin. "Give me that. I'll roll out the cookie dough. It'll release some of my tension."

"What happened last night?" She took a ball of ginger-bread dough from the bottom shelf of the refrigerator and handed it to me.

"You will not believe what Heather did to me. She invited me to her house, for a casual holiday dinner."

Diana's hand covered her heart and she gasped. "Spare me. How could she be so cruel and invite you to dinner?"

"Just wait. When I walked in the door, there were not one, but two guys sitting at the table. I got the impression they'd been waiting for me. They both smiled, and one actually patted the chair next to him."

"Let me guess." She tipped her head and put a finger on her chin. "You were late."

"That's not the issue here." I flattened the dough with a hard slap and smacked the rolling pin on it.

"You'd better let me do the rolling before you kill my gingerbread men. Get yourself some eggnog. Add some extra nog, too."

"I'm serious, Diana. One guy had yellow teeth that stunk as if he hadn't brushed in days. I don't think he'd brushed the three hairs on his head, either. The one that patted the chair was painfully prim and proper. He never relaxed or cracked a smile. Those three hours turned into the longest dinner party I've ever endured."

"Did you tell Heather you didn't appreciate her 'surprise'?" Diana raised her fingers in air quotes.

"Not exactly. I didn't want to hurt her feelings. She doesn't believe me when I tell her I'm not interested in a relationship. While we were rinsing the dishes, she asked me which guy I liked better."

Diana set the rolling pin aside and began cutting the dough into shapes. "Sienna, you and Mark split up over a year ago. Don't you think it's about time you dated again?"

It had been exactly thirteen months, eleven days, and oh, let's see, about twenty-one hours since my boyfriend had decided to move out of our apartment and into his new girlfriend's house. It wasn't something I could let go of easily. I'd been badly hurt, and I was scared of opening myself up to emotional pain again.

"Maybe I *will* have that eggnog." I turned around to walk

to the refrigerator and almost bumped into Brandon. My skin prickled as I breathed in the same air as he did.

He held out a baby bottle. "Could I have more milk? Little Andrew woke up, and now he's snuggling on the couch watching Spider-Man with me."

Way to melt a girl's heart. "I'll get you a new bottle." I put the empty one in the sink and got a new bottle out of the refrigerator. As I removed the lid to warm the milk, Brandon leaned back against the kitchen counter and crossed one cowboy boot over the other. His T-shirt couldn't hide his rock-solid abs. My cynical side went into high alert, warning me that someone like him was too much to hope for.

He's probably some grifter with an agenda.

"I'll take the bottle to Andrew." I twisted the cap back on, grabbed a plate of frosted cookies and carried both to the living room.

"Ooh! Look at the candy-cane cookies!" Grange left his post as Christmas Tree Gift Inspector and ran to the table. He picked up two cookies, handing one to Brandon. "Here you go, Uncle Brandon."

"Thanks, Buddy. Your mom makes terrific cookies, doesn't she?"

Uncle? Since when did my nephew call men he'd just met Uncle?

My niece opened the drawer of an end table and pulled out a deck of Uno cards. "Want to play?" she asked me.

"I'd love to, Emma. Playing a few card games with milk and cookies sounds terrific. Why don't you put on some jingle bell songs?" I said.

"It doesn't get better than this," Brandon said as he carried the cookies to the dining room table to join us in the game. I wanted to dislike him and I was ready to find any fault, but he was making it difficult to do so. His easy sense of humor made the card game the best time I'd had since long before Mark left me.

I'm an accountant because the concreteness of numbers and lists gives me a sense of order and safety. I like the same thing in my personal life, so I started a mental list of pros and cons for Brandon.

Pros: He likes kids, he's in great shape and he tells funny jokes.

Cons: Hard to think of any. Considering my decision to stay single, that's not a good sign. Make more effort to find some bad habits.

When Diana turned on the Christmas tree lights, and the kids complained that they were hungry, I realized we'd been playing cards and chatting for hours.

"Oh my goodness! It's almost six o'clock. Let me order a pizza," I offered.

The kids settled in on the couch to watch a holiday movie while they waited for the pizza to arrive. Brandon and I set the table.

"Since you're in the Air Force, you could be living anywhere in the world. Why are you here in rural Arizona?" I hoped he'd tell me he'd gotten into trouble so I could get my "Cons" list started.

"I came home early from a tour in Germany because my grandmother is sick. She's living with my mom, and I wanted to be close so I can help out as much as possible."

Double darn. He'd added another item to my "Pros" list. But he didn't stop there. He added two more "Pros" when he told me he loved skiing and cooking. Those things put him over the top.

"How about we get together next weekend and go skiing? This time of year the night skiing is spectacular."

I paused for a few seconds, pretending I might have something better to do. "I'd love to."

"Great. Afterwards, I'll cook dinner for you."

"What type of cooking do you do?"

"My specialty is a secret family recipe for green chili enchiladas." He leaned back in his chair. "Would you like me to make them for you?"

I breathed in deeply to calm the flutter in my heart. I had the same sensation I get when I'm at the top of a mountain, looking down at the ski run, the minute before I push off. It's a mix of excitement, fear and anticipation.

I nodded. "I'm ready."

"What did you say?" His eyebrows drew together.

A flush of heat rose from my chest to my cheeks as I realized I'd spoken my thought out loud. "I'd love to have enchiladas with you." At that moment, I realized I wanted to share enchiladas with this man for the rest of my life.

He smiled, a bright, warm smile that rivaled the lights on the Christmas tree behind him. I started falling down the mountain, slipping off the icy, snowy slope of my singleness.

The night ended far too early, and I left for the long drive home. As I backed out of the drive, Brandon stood in front of my sister's house, waving to me until Grange pulled on his arm and dragged him back into the house.

My phone rang almost as soon as I closed the door to my apartment.

When I picked up, his smooth voice came over the line. "Do you think tomorrow is too soon to have those enchiladas?"

"Unfortunately, it is. I'm going car shopping with my dad tomorrow."

"Oh." He couldn't hide the disappointment in his voice, which made me strangely happy. "Then how about the next night? You can show me your car, and I'll feed you."

As much as I already liked Brandon, this seemed to be moving too fast. I stalled and mentioned something about a busy week. We agreed to the dinner date the weekend before Christmas.

The week after Christmas we went skiing. I met his family in the middle of January. By Valentine's Day, I had fallen so deeply that in my heart I knew he was my perfect match. In March, we sent out wedding invitations for an April wedding.

"I've never seen two people fall so crazy in love at first sight," Diana commented as she helped me put on my wedding veil.

"I never believed it could happen." I turned away from the mirror and hugged her. "Thanks for the holiday blind date, Sis."

Twenty-five years later Brandon and I are still cooking together. His enchiladas are still just as good as the first time he made them for me. I still laugh at his jokes. And I'm still amazed at how our Christmas blind date turned out to be such a perfect gift.

Snowy Christmas in the Park

Cherie Carlson

————◦◦✕◦◦————

I had never seen so much silverware—six forks, six knives and six spoons per person, polished and gleaming and set in a proper constellation around the plate and on the linen napkin before me.

"How can we use them all during a single meal?" I whispered to my husband, Bill. He smiled back reassuringly. We settled in to our chairs at a round table for eight, nodded greetings to our table companions and vowed to give it our best effort. The wine was poured and the feast began. Leaning toward Bill as he sat next to me, I whispered, "Happy anniversary."

First up, a smooth and spicy carrot soup with crème fraîche. I ate slowly (certain that I had picked the right soup spoon), savoring both the creamy soup and the sumptuous scene that surrounded us. An elaborately printed menu described all the delights still to come. Shrimp and scallop timbale with horseradish and a cognac sauce. For the main course a Peacock Pie, a Boar's Head and a Baron of Beef. This Christmas feast happens only once a year. And this year was our thirty-seventh wedding anniversary.

I'd read about this event for years; the *Wall Street Journal* called it the "World's Premier Christmas Dinner." Held every December in Yosemite National Park, it began back in 1927. The nature photographer Ansel Adams produced it until 1973, and since then members of the Fulton family have continued the tradition, adding choirs and fine music, drama and frivolity to a feast and theatrical event that lasts close to four hours.

The setting is magnificent—the dining room of the Awahnee Hotel is transformed into a Gothic-type cathedral with stained-glass windows, a Parson and the Squire's table beneath. Actors wear period costumes with vibrant colors of purple, turquoise, rich black and scarlet, gold trim and velvet, fluffy sleeves and flowing fabric. It looks like an Italian painting come to life, the perfect setting for a romantic holiday dinner for any couple. I'd anticipated it for months now, and here we were.

"Comfy?" Bill nodded yes to my question. I reached over and adjusted his shawl-collared sweater, pleased with how handsome my husband looked. Most of the other men in the room were in black tie, but tuxedoes are no longer an option for Bill.

Planning a romantic getaway should be easy; just choose a place, book it and go. But life, particularly travel, is not as easy now as it was in our earlier years. Twelve years ago Bill became disabled. Now he's wheelchair-bound and that leaves it to me to do all the packing and unpacking, driving, checking in, tipping and carrying suitcases—the things most wives expect their husbands to help with. I also load and unload the wheelchair, help him transition from the car to the chair and then push him wherever we need to go. And we decided together that we needed to go to the Bracebridge Dinner for our anniversary. So there we sat amid all this silverware and countless courses to come. I offered up a silent prayer, a request for one perfect night in a romantic setting.

The three-day trip had gotten off to a lovely start. The day before we'd driven through the agricultural part of central California. Under a clear and sunny winter sky, I was delighted by the sight of Angus cows in field after field. I was raised on a cattle ranch and am still fond of the cattle my father liked to call "black roses." Closer to the park entrance, the road was lined with giant trees reaching to the sky, casting their green everywhere.

We'd reserved a little cottage with a spectacular view of the waterfall. Yes, it was everything I'd hoped. After unpacking our finery for the feast, we headed over to the Awahnee to scout out the scene for the big night to follow. Bill and I would both feel more comfortable if we had a chance to survey the scene beforehand and spot any potential pitfalls for the wheelchair.

The hotel's Christmas decor was suitably grand. A huge Christmas tree dominated the lobby, densely decorated with the glossy sheen of large red balls and silver ribbons. All around us were relaxed and happy winter vacationers, taking pictures of themselves in such an impressive setting and enjoying warm drinks by the enormous stone fireplace. Live music added to the gala atmosphere.

"Bill, this is lovely! I'm so glad we gave this a try." He quickly agreed, taking in the scene before him. Surrounded by a relaxed and friendly crowd of strangers in the lobby, we chatted pleasantly with one or two standing nearby. I can understand my husband when he speaks, but not everyone can.

"Yes," I repeated to him as we headed back to our cottage

for the night. "This is going to work out just fine. Tomorrow's dinner will be a dream come true."

The drive through the dark back to our cottage gave me a chance to review the route for the following evening. I am always on the lookout for what might go wrong. Sadly, there is so much Bill cannot do, and, yes, sometimes I am overwhelmed with the responsibility I have for both of us. But life is short, and we refuse to stay at home all the time and feel sorry for ourselves. God has given us an amazing world, and I want to do all I can to help both of us enjoy it.

Next morning we woke to an inch of snow on everything. The mountains were spectacular, and the waterfall right across from us sounded like it was dropping icicles. It was cold, white and beautiful. The huge trees now resembled white statues, reaching out to us with their branches like the arms of God.

Snow. What so many dream of for their Christmas can be a big challenge for us. Snow. Ice. Cold. Slippery. Instead of going to breakfast together, I bundled up and went out to pick up coffee and breakfast. Better we stay inside and simply enjoy the dramatic view from our window until night came.

Almost too soon, it was time to get ready for the long-anticipated Big Evening. I always plan at least two hours for preparation, but after those two hours, Bill looked so handsome! After thirty-seven years of marriage and a severe handicap, I still love and appreciate this man. Not every man would be game to go out in his wheelchair on a snowy evening in an unfamiliar place.

Off we went to the hotel and the Bracebridge Dinner in our finery. The trumpet blew a herald to announce the start of the dinner, and the assembled diners entered the hall of magic, music and amazing delicacies. Huge tables with tall candelabras stood before us. We were escorted to our places by the cast of players, dressed immaculately in colorful costumes.

The room grew dark once everyone was seated, and out of the darkness came a commanding voice.

Let all mortal flesh keep Silence
And with awe and wonder stand.
Ponder nothing earthly minded…
As the Light of Light descendeth
From the Realms of Endless Day…[1]

In the darkness I felt my husband's hand take mine and give me a gentle squeeze. Such a familiar touch after all these years of marriage. The lights came up again and the feast was on. Throughout the long meal, we hardly saw our plates removed before another one was placed before us with yet another tempting course. For hours on end we were transported into another time. The chorus sang with gusto. The jester made us laugh. The room was dressed like a medieval cathedral with stunning stained-glass windows and boars' heads. What fun to leave behind cares and concerns and real-life handicaps for a few hours and just enjoy life, the Christmas season and the happiness all around us. It was long and dreamy, it was romantic and sweet. And too soon it was over.

We left the warm and welcoming room with reluctance, heading back outside into the night and a cold sky. The drive home was only a mile or so—what could go wrong?

Driving slowly along the route to our cottage, I spotted an animal on the other side of the road. A large tan and furry something was blinded by my lights and standing stock-still.

---

1   Bracebridgedinner.com

I steered toward him so that Bill could help me decide what it was. Lights flashed behind me. The park police. I rolled down my window.

"Did you see it, too?" I said to the man who approached. "Was that a wolf or a coyote? I can't tell…" The officer tilted his head in confusion.

"Ma'am?"

"By the side of the road—didn't you see it? A big animal. I was trying to get a better look at it."

"Oh, we thought you were drinking. Could you get out of the car and do a few simple tests for us, please?"

It seemed that I had been driving on the wrong side of the road. I passed the test and climbed back into my car quite humbled.

"Happy anniversary, dear," I said to Bill for the second time that night, putting the car back into drive and continuing on. It was just a small blemish on that perfect evening I'd prayed for. But the night was almost over, and there had been no disasters.

Parking the car in front of our cottage, I went to get Bill's chair from the back. He opened the door to move onto the chair, and as soon as he set his feet down on the ice, he slid right to the ground. Dress shoes and ice—why hadn't I realized that would be a deadly combination? I can do a lot of things for him, but I can't lift Bill off the ground by myself.

"Hang on, I'll get help," I said, taking a deep breath to calm myself as I walked as fast as I safely could across the ice toward the hotel, hoping that someone would be available this late at night. Soon two security guards came around a corner, and together we got him up and into his chair and into our warm room. Thankfully, he wasn't injured; he had just a bruise and was very cold from sitting on the ice as I went for help.

For thirty-seven years now, we have lived and loved together and have only grown more patient with each other's faults and failings. We both believe it is a privilege to serve each other and that every day is a gift from God. That night, as we kissed and snuggled together, I held Bill, gratefully appreciating his eternal patience, his courage and his endurance. As I closed my eyes that night, resting in the arms of my loving husband, I thought back to the message in the closing song of the dinner:

Now the joyful bells are ringing.
All ye mountains praise the Lord!
Lift your hearts like birds awinging,
All ye mountains praise the Lord!
Now our fes'tal season bringing
Kinsmen all to bide and board.
Sets our cheery voices singing,
All ye mountains, praise the Lord![2]

---

2   Bracebridgedinner.com

Frozen Frisbee

Ruth Bremer

———◆◇◆———

Alex and I met in college and started dating in December of my junior year. But instead of calling it dating—not wanting to jinx it, I suppose—we just said we were "hanging out."

We "hung out" quite a lot in those last few weeks before finals and the holiday break, and whenever we got together it always involved some sort of unconventional activity. No dinner and a movie for us. We dressed up in goofy clothes and played a round of golf at the public course—although neither of us had ever golfed before. We walked along the train tracks at night sharing a sixty-four-ounce fountain drink. We cooked dinner on a barbecue grill at the park, using only a pocketknife and a spoon, and ate our baked beans straight from the jagged-edged can. So when we were invited to a Christmas party, we couldn't just show up on time with seven-layer dip like normal people.

It was the first major snowfall of the season, so naturally Alex decided it was a perfect opportunity to fire up the grill and barbecue some burgers. We agreed to meet up later that afternoon and cook a stack of hamburgers to take as our contribution.

The snow fell all day long, and we both got tied up running holiday errands on the snowy roads, so ultimately we had to scrap the burgers-cooked-outdoors idea. "So…we could make some punch instead," Alex suggested before leading me up and down the grocery store aisle grabbing 7-Up, cranberry juice and a bunch of fruit. "Do these folks even have a punch bowl?" I asked as we stood in line. He shrugged. "We'll find out soon enough."

Punch ingredients in the bag, we were on our way to arriving at the party on time. But to my surprise Alex soon pulled off to the side of the road and parked. "Are we there yet?" I asked, looking out the window at a snowy park.

Every December, the city put up an elaborate display of lights in the park along a major street near campus. It was impressive: huge letters that spelled out "Happy Holidays," Santa with his reindeer and sleigh, elves, skiers, snowmen, gingerbread houses and giant candy canes. I smiled. "Oh Alex, you remembered!"

A few days earlier I'd mentioned how much I loved that massive spectacle of festive decorations and looked forward to it each year.

He nodded. "I remembered. And I thought we could play a little Frisbee," he said, turning off the car and opening his door. Yes, I was touched by his thoughtfulness, but… "Um, it's really cold out there. And I am so not dressed for this."

"No problem! I have noticed that you seem to run on the cold side, so look at this…" Reluctantly I got out of the car. Shivering in the dark I peered into his open trunk. "I brought everything I had in the closet—something will fit you." Yes, he had an entire selection of extra coats, hats, scarves and gloves. "So, Frisbee then?" Yes, Frisbee. Why not?

Bundled up against the cold, we ran through the pristine drifts toward the display towering above us, casting its colorful lights onto the shimmering snow. We flung the Frisbee back and forth in front of the elves and candy canes while car after car drove by, on their way to dinner or the shopping mall or their own holiday party.

Soon enough our Frisbee game morphed into a snowball fight. I forgot all about being cold and just gave in to the fun. We laughed and ran around until the snow soaked through our shoes and our fingers grew numb and even Alex didn't want to be cold any longer. Then we packed it up and headed over to our friends' house with the heater blasting. We arrived at the party an hour late, out of breath, our clothes still damp from the snow. Punch bowl? No, but another guest did manage to find a big bowl that we could use to mix our ingredients.

Alex took me home after the party. "Tonight was great, Alex. Frisbee in the snow, amazing."

He looked at me closely. "Do you like doing crazy stuff like that?" he asked me. I told him I did. Not fully convinced, or maybe fishing to see if I wanted to go out on a "real" date, he continued: "You know, if you ever want to do something normal, like go to a movie or something, we could."

Really, I didn't. And so our "hanging out" turned into dating, then to engagement and finally marriage. Through it all we carried on with our adventures. Spur-of-the-moment scavenger hunts, an impromptu run through the sprinklers and, one summer evening, we had a romantic picnic in the median of the busiest street in town, until an emergency response team showed up, thinking we had been in an accident.

Perhaps it was inevitable that over the next several years our lives—and our dates—gradually became more conventional. We worked, raised babies, cleaned the house, paid the bills and we got tired. Too tired to play Frisbee in the snow or prepare meals at the park. Too worn out to come up with creative new ideas for the rare date night without the kids. We usually just went out to dinner. Every once in a while, we caught a movie.

Year after year at Christmastime, we decorated the tree, hung the stockings, wrapped presents, played holiday music and tried in vain to get all three kids to smile at once for the Christmas card photo. Life was good, but it was pretty darn conventional.

Sure, we've both changed since college, but some things remain the same. He's still thoughtful; I'm still cold all the time. And one common trait we share has remained the same: we're still drawn to the unconventional. We'd rather do something new than something safe. But normal is exactly what we had become.

Seventeen years after we played Frisbee in the snow among the twinkling Christmas lights, we decided to reject normal once and for all. Our kids were older and we weren't as physically tired, but we were still tired. Tired of the rat race, tired of playing it safe for the benefit of some unknown future while we missed out on the present. So we stopped. "Do you like doing crazy stuff?" he'd asked me seventeen years ago.

We gave away most of our belongings—everything that wouldn't fit in a fourteen-foot U-Haul. Alex resigned from his job, and we moved to a small mountain town in Colorado, a place where we had always wanted to live but had discounted as being too impractical. Immediately it felt like home. It's cold, of course, but with enough extra layers of clothing I think I can handle it. I started my own freelance business, and Alex now has a new job—with regular hours, no travel and no work to take home. We're living life on our own terms again, leaving some space for creativity, fun and whatever offbeat stuff might come to mind.

So now it is Christmastime in our new hometown, and all the surrounding towns are lit up with extravagant holiday light displays. I've been scoping out each one and think I have found the perfect place. I've put the Frisbee in the trunk, along with some extra gloves and hats. I'm just waiting for the right night. This time, maybe we'll even let the kids play with us.

The Christmas Visitor

Dawn Armstrong

———•◦❈◦•———

Sitting on the final suitcase, shifting my weight in all manner of awkward gyrations, arms and legs flailing, I slipped
to the floor with a thud. "Crikey, packing for an international
trip is never easy, especially with all these Christmas presents to manage." Three gray cats wound themselves wistfully
around my legs and the bags, the subtly skillful weave of their
scent hiding a secret message for me to come home soon. They
took turns sprawling across the clothes in the now-open bag
and swatting my hands as I tried to close it again. Realizing
that their efforts to abort this latest mission weren't working,
they resorted to one of their more successful ploys, looking
up at me in pitiful, sad-eyed unison.

Like the craggy teeth of a crotchety crocodile, the zipper
slid into place. The cats had lost their battle. For the past two
weeks, Silly, Willy and Billy had slept in, climbed over and
loudly voiced their catlike objections to the luggage, intui-
tively understanding that two big bags meant a longer-than-
normal absence. I ran my hands over each of the rescued
siblings, kneading and tickling them in reassurance. "Clever

kitties, don't worry. Mary Fe will be with you while I'm gone. Now, riddle me this: How am I going to get these bags down the stairs, on the shuttle and through the airport all by myself?"

Muttering to myself, I walked through the house performing a final check before heading for my flight. Glancing at the stove to make sure that it was switched to "off," I drew a line through another item on my list. *Is anything else out of place?* Noticing the poinsettia-painted cookie tin sitting precariously near a cabinet ledge, I moved the gift for my house sitter to the middle of the dining room table and readjusted the name tag. "I hope she finds this before my three rascals do!" The most adventurous of the three cats came running into the kitchen as if on cue. "You'll fit right into this family, Willy. We all love homemade chocolate chip cookies at Christmastime, especially Johnny. Every year we make them with his favorite recipe."

The aroma of hot cookie dough, warm chocolate chips and walnuts wrapped itself around me, a cloak of memories flooding in. I paused, gazing up at a picture of the handsomest of men. I rememorized the smallest detail of each adored feature to the finest degree. Plucking the vintage photo from its rightful place among loved ones on the dining room credenza adjacent to the kitchen, I gazed at the young man in uniform. His dark short-cropped hair; heavily fringed, twinkling hazel eyes; strong, yet kind features; clean-shaven face and saucy grin gave comfort even as I accepted the familiar longing that washed over me. "A couple times a year is not enough. I can't wait to be near you again. When I get to Australia, I'll bake a special batch just for you."

A ringing phone jogged me back into the present moment.

"Grandma, I was going to call you from the airport before

I got on the plane… Yes, I'm catching the usual flight from San Francisco to Sydney, and then a Regional Express hopper… I'm doing okay, was just thinking of how much I miss Johnny… You were just thinking of him, too? No, I'm not surprised at all…has he visited lately? I can't wait for your and Auntie's fresh mangos and vanilla ice cream!"

I hung up the phone with eager thoughts of the delicious food and relaxing holiday that awaited me Down Under. Mouth watering, I floated on visions of homemade succulent roast, flaky meat pie, creamy layered trifle, rich caramel tart and crisp ANZAC cookies. I mentally catalogued the long-awaited events that the next two weeks would hold: sleep in, tend garden, copy family recipes, cuddle a koala and, of course, catch up with scores of relatives at the holiday gathering.

My family is spread all over, and the annual get-togethers always include a thorough review of our ancestry. Every household attending brings a copy of the book compiled to document the intrigue surrounding births, deaths and great events leading back to the roots of our tangled family tree. The chronicles begin with journeys across the great ocean from England, continue with the first settling of long-past rough-and-ready relatives on the wild continent of Australia and end with the newest American additions. Every year we look forward to reliving our history, and particularly remembering those loved ones who bravely paved the way before us.

Australia, at last. The long plane trip had already begun to fade in my mind as I showered and snuggled down into my own special space on the veranda-turned-guestroom. New curtains and bed linens, I noticed. "Grandma Gloria and Auntie Mavis must have been busy," I said to the empty room. Early afternoon, and the house was warm. I was grateful for the ceiling fan, and anticipating the nighttime breezes the window-lined room would afford. I could hear the quiet sounds of country life in the neighborhood, happily reminding me of my upcoming visit with Uncle Merv to his cattle and cane farm. The voices of my grandma Gloria and her sister Mavis talking softly in the kitchen drifted in.

The two sisters had lived a lifetime of memories since Gloria, as a war bride at age nineteen, first left Australia for America. Separated for over fifty years with only one phone call a week to sustain them, they remained close. Having survived a spouse or two each, the sisters were overjoyed to live together in Australia once again.

My eyelids grew heavy and sleep was near, but I heard my auntie ask my grandmother, "Do you think Johnny will visit? Dawnie will be over the moon if that happens, but gutted if it doesn't. It will be a shame if he doesn't. I wouldn't want anything to put a damper on her visit."

Grandma Gloria answered quickly. "I'm sure of it. He hasn't disappointed her yet, and he stopped by last evening to check in on me. I bought him a new ornament this year, a dancing Santa. You know how much he loves Christmas." I smiled at what I'd overheard, and drifted off to sleep.

Like practiced runners preparing for an event, we three women settled into our starting places the next morning, tea in hand, warming up for a marathon of memories, hopes and dreams, set against a backdrop of communal meals, gardening and housekeeping. As if on cue, a slight, gray cat with weathered fur trotted onto the veranda, curled herself around my legs, gave a squeaky purr and settled down in her own special chair.

The crunch of wheels across a gravel drive heralded the

first of many cousins who would be stopping by over the next fortnight.

"We had to use the amphibian to get out here today," my cousin Danette announced as she and her daughters walked up to the porch. "Creek flooded the bridge, but the girls and I wanted to get a visit in before school starts back up."

She looked at me and smiled. "So, has Johnny dropped in yet?"

My spirits dropped, though I tried not to let it show. "Not yet, but Grandma bought a special decoration for him. It's a motion-activated Santa. At night when the house is as quiet and still as can be, right before she goes to bed Grandma hears 'Jingle Bells'…"

My grandmother and her sister exchanged a look. "Dawnie, we could use your help in the garden for a bit this afternoon. You can see the new bananas and pineapples that are coming in and we can pick some vegetables for dinner." It was clear that the sisters were trying to change the subject from who had already been by and who had not.

As the sunlight faded, all company departed, and the day came to a close. We three turned to our usual routine of feeding the animals, locking the doors, tidying up and individually preparing to hunker down together for an evening of television, nostalgia and precious moments. Gloria's urgent tone carried across the quiet evening air as we changed into our pajamas.

"Dawnie, you have a visitor."

Goose bumps coursed over our skin as we quickly converged in the middle of the house. Auntie Mavis and I looked at my Grandma Gloria expectantly. A cool breeze ruffled our nightgowns. Gloria nodded toward the back door, which stood wide open, porch light spilling in to illuminate the area around us.

"It's Johnny, isn't it? Where is he?" Auntie Mavis's face paled.

Gloria looked at me pointedly. "Apparently, your father opened the door to let the cats in, fixed the broken porch light and left us a gift."

Eyes widening, I gasped as I looked down at the table in front of me, and saw the family ancestry album opened to the very page chronicling the birth and untimely death of my father, Gloria's son Johnny. Though we were in the dining room, the sound of "Jingle Bells" drifted out from the sitting room.

Mavis looked at Gloria. "Heidi, the little gray cat, is asleep in my bedroom."

Gloria looked at Mavis. "And the big ginger kitten is lying on the porch chair outside. I can see him from here."

I looked at Mavis and Gloria. "It's Dad!" Running into the vacant sitting room, I barely noticed the wildly dancing Santa twisting and turning on his pedestal. Picking up my grandmother's matching family picture of my long-lost father in his military uniform, I twirled in a circle around the room. Eyes watering, heart exploding with love for him, I stopped and planted a breathless kiss on his still cheek. "Merry Christmas to you, too, Dad; I'm so glad you made it."

The sisters stood in the hallway, beaming joyfully. "We knew he would, Darling. Look above you." I looked up and was not surprised to see I was standing directly below the mistletoe.

First Christmas Kiss

Scott "Robby" Evans

———◦◦❂◦◦———

By mid-December, fog had hung over the northern California valley like a dripping gray shroud for more than a week. I was missing the clean white snow of Pittsburgh—it just didn't seem like Christmas without snow—and I was terribly homesick. More than once, I woke up crying, missing my dad and the life we had before my parents divorced. Every afternoon when I came home from school, I found Mom asleep on the sofa. I guess she missed the snow, too.

One night I was at the kitchen table doing my homework for high school. Mother was, as usual, asleep on the sofa. The table sat under the kitchen window and the curtains were open. I glanced up and noticed our downstairs neighbor, Heather, smiling in at me from outside in the hallway. Except for her glasses, I thought she looked just like Audrey Hepburn in *Breakfast at Tiffany's*.

I didn't want her to see my mother already asleep on the couch so early in the evening, so I hopped up and opened the window before she could get to our front door. Her little daughter, Emily, was, at four, too short to look inside.

"Hi, Robby. Doing homework?"

"Yeah. A little algebra."

"Oh. I hated algebra," she said. The cool, damp air rushed in through the screen, carrying her perfume with it. "I wonder if you could help me."

"You need me to babysit?" She was a young divorcee, and I'd watched her little girl on a few occasions.

"No, I need your muscles. On my way home from work, Em and I bought a Christmas tree. Can you help me carry it in?"

"I'll grab a jacket and be right down."

"You're an angel." She looked down at Emily and said, "Robby's going to help us put up our tree. Isn't that nice?" Nice for me, too, I thought, as I walked past my mother on my way to get my jacket. This would probably be the only tree I'd help decorate this year, as my own family's Christmas didn't seem to be shaping up that way.

On my way back from my room, I leaned over to check my mom. She was facing the back of the couch and her breathing was heavy, so I knew she'd be out for the rest of the night. I draped a faded afghan over her and, buttoning up my jacket, went out to try to grab a little holiday spirit.

The Christmas tree loosely tied to the roof of Heather's car was actually a shrub about five feet tall, far from the majestic seven-foot silver spruce we'd always had in Pittsburgh. But once I grabbed the trunk, I realized it was a substantial little pine after all. I hoisted the tree up to my shoulder.

"Wow," Emily gushed. "You're strong."

I smiled, realizing that the weight lifting I'd been doing after school was paying off.

Once we got inside Heather's apartment, I learned the real reason she wanted my help.

"I'd really like to have the tree in front of the window, Robby, but it means moving the couch out of the way. Could you help me move it?"

The couch sat under the window, facing the bookshelves and TV on the opposite wall. On a side wall was an easy chair and a little table and lamp and, opposite it, was the wall that led down the hall.

"So...where do you want the couch, then?" I asked. She looked around the small space.

"What if we move the chair over to this wall and put the couch where the chair was?"

It would be snug, but we could make it work.

The sofa was heavy—it was a hide-a-bed. We shoved it into place and slid the coffee table in front of it, after moving the little chair and lamp table to the opposite wall. I was sweating by the time we'd made room for the tree, which still rested against the wall outside the apartment.

Heather disappeared and came back with a metal stand and, after covering the carpet with an old towel, she positioned the stand under the window.

"Okay, Robby. We're ready for the tree."

Emily jumped up and down, squealing.

I opened the front door, grabbed the tree and maneuvered it into the stand with ease. Heather, crawling on all fours underneath the lowest branches, tightened the clamps that held it in place.

"Does it look straight?" she called from below.

I stepped back and stood beside Emily. "What do you think?"

"Pick me up, Robby, so I can see better."

I hoisted Emily into my arms and we looked at it together, wisps of her hair brushing my cheek.

"It looks perfect, Mommy."

Heather crawled out from under the lower boughs and brushed off her black slacks as she stood. She stepped to one corner, and then she walked around us and went to the hallway to check the view from there. She smiled.

"You're right, Em. It *is* perfect!"

The room had grown fragrant with the pine scent and, although a little cramped, it seemed very warm and homey. My buttoned-up jacket added to the warmth.

"Thanks, Robby," Heather said. She stepped over and quickly kissed my cheek.

I felt myself blush and grow even warmer under my wool coat. In my fourteen years, no girl had ever reached out to touch me in such a casual way.

"Well, I guess I should get back to my homework."

Heather reached out her arms and took Emily from me. "Can't you stay a bit? I was hoping you could help us decorate."

"Please, Robby," pleaded Emily. "Puh-leeze." Only little girls can draw a word out like that.

I shrugged. "Sure, I guess." Algebra could wait. My grades were okay in that class anyway.

Heather lowered Emily, who stepped over and hugged my leg.

"Let me grab the boxes out of my closet."

"Okay," I said. Feeling a little sweaty, I asked to use the bathroom. "Mind if I clean up a little?"

"Make yourself at home."

I splashed cold water on my face to cool down and then wondered if there was a way I could smell a tiny bit better. Glancing around the room, I noticed deodorant—Mennen—

and a small bottle of English Leather aftershave. I used both liberally.

"Wow, you smell good," Emily said when I walked into the living room.

Heather had put a record on—Andy Williams singing Christmas songs—and she was opening a box on the coffee table. She spun around and smiled, saying, "He sure does."

For the next hour, we decorated the tree as if we three were a happy little family. Heather asked me to put the star on top and string the lights, and she helped Emily hang ornaments.

We sang carols along with the record and shared stories as we worked. I told Emily about sledding down the snow-covered hills of Pennsylvania, and Heather promised we'd all go sledding up in the Sierra-Nevada mountains sometime during the break.

As we worked, sometimes Heather's hand touched mine, and she often smiled up at me with light in her eyes. Her perfume, the scent of the tree, Emily's giggles, the warm, dim little room—it was all so intimate, I could barely breathe at times. It was heady stuff for a high school boy.

When the tree was fully decorated, I plugged in the lights and Emily clapped and squealed. The greens and blues and reds and oranges converged on Heather's face. She looked radiant. At that moment, I felt older than fourteen, and she seemed younger than twenty-two.

Standing back, looking at the bright tree together, Heather put her arm around my waist, while holding Emily against her hip.

"It's the most adorable tree," she said.

"Santa Claus will like it, won't he, Mommy?"

"He'll love it," Heather assured her.

"You get more presents if Santa likes your tree," Emily told me, speaking with great authority.

I nodded. "I think I heard that, too, when I was a kid."

"Oh, Robby," she said, "thank you so much for helping us."

Emily yawned and said, "Mommy, I'm tired."

"Okay, Honey. Why don't you go to the bathroom like a big girl and then change into your pajamas, while I say good night to Robby."

"Can Robby tuck me in?"

"Oh, I don't know, Sweetie. We've probably kept him long enough."

"Please, Robby! Please tuck me in."

I shrugged. "Guess I can stay a little longer."

"You hurry, then," Heather said. She set her down and patted her on the bottom.

Heather turned toward me and put her hand on my arm. "If you've got to get back, it'll be okay." Study algebra, or sit in front of a Christmas tree with a girl who'd kissed me on the cheek? It didn't take me long to decide.

"Naw. I can stay a while."

Heather nodded and turned her attention back to her daughter. "I'll go help Emily get her pajamas on."

"Can I have some water?" I asked.

"Help yourself."

I went to the kitchen and filled a glass with cold water, which tasted great. Sometimes the simplest things are the most satisfying. A white-and-red candy, wrapped in twisted plastic, sat on the counter. I unwrapped it and plopped it into my mouth, as if I owned the place.

Then I noticed a piece of mistletoe on the table. Thin red ribbon was tied in a bow around the stem, and a new package of thumbtacks lay next to it. I stepped over and opened the package. Somehow I felt more at home in Heather's apartment than I'd felt in my own.

I stabbed the tack into the stem of the mistletoe just as Heather appeared.

"She's already asleep. She really wanted you to tuck her in, but I picked up her clothes from the bathroom and put them in the hamper. When I looked in, she was sound asleep."

"That's okay," I said. "I can tuck her in some other time."

Heather glanced at my hands. "So, you found my mistletoe."

"Yeah. I mean, I just figured it was one more decoration. You know."

Heather nodded. "Yes, I know." She grinned. "Where should we put it?"

I shrugged. "The hallway, maybe?"

She glanced up. "How about right here? Can you reach the archway?"

Reaching over her shoulder, I pushed the thumbtack into the plaster of the little archway that separated the hall from the kitchen. The mistletoe and the red bow now hung above us.

"Well?" Heather said. "Should we try it out?"

My heart raced as she rocked up onto her toes. Was this really happening to me? I bent down and closed my eyes. Our lips touched briefly. Hers were soft and warm, and my heart did a little flip inside my chest. I pulled away and opened my eyes. Heather's eyes were open, and she was smiling sweetly at me.

"You're so young, Robby. Just think how many kisses there are in your future. And whoever she is, she will be a very lucky girl to have you."

My heart was breaking. Couldn't that girl be Heather? I

wanted to stand under that archway for the rest of my life. But, no, I knew that was only a young boy's dream.

"Guess I should get back," I said weakly.

She nodded. "It's late, and you've got school tomorrow."

I looked at the beautiful lights of the Christmas tree for a few more seconds, then stepped toward the door and grabbed its cold handle. I opened it and stood there, hoping she'd insist I stay longer, but she stepped forward and said, "Good night, Robby."

When the door closed, I turned away. My heart was broken, but as I climbed the stairs to my apartment, I knew there would be other Christmases and other kisses in my future. There have been, but the memory of that first kiss still makes me smile. The soft kiss of a young, single mother struggling to find her place had been the best gift I received that year, giving me a small taste of what my future life would be as a family man with a tree and a daughter of my own.

The Scent of Pine and Candle Wax

Illia Thompson

————◆❖◆————

It had not been a good year for my small family of three. The trauma of an unexpected divorce had shaken my children and myself. Hamid was just twelve and Malina was younger by two years. The idea of moving somewhere new to start over held great appeal. With this in mind, I went on an autumn weekend visit to a small village near Carmel. Could this be a place for us to heal, I wondered, as I walked down the quaint streets and viewed the small shops.

Always a book lover, of course I needed to check out the library before deciding if this town seemed right. And that was where I saw it—the small sign on the library bulletin board that read "Preschool Director Needed." The interview for the position was to be held the very next day!

The interview was quickly arranged. Yes, all agreed that I fit the requirements well, but there were other, mostly local, applicants under consideration. I left my phone number with the interviewers, but tried not to get my hopes up. As I left town, I made a silent vow to myself: if I were to be chosen, my children and I would make the move. The phone rang two months later. "Can you start January 1st?" I could indeed.

Settling into a new community is always hard, but so much went well right away. The parent co-op offered me instant acquaintances so I was spared the difficulty of seeking out new friends. My talents were put to good use on the job, and I felt revitalized. Now, if only my romantic life would fall into place so smoothly, I thought. Friends in my former large suburb had warned me, "Don't move to a small community. They don't have many single men." My reply: "I only need one."

"I found the man I want you to marry. I found the man I want for a stepfather." This was my now-fifteen-year-old son, Hamid, speaking from the back seat of the station wagon as we returned from our first community Thanksgiving Dinner in the country.

"Hmph," I replied, focusing on the still-unfamiliar road home.

But he went on, adding a bit of support to his statement. "Really. He plays the guitar and sings and has an orange truck."

I dismissed his request, "Now, when we get home, go play outside before it gets dark."

My daughter, Malina, perked up at the mention of a guitar. "He sounds interesting, Mom. Why don't you give it a try?" It was true, I had started dating again, but I certainly did not need my son acting as matchmaker. He persisted and I finally agreed to ask his candidate, Locksin, to join us for a Sunday lunch. Lunch seemed harmless, as innocent as any time could be for carrying out my son's wishes.

Lunch, as it turned out, was delightful. The four of us seemed like an instant family, comfortably visiting over a midday meal and soon after singing and playing board games together. Locksin and I began to spend more time with each other, and I slowly felt the possibility of a new family in the making. But did he feel the same way I did?

This bachelor from southern California, who didn't even wear socks with his Topsiders and who was now working on land as a contractor after being at home on the sea, intrigued me. He of Viking ancestry. I of Mediterranean heritage. He, well over six feet tall, and I, barely five-feet-two. Both of us in our forties. There was an ease between us when it came to sharing our thoughts. Not long after we met, on the ride home after an outing in the nearby redwoods, I suddenly blurted out what was on my mind: "If you asked me to marry you, I wouldn't necessarily say no." Hmm, maybe that was a thought I shouldn't have shared, especially since he didn't respond at all to my statement. Complete silence reigned for the rest of the long two hours back. Locksin dropped me off at my house without a word and drove off into the night.

Two long weeks passed. The phone rang at last, with Locksin on the other end. "We have to talk." Over a quiet dinner in a restaurant, he reached across the table and held my hands while finally sharing his thoughts on the subject. "I love your children. I would love to be married. And I would love for us to have a child together." I took that as a proposal. "Yes," I responded quickly, squeezing his hands to seal the deal. We married six months after my son had arranged our first meeting.

Our first December seemed to arrive quickly after we settled into our new home. Hanukkah was my family tradition and Christmas was his family tradition, so of course we blended both the festivities and the worship. Candlelight in the silver menorah, colored lights on the evergreen tree. Traditional Hebrew prayers and Christmas caroling with neighbors. A wreath on the front door, next to the mezuzah, the small ceramic case that holds the Ten Commandments. Presents wrapped in the traditional Jewish silver and blue and Christmas gifts wrapped in red-and-green paper. And, of course, mistletoe hung from the rafters. That first winter as a new family, the roundness of my form showed clearly that our child would be present at our next December celebration. Our son, Lance, was born into a cradle of love. During the December holidays, wide-eyed, this baby took in all the lights. Every year throughout our marriage our blended celebration took place. Until a December came when Locksin was not there.

He'd come home from work early complaining of a stomachache, something unusual for this strong, healthy-looking man. Sixteen-year-old Lance left me a note, scrawled on the back of an envelope: "Dad's not feeling well. I'm taking him to the doctor's. Don't worry. I'm in charge of the situation. Love, Lance."

It was a quick year once his cancer diagnosis was made. For the last three months, his bedside became a place for stories and sharing with family and friends. Alone together in the evenings, my husband and I talked deep into the night, speaking our deepest truths. On an early June morning, when no one was around, he took his last breath. I later held his cool hand for the last time, remembering his declaration from years ago. "We hold hands well together."

For me, the following December lost its festive feeling. Locksin was gone. No Christmas tree. Christmas Eve found me driving alone past a small nursery. "Should I stop and buy something festive?" I wondered. Red would liven up my gloomy house, add a bit of brightness. The parking lot was deserted; everyone else had long since made their holiday purchases. I wandered through the quiet aisles, trying to decide on a small something. A lovely evergreen wreath sat alone. Pine? No, I needed to stick with something less symbolic of Christmas this year, I thought, shaking my head and walking past it to the poinsettias. Red ribbons tied around red sparkling pots. Just what my living room needs right now, I decided, picking up the one closest to me and heading for the cash register. I glanced down at the wreath again as I walked past. Maybe…but no. I wasn't ready yet.

Standing at the counter, I looked again to where the lone green wreath sat near the entrance. Maybe I did need it after all. Something to acknowledge my husband's love of Christmas. He wasn't there with me this year, but at least the house could smell as if he were.

"There's a wreath back there. Just sitting there," I said to the clerk as he wrapped the poinsettia in plastic to protect my car seat. He nodded and began to ring up my plant. Quietly, I asked, "How much is it? That wreath." Again, he paid no attention. "What's the price?" I finally said in a louder voice. "Here's your plant. Where is your car?" he asked. I pointed to the only one in the parking lot.

On the way out, he bent down smoothly and scooped the wreath up with his free hand, never breaking stride. "Merry Christmas," he said quietly, as we walked together to my car. "You can have it."

Startled, I protested. "Oh, but I can buy it. You don't have to give it to me."

"Nope," he said, shaking his head firmly. "It would give me great pleasure to give it to you. It's late in the season, and it needs a good home."

With a poinsettia dressed in red and the pine-scented

wreath filling my car with the familiar scent of Locksin's beloved pine trees, my holiday spirit revived at last. "Locksin, are you there?" I asked out loud in the car. "Did you do this, dear? Thank you for the wreath." I hung it by the front door, encircled by his love once again.

Song of Love

Dena Kouremetis

———•◦✕◦•———

There he is, in his tux up on the stage of our local performing arts center. It's our pop choir's fourth performance of the Christmas season. As I peek from backstage at the group singing "It's the Most Wonderful Time of the Year," I see my salt-and-pepper-haired husband, elegantly moving to the beat of this jazzy rendition, not knowing just how very smitten I am with his crooning and how thrilled I am that he loves being up there as well. Smiling and shifting my weight from one patent-leather pump to the other one, in anticipation of my turn onstage, I remember my childhood dreams of the perfect Christmas. It looked just like this. But for many decades of my adult life, Christmas was far from harmonious.

I came from a very close, fun-loving family. We laughed a lot. We traveled a lot. And from my earliest recollection, my two brothers and I made music together, encouraged by two piano-playing, singing, whistling parents. As we embarked on cross-country trips to visit our Midwestern relatives each summer, my brothers and I had our own little band going in the back seat of our family Mercury. One brother was the (voice-produced) bass player, the other was the drum section and I was the diva singer.

As I got older, singing became an important part of my life. My teenage insecurities kept me from auditioning for school musicals or singing in choral groups, so instead I learned to play guitar and imitate my folk-singing heroes of the 1960s in my own, private way. By the time I got to college and gained more confidence, I was sharing my love of singing with my friends, regaling girls in the dormitory with my doleful version of "Leaving on a Jet Plane." I spent a year in Greece during college, and I wowed my Greek relatives by strumming my guitar and singing Nana Mouskouri songs.

On my own in San Francisco after college, I joined my church's Greek Orthodox choir as an alto, learning to sing the beautifully arranged hymns that dated back to early Christianity. It was wonderful to engage in harmony with a group who shared my love of singing and, for many years, it would become my form of worship, lending me both roots to honor and wings to fly.

And then that part of my life suddenly grew silent. I'd married a man who seemed perfect for me. Our daughter came along very quickly, and we were delighted. In time, however, I found that many of the things I thought would never matter much to me began to haunt me. I loved to dance, but my husband didn't. I loved music of many kinds, played piano, played guitar and sang, none of which he felt capable of learning nor appreciated in me. I loved to write, but couldn't seem to get him to read. I was in love with the idea of flying and traveling; he was a white-knuckled passenger. Other differences in taste and especially temperament became evident as well and, before long, laughter faded for good in our house.

No matter how hard I tried, I could not reproduce the kind of joy I had experienced in my childhood home.

Christmastime, which had been one of the most special times of the year for me growing up, became a disappointing guessing game about which gifts might be returned. Gift giving was no longer about sharing in a cacophony of delight, surprise and appreciation. What had always been a wonderful time of the year became one of the most upsetting. And finally, after almost twenty years, it all came to an end.

Soon after settling into this new single phase of my life I received an invitation to a friend's surprise birthday party from another Greek-American family. In case you haven't heard, Greeks know how to throw parties. One of the people hosting the party was my friend's handsome brother George—someone I had seen occasionally throughout my married years at Greek festivals, weddings and picnics. I would dive into the long dance lines next to him because of his smooth dancing style and his knowledge of the dance steps for each type of Greek tune. My husband stood on the sidelines, watching, but never seemed to want to join in the fun.

I knew George, a San Francisco firefighter, merely as my friend's brother—a jovial, well-mannered man everyone seemed to love. Good-looking as he was, he had never married, and no amount of interrogating his sister about why he had remained single seemed to produce much of an answer. Now that we were in a more intimate social situation, however, I was able to observe him in a different way. Once the surprise part of the party was over, I looked on as he and his sisters joked and howled as they recounted childhood stories. They recalled lines from movies they had loved, talked about their parents and reminisced about the different places they had lived. Soon I heard two of the sisters harmonizing as they sang a song. It was magic. It felt as if a piece of home had surfaced in someone else's family, and I was just plain happy to be there.

By the end of the party, George was paying special attention to me, but I tried to shrug it off. The ink on my divorce filing was not yet dry, and I had been told by all my well-meaning friends to go it alone for a while. "Get to know yourself," they advised, "apart from being a wife and mother." Yet I was flattered to be getting a new kind of attention from someone I had always been curious about. George walked me to my car and asked if he could call me soon. Without a hint of hesitation, I said yes.

Once he picked me up to take me to coffee a few days later, George wasted no time in letting me know that he had always had a secret crush on me—that his gentlemanly ways, while proper, had merely masked an interest that went back to before my marriage some twenty years earlier. I was taken aback by his honesty and surprised that he would make himself so vulnerable. But I was also interested. And no advice from friends or family was going to stop me from exploring the possibilities of at least having a closer friendship with this man.

Apart from our Greek-American ethnic background, George and I had much more in common than I could ever have imagined. At the time, we (and our siblings) were both caring for aging, increasingly disabled parents who needed 24/7 care. George's mother suffered from dementia, diabetes and heart problems, while my father was failing fast with prostate cancer, abandoning his lifelong love of food and laughter after having lost Mom seven years earlier. Dad passed on shortly before my divorce became final, while George's mom continued needing care for the unforeseeable future. I understood from early on that I would have to share George with his commitment to care for his mother before he and I could truly be together. But apart from the challenges we faced, I was to find that this special man loved to sing and dance; had a private pilot's license; shared my love of travel, art and literature; and had a sense of humor that kept me in smiles nearly all the time we were together. It was an unbeatable list of made-to-order traits I could not easily resist.

Once the divorce was properly final, George began attending church with me, rejoining the choir after more than fifteen years of being away from it. To look over at the tenor section and see George's face as he blew secret kisses my way between Byzantine lyrics made me fall fast for this amazing man. After a year and a half of being together, we announced our engagement and set a date, knowing George would have to commute back and forth to care for his mom after we moved in together.

The wedding was divine. As the church filled with voices singing the ancient music of the betrothal and the wedding sacrament, George and I circled an altar table three times in what is called the "Dance of Isaiah"—signaling the first journey we would take as a couple. The sweetness of having discovered one another in midlife was special enough, but because George was pushing fifty and had never been married before, his relatives surfaced from all over the country to wish him well.

More than twelve years have gone by since that fateful surprise party where we met. George's mom passed away a year after our wedding and, not long after, we bought our first home together. The first Christmas in our new home George retrieved some carefully wrapped and taped storage boxes. Inside was a beautiful assortment of oversized glass

Christmas ornaments, most of which were mini-Santa figures he had collected over his bachelor years. Really? Honestly, a single man who collects Christmas ornaments? How adorable is that? I knew no small Christmas tree would do to display these lovely decorations, and each year I use a different combination of them.

But nothing would prepare me for the first Christmas we would sing onstage together. After having seen me sing in a large, well-organized choral group, George auditioned for it as well and got a place in the tenor section. Each year the group puts on a show of amazing Christmas music, both traditional and pop arrangements. For months we prepared for these musical extravaganzas, and we had to learn and memorize the music at different rates and in entirely different styles. And for months we sing and allow the Christmas feeling to envelop us, far longer than most folks get to enjoy it.

So here I am for the first time, gazing at my tuxedoed, dapper husband in the men's section. But it's always the same little ritual taking place. He catches my glance and, soon, a secret kiss gets blown my way. No matter what comes next in the song of life, I know I am with the right partner at last.

Another Christmas at Uncle Joe's

Jerry White

―◦◦◦◦―

"Jerry," said Marie, "I have a niece you should meet." Marie was a hostess at a nightclub I frequented in Fresno. "You two would make a great couple," she continued.

Well, what could I say? "Sure, I would be delighted to meet your niece."

Marie smiled and said, "Donna. Her name is Donna; I will ask her to come by on Saturday night."

Donna arrived at the club Saturday night with two of her girlfriends in tow—safety in numbers, I guess. As advertised, Donna was indeed a beautiful and charming young lady. I asked her on a date; she accepted. By the end of the first date I had proposed to her. There was no question about it—she was the one for me. It was the long dark hair, the soft voice, the warm smile and the eyes that sparkled with a mischievous glint.

"You can't be serious," she said when I proposed. I was very serious, but I figured it would take at least one more date to convince her. I knew what I wanted right away, but apparently she needed more time to reach the same conclusion. In fact, it would take years.

Donna's sister, Carolyn, was getting married soon after I met Donna. At the wedding I got to meet the entire family—and what a family it was. Dena, Donna's mother, was one of nine children, all of whom still lived in Fresno. Their yearly tradition was to gather at Uncle Joe and Aunt Norma's home for a Christmas Eve celebration, and then attend Christmas Eve mass at midnight. Christmas Eve at Uncle Joe's became a tradition for us, even though we were sometimes only dating on and off. Families with Italian heritage know how to celebrate religious holidays—lots of great food, laughter and hugs.

Four years after we met, Donna was working as a nurse in San Francisco and I was on orders for duty in Vietnam as a captain of infantry. We spent Christmas Eve at Uncle Joe's for the fourth time in a row that year, knowing that soon the tradition would be broken. Next Christmas I would be overseas.

After a few months in Vietnam I was reasonably sure I would not survive the one-year tour. I often thought that dying would be acceptable if only I could see Donna's smile, hear her voice and hold her hand one more time. Just one more time, that was all I asked from the war.

Soldiers who had served several months in Vietnam were entitled to a seven-day Rest and Recreation period outside the country. Married soldiers would travel to Hawaii to meet their loved ones. A few days before Christmas I saw a fellow officer and good friend, Lieutenant Chuck Boyle. He didn't look too happy.

"Why so glum, Chuck?" I asked.

"I was going to meet my wife in Hawaii for Christmas, but now she can't make it." He looked at me with a gleam in his eye. "Hey, Jerry, why don't you take my R & R space?

You're always going on about that nurse in San Francisco. Go visit her for Christmas."

"Great idea," I said. "But soldiers on R & R in Hawaii can't travel to the mainland, you know that."

Chuck thought about that for a moment before pointing out the obvious. "OK, so you get caught being AWOL. What's the worst thing the Army can do to you—send you to Vietnam?" He had a good point there.

Another Christmas with Donna at Uncle Joe's—the tradition won't be broken! I thought to myself. I immediately accepted his ticket. *Hawaii, here I come! And after that… I sure hoped the Army wouldn't notice…*

Arriving in Hawaii, I sat through an orientation at the military recreation center in downtown Honolulu. The presenter warned us all about the serious consequences for any soldier who tried to go to the mainland. I listened closely, and then caught a cab back to the airport and approached the Pan Am ticket counter. The agent was a young man about my age.

"A round-trip ticket at the military discount rate to San Francisco, please," I said.

"Can I please see your military orders, sir?" he replied.

Since I didn't have enough money to purchase a civilian rate ticket, I began with the story I had invented on the long flight from Vietnam.

"I understand the policy," I said, "but I have a wife and four kids in San Francisco, and I can't afford to bring them to Hawaii. I was hoping to be home for Christmas. It would mean so much to the children."

The agent paused, looked at the decorations I was wearing, and silently printed the ticket. He handed me the ticket, smiled, and said, "Enjoy Christmas with your family, Captain."

★ ★ ★

"Hi, Donna."

"Jerry?"

"Yes."

"Where are you?"

"At the San Francisco airport."

"What? San Francisco? How? I thought you weren't coming home until April."

"I wanted to see you and to keep the Christmas tradition of going to Uncle Joe's unbroken, so I went AWOL. I thought I would surprise you." Yes, she certainly was surprised.

We arrived in Fresno on Christmas Eve day. My family and friends and Donna's family were, of course, surprised and happy to see me. Being at Uncle Joe's for the family gathering was especially joyous for me. My three days at home were a blur of invitations, parties and holiday meals that I will always remember.

Joy, even Christmas joy, does not last long. After three days of festivities, the return to war was approaching quickly. Donna had to go back to work in San Francisco and I had to catch a flight to Hawaii without the authorities becoming aware of my unauthorized trip to California. Thankfully, I managed to once again slip onto a Hawaii-bound plane without incident, and from there headed back to Southeast Asia.

As I settled into my seat for the flight from Hawaii to Vietnam, I reflected on reaching the goal I had set for myself before I died. I had seen her smile, heard her voice and held her hand. Even better, I began to detect hints that Donna had, five years after my proposal, made up her mind to accept. As she dropped me at the airport, I noticed a tear slowly moving down her cheek as we said goodbye.

I managed to survive my final months in Vietnam. Donna and I were married soon after I returned home, and after forty-two years together, she remains the young lady whose long dark hair, soft voice, warm smile and mischievously sparkling eyes inspired a young soldier's secret Christmas journey home.

The Quiet Man

Margaret H. Scanlon

———◦◦◯◦◦———

Iwas facing Christmas alone for the third time. It had now been three years since my beloved husband, Dan, passed away. He and I loved the holidays and I had tried hard on my own to continue our traditions. I put up a real tree, built the miniature village underneath it and put the tiny train together. I baked all the family specialties and invited the children over for dinner—but it wasn't the same. It never will be.

We raised a large family together—three girls and five boys. And those eight children have now given me fifteen grandchildren. So a large crowd gathers at my house every year for the holidays and they all miss their "Papa's" presence just as much as I do.

That year, as usual, I attended the midnight mass at our parish church. The mass was, in fact, dedicated to my late husband, a bittersweet tribute and one that made me feel his absence all the more. Sitting in the smooth, wooden pew, I felt the music of the carols and the words of the sermon wash over me as my thoughts roamed back over my years with Dan.

We always called him the Quiet Man, a man more given to

gestures than words. And his gestures over the years had been memorable—a bouquet of flowers for no particular reason; small gifts that would quietly appear at the breakfast table. My favorite surprise was the evening he came up behind me and slipped a small diamond necklace around my neck. "Just a little something to make up for the bad times," he said as he fastened it in place. Oh, he could make me smile, that husband of mine.

Even after his death, it sometimes seemed that he was still with me. The first Christmas without him was the hardest. At least it was until he made me smile. How did he do it? As I drove home from church that day, consumed by my new loss, I decided that a little Christmas music might distract me. I punched the button on the radio and settled back, expecting to hear "Silent Night" or "Angels We Have Heard on High," the typical Christmas Day fare. What came softly over the airwaves was Andy Williams's rendition of "Danny Boy," a strange selection for Christmas Day. It was a cheer-up gesture from Dan, I'm certain of it. And it made me smile.

Sensing my sadness after the special midnight mass ended, one of my grandsons offered to come home and spend the night with me. I thanked him but decided instead to spend Christmas Eve alone with my thoughts. I went home to my gaily decorated–but–empty house and settled in comfortably by a cozy fire. One by one I read the lovely holiday cards and messages I had received. Instead of the sadness I'd felt on earlier Christmases, I had a feeling of peace. Before turning in that night, I quietly thanked God for all forty-six years that Dan and I had together.

Christmas morning dawned, and I set about preparing the house for the arrival of my family. My first task was to clean out the fireplace and lay a fresh fire. This had always been

Dan's favorite job; he took particular care to build a long-lasting fire, with the logs and kindling placed just so. I tried to take the same care, scraping out the burned chunk of wood from my fire the night before and sweeping out the ashes before setting the wood and kindling inside. I would wait to light it until the children and grandchildren began to arrive.

My daughter Ginny was the first to appear. She cooked up a sumptuous breakfast of scrambled eggs, bacon, toast, rolls and freshly ground coffee. I put our holiday ham in the oven and sat down to enjoy this early-morning feast with her.

As we began to eat, Ginny said, "Gee, Ma, that's a great fire you built."

"Fire?" I asked. "What fire? I haven't started it yet. It's for later this afternoon."

"Well, turn around and look," Ginny urged. And turn around I did. There was the most beautiful fire blazing away in my fireplace, a fire that I hadn't struck a match to. It was one of Dan's fires.

My daughter and I sat together in the kitchen, marveling at the scene before us. Once again, it seemed the Quiet Man was watching out for us, showing us with one of his small gestures that he was nearby and thinking of us. The warmth of the fire that year helped me melt away more of the sadness that my family still felt about the loss of their father. For now we knew that as lonely as we were without him, he was trying to let us know that we were still in his heart.

The Christmas That Almost Wasn't

Kathryn Canan

———◦◦◦———

"And cancel Christmas!"

This line, snarled by the Sheriff of Nottingham, is the only line I remember from the movie *Robin Hood: Prince of Thieves*. For years now I've been tempted to cancel Christmas myself.

I'm not sure when I became a grinch. Certainly I remember the magic when my children were small—tackling an elaborate gingerbread house, staying up half the night assembling bikes and writing letters from Father Christmas. I had the energy and time to crochet, cross-stitch and do needlepoint on Christmas ornaments and stockings, send personal, handwritten cards, and make or buy the perfect gifts. As an early music specialist, I delighted in discovering medieval and Renaissance Christmas music never heard in the malls, and I loved sharing this ancient music in any performances I could arrange.

Family recipes from both sides melded together to become our own traditions. Spritz and sugar cookies, almond crescents, nut butter snowballs, gingersnaps and homemade fudge were all essential. When my parents visited, they brought Springerles from our German heritage; these never caught on with the rest of my family, but I appreciated the ritual of dipping the rock-hard anise bricks with quaint pictures into coffee. Christmas breakfast had to include homemade sourdough cherry rose rolls and the oranges from our stockings, and dinner, where I resisted a menu set in stone, still had to include Yorkshire pudding and strawberry Jell-O with crushed pineapple.

The handmade stockings became the hallmark of our Christmases. They weren't just for the kids; Dave and I had them, too, and filled them for each other. As we all grew older, they took on themes. Last Christmas our younger son, Tim, on the path to becoming a cardiologist, got a bacon-themed stocking, including a tie he could wear under his white coat. Guests got them, too; when my sister Patricia visited us in California for the first time, I crocheted her a stocking and filled it with California avocados and kiwis. Trouble was, the stocking kept stretching as I added weight to it, and it morphed into the legendary Avocado Monster.

I think now that I was a victim of my own success. The problem with creating so many heartwarming Christmas traditions is that my family grew to love them—all of them. Some things need to change as children grow up and the family changes, but Christmas traditions are not conducive to change. It seemed to me, as the years went by, that the Martha Stewart Christmas I always tried to create morphed into National Lampoon's *Christmas Vacation,* with nearly as many disasters.

Now that my children are grown, they are home for only a few days during the holidays. I don't want them to waste that time shopping; I want to spend time together. One year

I took my two sons skiing the day after Christmas. It was the only day that week the weather was perfect, and as we headed up to the Sierras, we felt as if we were driving into a Christmas card. We arrived at the hill by 10:00 a.m. and managed to find a parking place within two miles of the lift. Tim and I had our own equipment; Jon, who had flown down from Seattle, needed to stand in the rental line—he didn't receive his skis until 2:00 p.m. Then he had to stand in another line to trade his full-day pass for a half-day pass. We don't go skiing during Christmas week anymore.

Gifts for our children now have to fit in carry-on luggage. We avoid the problem somewhat by giving gift cards and finding new ways to wrap receipts for gifts shipped directly to their homes—creating strange ways to use paper bags and duct tape is another tradition—but it's hard to evoke the same magic on Christmas morning these days. In fact, I increasingly resist the whole commercial aspect of Christmas. I avoid the malls and make a spiritual practice out of not shopping on Black Friday.

As a musician, I'm sensitive to noise—including bad Christmas music, which starts before Halloween these days. Even my initial enthusiasm for unusual medieval and Renaissance carols has dimmed. (Must we play "Ríu Ríu Chíu" again? The tenors never come in on time.) The last time my consort played for a party at a winery in a replicated castle, we had to fend off grapes shot from spoons the guests had turned into mini-catapults. Christmas spirits can be a problem in the entertainment world.

Our daughter, Robin, became an accomplished pastry chef by the time she was twelve. She began to concoct amazing variations on everything in the cookie cookbooks we owned. Of course, we couldn't do without the traditional favorites, so we kept adding to the cookie repertoire. I bought a freezer, donated freely to every December gathering I attended and invested in cute tins for gifts of baked goods. I did compromise and get rid of the Springerles the year that rats found the dough chilling in the attic because the refrigerator was too full. I still had to get out the low-carb vegan cookbook every January to recover from the sugar high.

On Christmas Eve, Dave and I used to be able to cook and clean up dinner, go to a candlelight service, visit the Grinch and set visions of sugar plums dancing, put the kids to bed with a lullaby of Kermit singing carols with John Denver, assemble half a dozen toys, fill the stockings, arrange the presents under the tree, compose a letter from Father Christmas à la J.R.R. Tolkien for the mantel, fall into bed around 3:00 a.m., and still wake up early enough to make the cherry rose rolls before the kids clattered downstairs to the stockings. As the kids (and we) got older, it helped that they slept in longer and Father Christmas wrote his final letter to them, but the toys got more complicated, the assembly instructions were outsourced overseas and somehow we lost the ability to stay up past ten. And church? We got tired of hot wax burning our fingers while we forgot the words to "Silent Night."

The crowning glory of our Christmas disasters, however, has been the perpetual tree argument. We don't have a fake tree, and we never will. When we first moved into our house with cathedral ceilings, we happily trooped up to the foothills and brought a fifteen-foot tree home on the roof of our minivan. There were a few problems—most stands are made for eight-foot trees, and we had to accept that the topmost string of lights would always fail within a day. It got harder when we traded in the van for a Honda Civic, but we made do: we paid a high school boy with a pickup truck to deliver it, borrowed or rented a truck or bribed a neighbor with a bottle of wine (he didn't want a tin of cookies). We put the tradition on hold for a couple of years when the tree nearly fell on Robin as a toddler, but when she got old enough to dodge a potential accident the monster trees resumed.

And then we got Psycho Cat. We'd had a cat before, a nice, benign cat that knew how to go outside when necessary and was pretty laid-back about everything. He liked to sleep under the tree, and even the lowest ornaments were safe. But after Frodo died, we picked out an orphaned kitten, a calico Manx who was easily frightened and hated change. Bringing a fifteen-foot tree into the living room and covering it with lights and ornaments was change. She also never learned the difference between a throw rug and a litter box, or the difference between a Christmas tree skirt and a throw rug (please apply the transitive property of equality here).

One year, it seemed that all of the negative aspects of Christmas hit at once. Jon had married our beloved new daughter-in-law, Ramona, in August, and we had enjoyed Thanksgiving with them. But it was her parents' turn for Christmas and they were in Denver, a thousand miles away. Dave's father, James, had died in September, and we were still deeply grieving. My Civic had been rear-ended, leaving my back and neck temporarily sore. Tim, now in medical school, was rarely awake during the few days he was home. The recession had hit, and since music lessons and live music are expendable expenses, I had no income that month. I was feeling especially anticommercial anyway; I even dragged my husband to a workshop on simplifying Christmas, but the workshop only accentuated our irreconcilable differences about the holidays. We loaded up the credit card anyway, put up the insanely tall tree and tried to keep Psycho Cat out of the living room.

Christmas came and went despite the gloom, and on December 28 Dave and I awoke to celebrate our thirtieth anniversary. We took our coffee into the living room for a peaceful, romantic morning alone, but another smell was fighting with the odors of pine and cinnamon. I threw the tree skirt into the washer and began to clean up the rest of the mess. I had to lift up the plastic mat we had placed under the tree to protect the floor, and suddenly we had a much bigger mess to deal with. Fortunately all those crocheted and embroidered ornaments weren't breakable, and the tree missed the lamps on its way down.

Just when I felt the whole season deserved to be swept under the rug, Robin came running down the stairs, several hours before she usually got out of bed during vacation. She waved her cell phone at us. "Jon says to check the porch for a package!"

She opened the door, and there stood Jon and Ramona.

Sometime in the middle of all the hugs, Jon explained, "We're spending New Year's Eve with friends in San Francisco, so we came a couple of days early to celebrate with you. Happy anniversary!"

The newlyweds were glowing with the joy of their first Christmas as a couple, and their love transported us back to the early years of our marriage. We remembered our tiny Chicago apartment, and our first Christmas away from our families in Montana. We'd bought a small, dangerously dry tree in a drab city parking lot and covered it with generic ornaments from Woolworths. A thunderstorm on Christmas Eve destroyed any hope of a white Christmas; without a car, we splashed through the streets and shivered through a service in an unfamiliar church. And yet, that first Christmas, we also had our new baby son, whose eyes were glued to the sparkling lights. Jon was happy just playing with boxes and ribbons and getting his first taste of solid food. Now, with our family together again, welcoming Jon's new wife into our traditions, Dave and I realized that all of the "disasters" from thirty years of Christmas had transformed into good stories, a tapestry of shared memories that hold us together.

Since then, Christmas has regained its magic. We replaced the Civic with a small SUV that can carry a twelve-foot tree, and we gave three boxes worth of ornaments to our children for their own trees. I plan to make a new tree skirt in memory of Psycho Cat as soon as I finish cross-stitching Ramona's stocking. Robin's culinary experiments have expanded beyond dessert, so I have ceded control of the kitchen to her. We cut down on the cookies so we can enjoy Grandpa's favorite rum and orange juice with our adult children; we also treasure even more the time we still have with our mothers. We haven't yet missed a Christmas with the new doctor in the family, which has to be a miracle, and we've adjusted to the rhythm of sharing Jon and Ramona with her delightful parents. We're beginning to look forward to assembling toys and writing Father Christmas letters for as yet mythical grandchildren. When they do arrive, Christmas will move to their house, where they have room for a twenty-foot tree.

I'll bring the Springerles.

The Christmas Tree

Neva J. Hodges

———◦◦◦◦◦———

What had I done? The forever vows my husband and I exchanged in a wedding ceremony a few hours ago took on a new meaning. Changing from my travel clothes into my wedding nightgown on what I'd always believed would be the most romantic night of my life, the calm and sure belief that Jim was my true love deserted me. There was so much I didn't know about love and marriage. I looked around the small motel room. And romance? When would that start on this honeymoon?

Both Jim and I were raised in a strict religious environment, and even though the sexual revolution of the sixties pervaded our culture, we waited for our wedding night to consummate our relationship. However, stolen kisses and deep caresses highlighted our dates.

Jim proposed in June 1966, when he stopped to see me at my parents' home in Pueblo, Colorado, on his way to a six-week geology field camp. That same day, he said, "Let's look at rings." I couldn't believe it. We drove downtown and walked into a jewelry store. Jim told the owner I could have whatever I wanted. A simple one suited me. It had a quarter-carat diamond set in a half loop of gold. Jim later told me he was afraid I would choose the most expensive ring in the store. My taste fit his budget, though. Then Jim told the storeowner he didn't have the money and that he was a college student. I held my breath. "No problem," the owner said. "You can make monthly payments."

In the car, Jim slid the ring onto my finger and pledged his love to me.

After he left to meet his fellow geologists in Utah, I dreamed of a June wedding a year later—time enough to save money and plan the details. My parents could not afford to pay for the wedding. I left my hometown to look for work near Jim's college in Golden, Colorado. I stayed with a friend until I had a job and enough money for rent.

I searched for a place to live and found a small in-law unit at the back of the landlord's house. At least it was private. My fiancé, though, upped the ante. He wanted the wedding during his semester break. I told him I needed time to plan. His persuasive powers carried the day. He was practical and said, "I'll have a new job after graduation and I don't want to move and get married the same month."

We chose December 23 for our wedding. Young and in love, we didn't consider that people might have other plans for the Christmas holiday. Each week before we married, Jim stopped by the little house we would soon call home and gave me a greeting card. I loved seeing him, but the cards disappointed me. They were humorous. I wanted the romantic, serious ones that pledged undying love. The words didn't match the passion we experienced every time we met. I wanted more.

I proceeded to plan our wedding, which was less than four

months away, even though I worried that we were missing the romance I wanted. Many weekends I rode the bus from Denver to Pueblo, my hometown, two hours away, to choose my wedding dress, arrange for a photographer, secure my attendants and buy the cloth and patterns for their dresses. I lived paycheck to paycheck and bought less food to save money for the wedding expenses. By the time I bought my gown, I was a size eight, from a twelve. Even though I was hungry at times, my wedding dominated all that I did. A coworker saw how thin I had become and said, "Are you eating?"

I assured him I was.

The night of the rehearsal arrived. I was fine until Jim and his groomsmen teased me, laughed and in general had a good time. Tense and serious, I said, "Knock it off, you have to pay attention." They laughed, which added to my angst. I wanted a perfect wedding and, therefore, I needed a perfect rehearsal.

During the confusion, one of Jim's brothers slipped out and came back with hamburgers for everyone. It suddenly dawned on me. My fiancé hadn't planned a rehearsal dinner. Some people had driven two hours to get there and were returning home that night. They would come again the next evening for the wedding. My future husband hadn't read the bride magazines, and I later learned that he didn't know what his responsibilities were, except for choosing the groomsmen and arranging for the honeymoon.

Calm overtook me by the next morning. I rested in the afternoon and anticipated what it would feel like to have Jim make love to me that night.

Incorporating the beautiful colors of Christmas for my wedding, my attendants wore empire waist dresses, which matched the style of my white wedding dress. Their bodices were deep pink satin and the long flowing velvet skirts were deep rose. Fragrant with evergreen sprays, the floral baskets held a mix of carnations the color of the bridesmaids dresses. The containers sat on pedestals next to the white arch under which we were married. Everything went well during the ceremony until the moment we faced each other and listened to our vocalist sing "More." As the song filled the church sanctuary, I felt Jim sway—was he about to faint? I held his hands tight and pulled him closer to me. "Don't faint," I whispered. He unlocked his knees and the moment passed. Relieved, I turned my attention back to the ceremony. We said the vows we had memorized and waited for the final sentence, "You may kiss the bride." And now, to the honeymoon, the moment I'd longed for these past few months.

We drove to Colorado Springs for our first night, fooling the guests who had decorated Jim's '58 Chevrolet with cans that dangled and rattled and the words "Just Married" written in shaving cream on the rear window. We took his parents' car instead for our trip to explore the snow-covered Colorado Rockies. Yes, I did overcome my wedding night jitters, all doubts fled. But another problem soon troubled me. All the time we'd been planning this wedding, it never occurred to me to plan something for Christmas. I'd been so focused on dresses and flowers and vows. How would we celebrate our first holiday in a sterile motel? I turned to Jim that morning and admitted my mistake.

He looked at me and smiled. "I'll be right back," he said, closing the door to our room behind him. Another funny greeting card, I guessed, watching him from the window as he headed to the car. The romantic atmosphere of our wedding ceremony seemed to have faded quickly.

I guessed wrong. Jim opened the door to the room and dragged in a four-foot-tall, undecorated Christmas tree.

"Merry Christmas. I put this in the trunk and thought we'd take this along with us on our trip. That way we can put it in our room every night." My husband. He was a romantic, after all. Who needed sentimental cards when the man I married could surprise me with a special gift? And after forty-six years together, he surprises me still.

Enchiladas, Hold the Beer

Pam Walters

Holidays are a time for nostalgia, merriment and good cheer. We clink glasses and remember the past. We salute the present. And we toast each other for happiness and good fortune in the new year. But here's a sobering thought. How many people are merely putting on a party face? While most folks are wishing for lavish presents under the tree, some people are simply wishing for a way out of their emotional pain. To many people, a certain kind of personal freedom would be the most loving gift they could give to themselves.

By the time I was eighteen, I was drinking excessively. It started innocently enough in high school, yet I already knew that drinking meant more to me than it did to my friends as we snuck booze from our parents' liquor cabinets and shared it in the back of someone's car. I behaved differently than they did when it came to liquor, and I knew that my friends thought I was beginning to have a problem as well. I could tell by the looks they gave each other when I wanted to keep drinking after everyone else had stopped. As the years went by, my dependence on alcohol increased, and by the time I was forty, alcohol wasn't just important to me, it was the only thing that mattered. I was head over heels in love, having a long-term romance with alcohol.

The day my world came apart, and the day it came together, was the day after Thanksgiving in 1989. It was my personal "black Friday," the day I hit bottom.

Thanksgiving had been just another miserable holiday for me. I spent it alone, holed up in my fancy condo on the north side of Chicago. I sat in my comfy white chair—a big tumbler of vodka in hand—overlooking Lake Michigan. It was only 2:30 in the afternoon, and I was already far too drunk. I was a daily, maintenance drinker by then and—although I started drinking in the morning—I usually paced myself so that I wouldn't pass out until around 9 p.m. But not this day. I had totally overshot my mark. What was I going to do? I couldn't stop drinking; I couldn't even slow down. And if I had a couple more, I'd surely pass out in the chair. Somehow the idea of passing out in the middle of the day was horrific. I knew I was a bad drunk, but not *that* bad.

And then something happened. Some people call it a moment of clarity. But right then, I knew the jig was up. My life passed before my eyes. I sped through the years of hopping from one advertising agency job to another—a jump ahead of getting fired for lack of performance, lack of attendance or lack of anything resembling a good attitude toward my coworkers, my bosses or the clients. I drank that promising career away, and now I was unemployed yet again.

I had never been married…never had any kids. I ticked off my list of unhealthy love interests that mostly centered around us getting drunk or getting high. I was estranged from my parents and other relatives. I had no girlfriends and the couple of men friends I had were only drinking buddies. And they'd pretty much given up on me, too.

I looked at all the mistakes I'd made, the harebrained schemes, the moves to different cities. Running…always running away from something or someone, some bad decision, the wrong job or the wrong relationship. Running away from my dysfunctional childhood. Oh, I could always drag out that old drama and try to elicit a sympathetic ear. But somehow all the running away from the truth about myself stopped and started in that white chair, in the middle of the day, the day after Thanksgiving.

I looked around my beautiful living room. Everything became slightly out of focus. I couldn't really hear the TV—my constant companion. It's as if my whole world were put on mute. I felt weightless in that chair. And I knew *this* all had to stop. I knew my entire life and everything that had happened was centered around my alcoholism; the key to me was alcohol. I faced it and, for a split second, something in me surrendered, and I opened myself up to possibilities. I whispered, "Now what?"

Suddenly the phone rang—this didn't happen often. And then someone was buzzing me from the downstairs lobby—this *never* happened. I picked up the phone. It was my old boyfriend, Tom. We were together for a couple of drunken years, and then he decided to get sober. I asked him to hold as I went to the intercom. It was a nurse I'd met at one of the AA meetings I attended as Tom's "significant other."

Between the two of them, double-teaming in an intervention, I agreed to check myself into a treatment center. As the phone calls were placed and the arrangements made, I sat in wonder that all this was unfolding in front of me, and that I was actually going along with it. Could I really break up with the bottle? Could I leave this long-term relationship behind?

Several days later, I found myself walking up the steps to a twenty-eight-day recovery center. I was still in shock at what was happening, but I kept putting one foot in front of the other and, thank God, I never turned away and bolted for the door.

The weeks passed and slowly the haze lifted. I saw myself clearly, probably for the first time in my life, but not with anguish, remorse or guilt. I saw that I was a sick person. I had a disease. Yes, I did things that were stupid and destructive, but they were knee-jerk reactions—the result of operating under the heavy cloak of alcoholism.

My life lay in front of me—blank pages yet to be filled in. I had no script, no plans and no big ideas. The day of the "big idea" was over. I was just taking it one day at a time. One revelation, one insight at a time.

And I was about to face my first sober Christmas. I was glad I was in treatment. At least I wouldn't be alone.

The administrators and counselors were dissuading us from making a big deal about Christmas. Why? Because the holiday symbolized too much nostalgia. It brought up too many emotional triggers. As a result, there were no Christmas decorations, and we weren't allowed to accept gifts or cards from the outside. For dinner Christmas Eve, we had tuna noodle casserole. Not exactly your traditional holiday fare. After dinner and a low-key group session, we each retired to our rooms.

But in the middle of the night, I was wide awake. It was Christmas, after all. A day in which gifts from the heart are given and received. How could I express the love that was developing inside me, not just for my sober self, but also for those who were helping me on this difficult journey? *There*

must be some way I can show them, I thought as I quietly pad-
ded around the facility. I poked around until I hit the laundry
room. There on long bars, hung up high, were dozens of my
housemates' blouses, jeans and T-shirts. Bingo. I'd found it.
There was a way I could put my love into action.

So at 3:30 on Christmas morning, I ironed everyone's
clothes. I didn't tell them who'd done it. It was my secret
gift to them.

That Christmas day was the same as all the others in that
twenty-eight-day center. Morning meditation, group therapy,
individual counseling and so on. And for Christmas dinner,
we were served enchiladas. We all laughed and spontaneously
said: "Hold the Corona."

That was twenty-three years ago. It's hard to believe; it's a
miracle, actually. I never looked back, not once. I just stared
straight ahead at my unknown future. One step in front of
the other, one day at a time. And miracles have happened to
me *beyond my wildest dreams.* Unbelievably wonderful things
have occurred. I wouldn't even have dreamed to ask for what's
happened; I would have shortchanged myself. But the most
important gifts I've received are the gifts of freedom, serenity,
peace of mind and true joy. Getting sober was the most loving Christmas present I have ever received, and yes, it came
hand-delivered from me to me.

Perfect Record

Lelia Kutger, as told to April Kutger

———————— ◦•❯❮•◦ ————————

There was a fierce blizzard in the days before Christmas in 1951. We were snowed in in Morrisville, Pennsylvania. Snowplows had left four-foot-high drifts blocking the driveway. We had our tree, but, according to tradition, would not decorate it until Christmas Eve. The presents for the girls were stowed in the trunk of my big, old Packard. It was all up to me this year, just as it had been for our daughter JoAnne's first Christmas some years before, during World War II. That was the year I got the telegram.

Joe was a navigator for the B-24 bombers dropping their payloads over Germany. I feared for his life every day, but my precious baby girl diverted my attention from missing her father. JoAnne was born in September 1944, nine months after Joe's and my first Christmas together. I hadn't seen him since that Christmas. I had sent pictures of our baby girl to Joe, but I hadn't received a letter from him since a short V-mail, bursting with joy and relief that his first child had been born safely. I wished so much that he could be with us for JoAnne's first Christmas, but it was the same for me as for most of the women I knew. The men were off at war.

It was November 30 when the boy who worked at the drugstore rode his bike up to the cottage we rented near Fort Dix, New Jersey. JoAnne was asleep in her cradle and I was folding diapers, stiff from drying in the cold air.

"Ma'am," he said with a small nod. He was holding a yellow envelope in his hand. A telegram. I sucked in my breath, but didn't make a sound. The boy pushed the envelope toward me and repeated, "Ma'am." I took it from his gloved hand and, for some absurd reason, I said, "Thank you." I handed him a quarter from my coin purse and stood in the open doorway, staring into space. It was several moments before the chill air made me realize where I was.

Clutching the telegram to my breast, I sat down on the navy-blue-velvet couch my parents had handed down to us. I couldn't open it. I went to the kitchen to reheat the morning coffee. It would taste bitter, but my mouth was already bitter. I swallowed a big gulp. Suddenly I was in a cold sweat and shaking. I ran to the bathroom and threw up. "This is absurd," I said to myself. "I don't even know what's in the telegram." But I knew. I went back to the kitchen and sat down again, slipped my thumb under the envelope flap and gently pried it open as if it were an ancient papyrus artifact.

"LT JOSEPH P KUTGER MISSING IN ACTION STOP." I stopped.

Five months after that lonely and anxious time, not knowing if Joe was dead or alive or, as proved to be true, a prisoner of war, the war in Europe ended. A month later Joe was transferred to a stateside hospital. The following Christmas I was four months' pregnant with our second child. Joe was healthy and had gained back most of the weight he'd lost in prison camp. On Christmas Eve he gave me a gold crucifix. He told me it should remind me that I was never alone, because God was always with me. I cried and said, "It's beautiful, but I want *you* to always be with me." Joe held me in his arms and said he would never miss another Christmas. I knew he might not be able to keep that promise. But now it had been six years, and he had.

In 1951 Joe was stationed at Godman Air Field near Fort Knox, Kentucky, more than seven hundred miles from where the children and I lived. I hadn't seen him for three months, but after a lot of finagling, trading duty assignments and finishing his training assignment ahead of schedule, Joe told me he thought he would be able to make it home at least for a few days. He was going to hitch a couple of rides on puddle jumpers that would get him to Millville Air Field in New Jersey.

Then the blizzard blanketed the East Coast and another one was expected. Joe called to say, "There's no way I can get there, Honey. I'm really sorry. I wanted to keep my promise. I did everything I could to make this happen."

"Oh, Joe," I cried.

"Honey, I'm sorry. I can't help it."

"What about the girls? They've been counting down the days until you'd be here."

"You know I would if I could, but there are no flights operating. It's just not possible."

"I can't do this without you, Joe. I can't make Christmas without you."

"You have to, Lee. You have to be strong and make everything about this Christmas the same as always. Make sugar cookies. Decorate the tree on Christmas Eve. Open the presents in the morning. Serve roast beef for Christmas dinner…"

"Oh, Joe, I feel like I did when you were shot down in '44. I need you."

"I know you can do this, Hon. Are you wearing your crucifix? Remember, you're not alone. God is with you."

"I hate it when you tell me that whenever I'm missing you too much. I don't want God. I want you." I caught my breath and said, "Sorry. I didn't mean that. I do want God. It's just that I want you so much."

"It's going to be okay, Sweetheart."

I blew my nose and modulated my tone. "I know. I can do it. Don't worry," I told him, even though I didn't feel that way at all.

"That's my girl."

With the driveway packed in, we couldn't get to church on Sunday, and the weatherman forecasted a new storm by nightfall. I hoped my brother, Ralph, would be able to make it on Christmas Day. I always counted on Ralph to be there for me when Joe was gone.

It did not snow Sunday night, and I got my hopes up that we might be able to dig out soon. On Monday, Christmas Eve morning, a friend of Joe's showed up with a pickup truck and a plow.

"Pete," I yelled from the front door, "what are you doing here?"

"Joe called me, so here I am," he laughed. My sweet husband. Taking care of us even when he was hundreds of miles away.

"Thank you so much, Pete."

"I'm happy to do it, Lee."

"Come on in for a cup of coffee."

"I will when I'm finished."

Pete cleared the driveway, the front steps and the walkway,

as well as a path to the garage at the edge of the woods behind the house, which made it possible for us to keep one of our traditions. We always cut evergreen boughs to decorate the mantle and banister and a few to burn in the fireplace to give the house the wonderful smell of burning pine needles and the popping sound of pinecones.

A short time later, my very devoted milkman trudged through two-feet-deep snow to deliver three quarts of milk, a pound of butter and a dozen eggs. Another dilemma resolved. I had the ingredients I needed to make cookies. I handed him a Christmas card with $2 in it. Before he left, he said, "You're lucky to have power."

We had radio reception, too, so we could listen, as we did every morning, to Don McNeill's Breakfast Club. I did the dishes and the laundry, and the girls marched around the table when Don told them to. By 11:00 a.m., the sky was heavily overcast and the neighborhood was eerily silent except for the occasional sound of a tree branch breaking. The storm was on its way.

The night before I had told the girls their daddy could not come for Christmas. They were crushed, but soon they stopped crying and then whimpered into sleep as I sang to them. They had seemed fine all morning, but now I could tell they were not taking it well. They were ripping around the house like monkeys that had escaped from the zoo. Whooping and hollering. Arguing and taunting and fighting. JoAnne teased April. April cried and hit her. JoAnne ran to me to tattle. Finally, I said, "Naptime! And separate bedrooms!"

"I get Mommy's bed," JoAnne shouted.

"No, me!" April whined.

When there was silence from the second floor, I lay down,

too. I slept fitfully until I heard little voices calling, "Can we get up now, Mommy?"

After peanut butter and jelly sandwiches and hot chocolate, I bundled the girls into their snowsuits. Fresh air would be good for all of us. "Come on. We're going to cut tree branches and put big red ribbons on them."

"Can I help, Mommy?" April asked with great enthusiasm.

"Of course, Honey. I want you to tell me which branches are the best."

I got my garden shears, and we tramped through the snow to the woods behind the house. It was hard for my cherubs to make their way through the deep snow, but we followed the path Pete had plowed.

"I'm cold, Mommy," my little towhead April cried after we were out for a few minutes.

"We'll go in soon, Honey."

JoAnne, my stubborn and determined girl, said, "Can't we stay out and make snow angels?" Before I could answer, the first new flurries began to fall.

As soon as we were inside, I called Ralph. "Why don't you come now? Stay overnight with us. The roads will be impossible in an hour." He was silent. "I have pork chops for dinner," I coaxed.

"I was on my way to a friend's. His parents came down for the holiday."

"Please, Ralph." I didn't want to be alone.

"Okay, Sis. Do you want me to pick anything up on the way?"

"I can't think of anything—just get here before it's too dangerous."

Ralph made it to us just as the early winter twilight fell. He scooped the girls up and threw them in the air as they screamed and giggled. I heated up my hard cider for the two of us, something Joe and I always shared on Christmas Eve.

"Thank you," I told him. "For everything." We shared a smile.

After dinner, the four of us gathered around the tree. "You girls do the low branches, I'll do the middle and Uncle Ralph will do the high ones," I announced. When we were finished, Ralph carefully placed an heirloom angel in a white satin dress on the very top branch. JoAnne and April clapped and oohed and aahed; their eyes shining with the reflection of the Christmas lights.

"And now it's time for bed, girls," I said. They were wearing matching red plaid flannel nightgowns and fluffy slippers. Joe's and my little angels.

"I wish Daddy was here," JoAnne said, tears starting to fall.

"Me, too," cried April.

I hugged my girls and said, "I wish Daddy was here, too. But we'll be okay."

"I'll take them up," Ralph said, his hands reaching out for theirs.

"Thanks, Ralph. I'm beat." I gave each little forehead a good-night kiss and leaned back on the couch.

Ralph stayed downstairs with me until midnight, and I think we both got a little tipsy. We had been listening to Christmas songs on the radio and sharing stories of our childhood. I blubbered as I told Ralph how much I missed Joe, especially at Christmas. "It's just like the war. I went more than a year without seeing him when he was a POW. At first I didn't even know if he was alive."

Ralph had heard the story many times. He always listened sympathetically, but not for too long. He started making fun of me and my tears and my memories. "You are not going to look like a merry Christmas girl with those swollen eyes and mascara running down your cheeks." I laughed and wiped my eyes. "How do you think Joe would feel if he saw you like this? It's bad enough that he can't be here, but then to think you've become completely discombobulated in his absence." Now I couldn't stop laughing. "Soused and sobbing on Christmas Eve. Or is it Christmas morning?" he said as he looked at his watch. "You're not the woman Joe married, I can tell you that. Pull yourself together, Sis!" Ralph grabbed my shoulders and shook me in jest. I was laughing so hard I thought I would wake the girls.

After Ralph climbed the stairs, I lay down on the old blue-velvet couch—Joe's favorite place to nap. I turned the radio to a station that played the Hit Parade. Everything from Johnnie Ray's "Cry" and "Too Young" by Nat King Cole to Les Paul and Mary Ford's "How High the Moon." I loved that one. Joe said he played it on the Officer's Club jukebox because it made him think of me. I couldn't help shedding a tear. I wondered if Joe was listening to it now.

As I held my "missing Joe" crucifix between my thumb and forefinger, I prayed the prayer I had repeated so often when Joe was a POW. "Keep him safe, Lord. Bring him home to me. Take care of him. Keep him warm. Let him know how much I love him. Bring him home safe and sound." As I drifted off, I imagined I smelled Joe's hair cream emanating from the doily on the couch's armrest.

Only minutes later, I woke with a start, but then lay dead still. Someone was jiggling the front doorknob. Then I heard the floor creak in the hallway. Oh, dear Lord, protect my children. My heart was pounding so hard I thought it would explode. I was afraid to breathe. A burly man walked slowly, silently, toward the center of the room where the tree lights twinkled. I didn't move. The figure turned toward me.

"Oh, my goodness! Joe!" I gasped as I jumped up.

"I promised you I would always be home for Christmas." He leaned over and kissed my forehead, then my eyelids, then my lips. "Don't cry, Honey," he said, wiping away my tears. "I only have a few hours. Let's make the most of it." He zipped himself out of his thick shearling flight suit and boots, which added twenty pounds to his frame, and sat down beside me.

"Did you make your hard cider this year?" he asked, rubbing his cold, red hands together.

"Of course." I kissed every square inch of his visible skin. "Joe, you're freezing," I said, my arms tightening around his shivering body.

"You're right. I *am* freezing. I'll tell you about it after I get my hands around a warm mug of cider."

Once he was settled and warm, Joe told me how he got home. "I borrowed a car from a pilot who couldn't leave the base. A Fiat. Tiniest car you've ever seen. Italian. Not built for snow. It had a broken heater, but I decided to go for it. I wore my flight suit to stay warm."

"But Joe, if you broke down on an empty road, you could have frozen to death."

"I was okay until I got to Pittsburgh. Then the driver's side windshield wiper broke. I had to drive with my hand out the window to clear off the snow."

Armed with nothing but a thermos of coffee, he drove for twenty straight hours, through a raging snowstorm. He was never able to go faster than 45 mph, often a lot slower. Then the car simply stopped in one of the tunnels. It was only a matter of reconnecting the alternator wire, but if there had been other cars on the road, he would have caused a pileup.

As thrilled as I was to be nestled in Joe's arms, the thought of what he had done to get home terrified me. "Joe, you shouldn't have done it. You could have gotten killed."

"When I got home from the war," Joe whispered, "I made you a promise that I'd never again leave you alone on Christmas. My record's been perfect so far. I didn't want to break it. And the look in your eyes makes it all worthwhile."

Giving Shelter

Melissa Chambers

------◆◇◆------

It was that time of year… I was busy preparing for Christmas, getting the tree up and trimmed, decorating the house, shopping and attempting to hold the attention of thirty fifth-graders for six hours a day. It was also a time of discovery; just a few weeks before my boyfriend had moved in, and we were still learning what that was like. We had so much in common, Charlie and I—a love of animals, books and political discussion. Life was wonderful, and I suspected that he was starting to think about marriage. But…were we really a perfect match? I'd made a mistake once before, so how could I be sure I wouldn't make another one?

This holiday season, rather than donating to a local animal rescue, as I had for the last few years, I had decided to become involved in animal rescue myself. "Great idea," Charlie had said when I told him about my plan to drive a few hours down to the Central Valley with Susan, a new friend who volunteered for a local rescue, and "pull" a couple of dogs from an overcrowded shelter she'd learned about. The plan was that we'd bring the dogs north to our town and we would have them spayed or neutered and foster them until new homes were found for each of them. It was a long drive, through areas known for thick "Tule fog" this time of year. "Getting the dogs is wonderful," he'd said, and then added, "but wait until the fog burns off before you get on the road."

As the day grew closer, I was more excited about our rescue mission than I was about the approaching holiday. For the last week, every evening, when I should have been wrapping presents, I had instead been looking at the dogs on the shelter's website. A few days earlier I had decided to pull an adult Chihuahua and notified the shelter of my intent, but then had received word yesterday that she had not survived a bout of kennel cough.

Lying awake in bed that last night, reviewing everything I needed to pack in the morning for the trip, I kept seeing the big, scared eyes of the little blond Chihuahua. I'd already become attached to her just by seeing her picture. I felt it was my fault that she had died. What if I had taken off work and gone down there a few days earlier? Would I have been able to save her? I'd never had an animal's death on my conscience before. As I tossed and turned, unable to quiet my thoughts enough to sleep, I realized what I would be doing tomorrow was playing God. The dogs I chose to bring back with me would be given a chance to survive. I knew that, but somehow had not connected the dots and realized that I would pretty much be sealing the fate of those I left behind. After that unwelcome epiphany, I didn't think I would sleep at all, but I must have succumbed at some point because I was awakened from a deep sleep by the alarm at 8:30. We planned to hit the road about 1 p.m., which left plenty of time to pack everything and for the fog to burn off.

Traffic had been heavy with holiday travelers, but luckily there was no fog. Susan called the shelter to let them know we would not be getting there until after they had closed for the day.

Our first stop once we reached the shelter was the isolation ward for sick and injured dogs. A tiny ginger-hued Chihuahua puppy with caramel eyes peered out at me from the first cage I saw. One of his front paws flopped uselessly from the joint, but that didn't stop him from plastering himself against the bars of the cage and sticking his long pink tongue out to lick my hand. A shelter worker in the room looked at his intake card and told us, "We don't have a vet here, so he'll be put down in the morning."

"Oh no, he won't," I responded, lifting him from the cage and wrapping my coat around his wriggling body.

A few cages further down we saw a dog that looked like a Jack Russell Terrier, but with very short legs, that seemed to have swallowed a watermelon. Because she was pregnant, she was also scheduled for euthanasia the next day, we were told. Her tail beat the air like a metronome as she threw herself at the bars over and over in an effort to get to us. Vanessa, as her kennel card identified her, was in a crate and ready to go in moments. *Surely Charlie would understand why I couldn't leave her, wouldn't he?* I asked myself.

The main kennels were so loud that conversation was impossible. This part of the shelter had openings to small outside areas attached to each kennel, and the icy December wind rushed in. I huddled deeper in my coat and gaped at the packed kennels whose floors were wet from when they had last been washed. With no way to get off the wet floor, the dogs were huddling together in piles, trying to get warm.

I blinked tears from my eyes as I thought of Charlie and the three dogs we already owned, at home, warm and safe. This time of the evening would find them snuggled together on the living room couch, the cheerful glow from the lights of the Christmas tree in front of the window competing with the blue light of the television across the room. Our dogs each had a Christmas stocking hung from the bookcase, between Charlie's and mine. On Christmas morning they would be filled with chew toys, carrots and tiny tennis balls. At night they slept upstairs in the bed with us. Each had his or her special spot, and woe to the dog that tried to muscle in on another's territory. The dogs were all mine, but when Charlie moved in, they were ecstatic to have someone else to lavish attention on them. All had been adopted from rescues. I hoped they had forgotten that part of their lives, now that they were used to being warm and dry and fed and loved. How many of the shivering dogs surrounding me now, I wondered, would get the chance to be part of a family again? There wasn't one of them that didn't deserve to have its own stocking filled with treats to devour on Christmas morning.

At least I could make a difference in the lives of a couple of them today. Last night over dinner I had promised Charlie I would pull just one or two dogs from the shelter. Small Chihuahuas like we had at home, because the Central Valley shelters were overflowing with them. I promised him they wouldn't be any trouble. The amount of money I spent getting them spayed or neutered would be the amount I asked for their adoption fee, so they would not be a financial burden. "You will hardly know they're here before they'll be gone and in their new loving homes!" I'd insisted this afternoon as I shrugged into my coat.

"Just be safe and let me know when you're heading back," Charlie replied as I gave him a quick hug and headed for the door. Now I realized that I could not keep my word. I had lied to him. At the time I had thought I could save just two dogs. I had already chosen two, and one was going to deliver puppies any day! Charlie trusted me. I knew how important honesty was in a relationship. Should I call and ask him if he would mind if I brought home more than two? Could I even leave the shelter with just these two dogs? How would he react when he found out I had broken my promise? Adding two dogs to our home, even temporarily, would be a bit stressful. More than two, more stress. What kind of reaction could I expect? Would he be angry? Feel he could no longer trust me to keep my word? Would he move out, leaving me to spend Christmas alone?

These thoughts chased around in my head as I surveyed the small faces surrounding me, begging me with their eyes, reaching for me with their tiny paws, each asking to be saved.

I texted Charlie when we left the shelter and headed back up north but didn't mention anything about the dogs I was bringing home. It was almost 1 a.m. before we made it back to Sacramento. After dropping Susan and her new foster dogs off, I headed home, part of me eager to be back, another part wanting to delay having to face Charlie and tell him what I'd done.

The lights of our Christmas tree were still on, clearly visible through the front window as I pulled into the driveway. I wished I could leave the dogs in the car while I went in and prepared Charlie, but the night was much too cold. As I began carrying in crate after crate I told him in bits and pieces about what I had seen in the shelter: the cold wet kennels, the pleading faces of the dogs, the impossibility of saving only two. His eyes wide, Charlie listened without saying anything and eyed the growing number of crates I placed next to our

Christmas tree. When the last crate was inside I stood before him, and said, "That's why I brought home eight dogs, rather than just two, as I promised." By that time the long day had caught up with me, and I was swaying on my feet. Charlie took me in his arms and wrapped me in a warm embrace. He looked down into my eyes and said, "Melissa, don't apologize. I would have brought home more." I hugged him back as hard as I could. No man could have said anything sweeter. I had made the right choice at last.

A Christmas Letter to My Wife of Fifty Years

Jack Skillicorn

—•◦◦◦•—

My Dearest Sandy:

It's that time of year again. You've just headed out to the store to stock up on holiday treats, and here I sit to begin the process of writing our annual holiday letter to friends and relatives. This year I am having a difficult time concentrating, though. It could be the glass of our favorite wine that I've just poured, or it could be that every few minutes I look up from the page and focus on our newly decorated Christmas tree, hung with the ornaments we've collected, homemade strings of popcorn and the golden star we use every year at the top of the tree. Yes, I know most wives don't think their husbands notice these kinds of small details but, Sandy, I do.

This holiday letter should be easy to write: after all, the formula is a well-worn one—a few paragraphs and some photos from trips we took, family updates on the kids and grandkids, throw in a few pet stories and voilà, I'm done. Or sometimes letter writers like to reminisce about holidays past. That should be an easy one to pull off; I have memories from fifty Christmases past to draw from…but no, this afternoon all I can focus on is you. Us. Our life together, as symbolized by a warmly lit and glittering tree. To heck with the Christmas letter—I'll send two next year instead. This letter, Sandy, is for you.

That gold star perched at the top of the tree? It takes me back fifty years to you, our young daughter, Jeanette, and I celebrating Christmas together for the very first time as a newly made family in Massachusetts, snow on the ground and frost on the windows. With you in my arms and smiles on our faces, we watched a five-year-old delight in her presents. It was my first moment as her father, and I remember it so clearly.

And the peacock ornaments there on the branch near the window—I know exactly where they came from and when. 1965, Thailand. You came from California to visit me when I was stationed at the Ubon Air Force Base. You arrived in Bangkok after giving me very specific instructions not to waste a day of my leave coming down from Ubon just to meet your plane. Instructions I, of course, ignored! Watching you walk off the plane and seeing the look on your happy face when you saw that I had ignored your instructions was worth it. Holding you there in the airport wasn't half bad, either. The blue, red and yellow cloth peacock ornaments are from a local marketplace in Ubon. I remember you wrapping each one to put in your suitcase when your visit ended all too soon. More than fifty years later, the colors are still vibrant, and so is my memory of you in that moment.

The small brass photo ornament in the middle of the tree, that is from 1968 in California. Our daughter Margaret was only three months old that Christmas. Is there ever a better present under the tree than a newborn baby in a red-velvet jumper and a white blouse with a lace collar and a Santa cap?

That clear glass ornament up there, near the top of the tree, filled with sand and seashells? Of course it is from 1979 in Maui. Moonlight walks on the beach, just the two of us walking hand in hand through the surf. What a trip—it is no wonder that we try to go back as often as we can.

I could go on and on, through each of the ornaments that we pull out of the box every year, dust off and then hang together as Christmas music plays in the background and the smell of baking cookies wafts in from the kitchen.

And now here we are, in our fiftieth year together. Such amazing memories, yes, but even more amazing will be the happy times and continuing romance in the coming years. Who knew, so many years ago, that it would turn out this well? I did, Sandy. I knew. I knew it when we bought that gold star, when we first held our children together, when we walked on beach after beach. Day in and day out, I knew. Christmas only comes once a year, but our long romance is never ending.

Your husband,
Jack

The Crumpled Card

Julaina Kleist-Corwin

————◆❍◆————

The cold December Saturday amplified the chill in my body. I raised the thermostat in my San Francisco Bay home, and the heater roared warmth. But it didn't help. I paced in circles around my luggage and in straight lines down the hall. The shiver of anxiety wouldn't stop. I expected a phone call from Mitchell at any moment.

We had attended a health conference in Paris, and it had been a romantic trip, blended with business. When we returned to the airport's extended-stay parking lot, we kissed. Then he opened the door to my Nissan. I entered and rolled down the window. He kissed me again before he walked to his car nearby. We waved goodbye through our car windows and drove our separate ways.

No sooner had I arrived home that afternoon then I dropped my bags and raced to the phone to check for messages, expecting to have already heard from him. Nothing. No message. Nothing then, and nothing in the days since. Had he already forgotten our two weeks together in the dreamiest city in the world? My bags still sat there on the rug where I'd left them. Still packed and unattended. In the time I'd been home I still hadn't had the heart to open them and face the reminders of Paris and, him.

This had to stop. I called my mother to come over and help me unpack. The doorbell rang, we hugged at the door and I offered her a cup of coffee.

"No, thanks. It's too hot in here." She took off her white Christmas-decorated sweater and pushed up the sleeves of her turtleneck. In winter, she always wore monochromatic navy-blue clothes, except for a few white holiday tops. I turned down the thermostat. No need for heat when my mom always brightened the cloud of gloom. We both knew I was capable of unpacking one bulging suitcase and a small carry-on by myself, but she didn't question me. She could recognize a distraught daughter and would stay calm until I explained. I opened my luggage and dug among my now-wrinkled clothes to find the souvenir of the Eiffel Tower I had brought back for her. I skirted the topic of Mitchell by asking what she had done during the time I was gone.

She summarized two weeks in two minutes and then nudged my elbow. "So, tell me, what did you do together? Did you sightsee with Mitchell, or did you have to go on guided tours with the conference group?"

Of course, she actually wanted to know if Mitchell and I had made commitments. Her mantra the last few months repeated in my head, "Divorced for three years, it's time you settle down with a good man." She was right. I was ready. Best of all, I had found Mitchell. The day we met less than a year ago, I fell in love with him. I thought that by now he cared for me in the same way.

"We went with the group to the Louvre, the Arc de Triomphe, Montmartre and Notre Dame." I didn't tell her we'd ditched the group at the cathedral in the late afternoon and had the best time finding a picturesque restaurant for dinner. I also left out the part about the boat trip on the Seine to see the lights on the Eiffel Tower.

I brought the lightweight laundry basket closer to us. She had her arms folded; her patience with me clearly dwindling fast. Tilting her head to one side, she raised her eyebrows with a silent question. I shrugged in a silent response. "Am I keeping you in suspense?" Two pairs of folded jeans remained in the suitcase, which I picked up and held to my heart. "I bought these on the Champs-Élysées. Oh, I do love Paris."

"Loving a city is different than loving a man." Her voice had a discouraged tone, and she shook her head. I had dumped my suitcases' contents on the bed, and she sorted the blouses into hand-wash and machine-wash piles.

"Being in Paris together confirmed how I feel." My eyes welled up from the worry that maybe something had gone wrong on his end. What could it be? I grabbed my travel-sized cosmetics bag and went to return the items to the ad-joining bathroom. I didn't want my mother to see me cry.

I talked louder from there, so she could hear me. "Mitch-ell and I had a day and evening to ourselves. We went to the Musée d'Orsay to see many of the French Impressionist paint-ings I've studied and admired for years. They were awesome. Then we took the speed train to visit one of his colleagues who served us dinner at his home in Vendôme. The family didn't speak English, but we managed to communicate with pantomime." I didn't tell her how I'd cried bittersweet tears in the restroom on the train back to Paris. We would fly home the next day, and I didn't want the trip to end.

I carried the empty suitcases to the garage door. I was also carrying an empty heart. "I'll put 'em away later. Thanks for your help. It would have been a lot sadder to unpack by myself."

She put her hand on my forearm. "Sad? But, Honey, I thought you had a romantic trip."

"I did. It felt like a honeymoon. But he hasn't called at all since we got back. Maybe, for him, it was just a fling." I plopped onto the living room love seat, and my mother took a seat on the wicker chair, her lips pressed together in a tight line.

The look on her face made me crumple inside and brought my sobs to the surface. She got up and wrapped her arms around me, comforting me as only a mother can. "Maybe he's busy at work. Maybe he had to catch up after being out of town."

I had thought of that, too, but even busy people have time to text. "I thought I'd send him a Christmas card, but he's Jewish and I don't want to make a religious mistake."

"A card? Why not just call him yourself?"

"Never. I have to know that he wants to be with me. I wouldn't want him to see me again just to humor me or to feel as if he has to make up an excuse not to see me again."

We ate chocolate ice cream, and I shared more stories about the Parisian places I'd visited. When she left, I pulled the blank Hanukkah card I'd bought out of my purse. Yes, I had already bought him a card for his upcoming holiday. It was generic and distant. Not something I'd give to a man I wanted to marry. I signed my name without love or best wishes, just my signature, and I wrote his address on the envelope.

I didn't mail it, though. The card stayed in my purse, the envelope bending and the corners crumpling more each day. I couldn't bring myself to drop it into the mailbox. Work wasn't enough of a distraction for me. Flashes of scenes from Paris kept popping up, and I missed Mitchell more than I would ever have guessed. I wrote out Christmas cards to my friends and family and mailed them all, but still the Hanukkah card withered in my purse.

Ten nights passed without a word. That night I brought out my tabletop artificial Christmas tree. I turned off the house lights after 8 p.m. and stared at the twinkling clear bulbs wrapped around the branches, imagining the tree to be the Eiffel Tower. I remembered the hum of the boat's motor as we glided on the smooth river. Mitchell had wrapped his strong arms around me as the sparkling tower came into view in the distance. We floated closer to the magical lights, and I put my head on his shoulder. He kissed my forehead several times. When we reached the tower in all its brilliance, we embraced, and I was sure a lightning bolt of energy connected us.

I must have been wrong. Ten days after that magical moment, I was alone in my house with a twinkling fake tree.

The next day I shuffled through a mall in a throng of excited shoppers. There were a few Christmas gifts I needed to buy for friends and family. I carefully avoided the men's section at Macy's. I looked away when I passed display windows filled with glittery engagement rings.

Dumping my packages on the kitchen table, I went straight to the bathroom to run a hot tub. My day was done. A bath and an early bedtime—that was all I had to look forward to. The phone rang at about 6:30 p.m. I wrapped my pink terrycloth robe around me and reached to answer it.

Mitchell's voice greeted me. "Are you ready to celebrate the holiday tonight?"

What? He sounded like I was supposed to be remembering a prearranged date. My heart pounded. "Tonight?"

"Did you forget? Remember I said I wouldn't be able to see you for a while but that we'd have dinner on Hanukkah?"

No, I didn't remember him saying that. I certainly would have remembered. Nevertheless, he sounded sincere; maybe he thought he had told me. I stifled my surprise with the first thought that came to mind. "I guess I didn't realize Hanukkah started tonight." Since returning from Europe, though, I had marked the days on my wall calendar. I knew the Jewish holiday had arrived, and I had been ready to toss that Hanukkah card in the trash.

An hour later, we met at the Holy Land Restaurant on College Avenue in Berkeley. He gave me a tight hug and seemed happy to see me. This was the man who hadn't called? It didn't seem possible, but yet... We chatted about Paris and work, ordered matzo ball soup and falafel. When we finished our meal, Mitchell reached for my hand and his deep brown eyes teased me as if he had a surprise. Then he pulled out a present from his pocket and put it into my hand, with an expression that chased away all my doubts. "Happy Hanukkah, Julaina."

I mumbled a thank-you. My face burned with embarrassment. "Um, I have this card for you, but, um, it's not in very good shape. I've carried it around for days." I retrieved it from my purse and placed it on his side of the table.

He smiled and nodded toward the gift he had given to me. The wrapping paper had the Star of David on it. I took his nod to mean I should open it. I struggled with the ribbon and tape on the five-inch-square box. When I opened it, I gasped. A multistring necklace of small jade beads lay on a bed of cotton.

"It was made in Israel." He shifted in his chair. "I worried it wouldn't arrive in time. I didn't want to spoil the surprise, and I knew I would tell you about it if I talked to you before tonight. It was a long wait. Eleven days were too long without you."

From across the table I nodded numbly, fingering the beautiful necklace.

He opened the envelope I had brought, acted like there were no bent corners, and read it. His face beamed, but I wondered how a card could compare to the treasured necklace.

Mitchell rose from his chair and came around behind me, gently clasping the strings of Israeli jade around my neck. This precious gift was the first of many necklaces he gave me for every holiday that came along. On my birthday that year, he gave me an engagement ring and a year later, we were married. I found gifts for him, too, but I've never given him another Hanukkah card.

We celebrate two holidays every December. I plug in my tabletop Christmas tree, and he lights the candles on the menorah. We share my pretense that the tree is the Eiffel Tower, and he says the flames on the menorah's candles represent the love we have for each other. And the best part about being married to Mitchell? He's never kept me waiting again.

A Box of Memories

Christina Richter

--◈◆◈--

We had passed the seven-year itch, but it was looking as if we might hit the ten-year ditch. My husband and I were both working full-time, juggling kids and family responsibilities, leaving no time for romance—let alone a nice discussion once in a while. Christmas was coming, which meant yet another activity was added to our already full lives.

Even though we were busy, little girls have a way with their fathers, and our daughters were no exception. Audrey and Anna, six and four, were especially fond of their papa, and he was completely smitten. Whenever they were together, the three of them would talk endlessly. But I noticed lately their chatter occurred only when I wasn't in the room. I knew they were up to something!

Secrets were not easily kept as we lived in a very small house back then. The little one-bedroom post-WWII bungalow was advertised at 1,200 square feet, but in reality it was barely that size. It had a cute front room with '40s-style casement windows, a tiny dining room attached to a galley kitchen and a walk-through room to the back porch that you might call a den. The spot dubbed as the laundry room only had space for a washing machine, so our dryer had to service us from the back patio.

The house didn't afford much privacy, but there was one place that was entirely the domain of my husband—the garage. It was actually quite spacious for the size of house, and Mark set up his office in its confines. Not that he needed an office; he just needed his space. I didn't venture into that area much; among other things, I was too busy with a full-time job and being an involved mother of two active daughters to notice what happened in the garage. In fact, it usually came as a relief when he and the girls were occupied in "Hubby's office."

The fall of 1996 was rather chilly in Southern California, so the garage door remained closed much of the time. I noticed around Halloween that the three of them were behind that door more than usual. The day I knocked and asked to come in was the day I was certain they were scheming something. All three of them responded, "You can't come in!" I knew better than to ask why, so I announced that dinner would be ready soon and walked away.

They sat down at the table full of giggles. These three had a secret and, judging by their dad's face, they weren't about to give up many clues. "What are you up to?" I asked very pointedly to the older of the two.

Audrey looked at her sister. "Noooothing!" Knowing I might get something out of them if I pressed, their dad quickly changed the subject. Dinner proceeded as usual and the subject was easily lost in the chaos of everyday life.

Before I knew it, Christmas was just days away. It seemed my job was demanding more of me than usual, but it could have just been the life of a full-time working mom at the holidays. Report deadlines, school parties, holiday cards, Christmas gifts and tree trimming all added up, and the days flew by.

I had no idea what to get my husband that year. He was just as busy as I was, so we hadn't really discussed gifts. At the last minute I settled on some clothes and a few other meaningless items. I didn't even think about feeling guilty. I was just getting through this year by crossing things off the to-do list. The presents were purchased, wrapped and under the tree. Check. I was ready.

Christmas morning is by far one of the best times for memories in our family. Glittering decorations complete with a tree filled with homemade ornaments, Christmas music and an aromatic breakfast in the oven provide the setting. Our excited eagerness and laughter provide the memories. As we gathered that December 25, it was no different. The girls and their father were especially full of smiles that morning.

Gift giving proceeded as usual. Noisy tears of wrapping paper, squeals of delight and appreciative, loving hugs filled our morning. The last present under the tree had finally been opened and the girls looked at their father in anticipation. Did he really forget to get a gift for me this year?

He looked at me and asked the girls if they were ready. In unison they replied, "Yes!" They grabbed my hands, made me close my eyes and led me out the front door. I heard the garage door opening and a quick shuffling. As I stood with my eyes closed, I wondered what in the world they could have in the garage for me. Then I was instructed to open my eyes, and there it was! The most thoughtful, sweetest gift anyone had ever given me!

Mark was into woodworking and had planned with the girls and made a beautiful, exquisitely constructed cedar chest! The looks on their faces told me how proud they were, and the three of them smiling at me told me how lucky I was. They showed it off to me: the cedar-lined inside complete with brass hinges, how the lid closed so snugly and the beautiful footings. The best part, they told me, was on the bottom. As the three carefully tilted the chest, I saw the wonderful inscription.

To me, from my hubby, a forever note that will always serve to remind the cedar chest's owner that it was a gift of love. No matter its contents or where it resides, my cedar chest will always carry with it the memories of that wonderful Christmas morning, when life slowed down a little, and the caring nature of family once again made a beautiful memory.

Déjà Vu Christmas

Paula Munier

---◆─◇◆◇─◆---

You can blame it on Hurricane Irene. At the University of Connecticut, my son Mikey lost power for a week at the house he rented with his college buddies. Back home at the little lakeside cottage in Massachusetts where I raised him, I had no lights or fans or water for five days of sweltering August heat. And out West in the air-conditioned cool of Phoenix, my ex-husband Michael worried and waited for his son to call him back and let him know he was okay.

That was his first mistake. Well, hardly his first mistake—more like his hundredth, thousandth, millionth mistake over the course of the twenty-five years in which I'd known him. But who's counting.

Teenage boys do not return phone calls. Given sufficient motivation, they may deign to return a parent's text via their smart phone, that motivation typically being the threatened loss of said smart phone.

But apparently Michael hadn't figured that out yet. So, in desperation, he broke the first of the many unspoken rules that had governed our relationship since we divorced nearly a dozen years before.

He called me.

This was highly irregular. All our communication was initially conducted through lawyers, and then, eventually, as passions and prejudices faded, through the occasional email. Phone calls were only permitted when Mikey was 35,000 feet in the air, hurtling toward one coast (mine) or the other (his), and the plane was late.

But Mikey was not en route at the moment.

I was sitting in my bed alone in absolute darkness, bored and hot and aching for a cold shower, when I saw the words *My Ex* appear on my cell as the first ring shattered the dark silence of the night. (Originally, the words that indicated my ex was calling were, shall we say, less neutral, but Mikey noticed and reprogrammed my phone. Like many children of divorce, he is, within the context of our broken nuclear family, the smart one.)

I was not pleased.

But after acknowledging that a natural disaster may indeed trump a delayed flight, I picked up, bracing for the sound of the only voice on the planet that could strike me dumb with fury.

"It's me," he said.

"Uh-huh," I said.

"Are you all right?"

"Fine." *Fine.* Every woman's favorite four-letter word.

"With the storm, I thought—"

"Fine," I repeated. "No power but fine."

"And Mikey? I haven't heard from Mikey."

"He doesn't have power either, but he's fine."

"What can I do?"

I bit back the wicked words that bounded into my throat and swallowed my bitterness. "Nothing. Really. We're fine."

My ex paused. "So I'm guessing everything's fine."

I laughed.

He always could make me laugh. It's not that he was really funny; *funny* was not the first word most people would use to describe an intense, taciturn guy like Michael. But whenever we were together, he had a tender way of teasing me that disarmed and charmed me every time. That playfulness, coupled with a passion that never failed to surprise and delight us both, made ours the one relationship we'd come to measure every other against. I'd had a husband before him and a couple of almost-husbands after him, but Michael remained the one significant other in my life who felt like home.

You can never go home again, which is why I'd moved to Massachusetts when we broke up. I took his son with me, and broke Michael's heart a second time. I did what I believed I had to do to save us from one another; in the end, all that playfulness and passion couldn't offset the mundane challenges that can undermine any couple—communication, money, teenagers. We both had kids from our first marriages, and they weren't exactly thrilled when we got married. And though they *were* thrilled when we had Mikey, even he couldn't save our not-so-blended family.

With enough time and distance, I thought I'd get over Michael. And I thought Michael would get over me—or die trying, as men are wont to do. But when he went off and got married to a Skinny-Mini-Me, I wasn't so sure.

Now he was single again—that marriage having died an inevitable death (she says with some satisfaction)—and I was single still. He was alone in his bed—and I was alone in mine. He was teasing me—and I was laughing.

You know what happened next. We talked all night and all day and all night again. He said he was sorry and I said I was sorry and he said he'd always loved me and I said I'd always loved him and he said we're older and wiser now and I said: *Are we really?*

By the time the lights were back on, so were we. More than a decade of rancor and regret forgotten as we reminded each other why we'd been so good together all those years ago. Flush with muscle memory, our hearts remembered what our brains had vowed to forget. Over the course of two months and a million phone calls, texts and emails, we were in love. Again.

It was like being struck by lightning a second time; already inured to the shock, we felt only a strong afterglow. And in the warmth of that afterglow, we made plans. Serious plans. We arranged to meet face-to-face somewhere in the middle of the country after Christmas for what would be only the third time in eleven years—a sort of trial run. In the meantime, Michael started looking for a new job on the East Coast.

In a mere matter of days, he garnered the interest of a big firm. They were flying him out for an interview. By now it was early November—and Christmas was just around the corner. Christmas, the time of year when I was the most sentimental, the most vulnerable, the most emotional. The time of year when I was most likely to do something very, very stupid.

We didn't tell anyone.

"I want to keep us to ourselves for a while," I told Michael, but in truth I was too scared to tell my friends or family, most of whom had held my hand through the divorce, the custody battle and the acrimonious aftermath. I wanted to live in this lovely bubble a little longer.

Then the past weighed in—and I panicked. Driving to

work in my Jeep the day before Michael was due to arrive for his interview, I played our song, which I am embarrassed to admit is that lame Foreigner song "I Don't Want to Live Without You." (What can I say; it was the eighties.)

I was giddy at the thought of seeing him. Too giddy. Dangerously giddy.

I'd felt this way before—and it had taken me a lot of years and a lot of yoga to get over it. What was I thinking? I flipped off the iPod and burst into tears. Sobs, really. I wept so wildly that I couldn't see the road.

There was a Dunkin' Donuts on the corner. (There is a Dunkin' Donuts on virtually every corner in the great Commonwealth of Massachusetts; we invented it.) I pulled into the parking lot and sat there, engine idling, until I'd cried myself out. Then I texted Michael: Tell me this is real.

He texted me right back: It's real. C u tomorrow.

I took a deep breath, and then did what any self-respecting woman planning to win back her ex would do: I called in sick and went and got a mani-pedi.

The next day I was at the airport early. Twitchy, jittery, silly. It was unseemly in a woman my age. I was a grandmother, for God's sake.

I closed my eyes and thought of my granddaughters. I smiled to myself.

I opened my eyes, and there he was. Long and nearly as lean as he'd been when I'd married him twenty-five years before. Well, that was one of us. I smiled to myself again.

Michael loped over, his dark blue eyes never leaving mine. He grinned, took me in his arms and that was that. Once again, he was the man who'd called me his Marilyn Monroe—and I was the woman who'd called him my Heathcliff.

★ ★ ★

He got the job. The offer letter came December 9, the same day I got laid off. Serendipity? Karma? Blind luck? Whatever you called it, to us it seemed as if this was meant to be. I was home with nothing to do but worry, so I made the ultimate sacrifice and started clearing out closets to make room for Michael. A week later, he packed up his truck and started driving east.

It was time to start telling people. First, our son, Mikey, who was still away at school. I would've preferred to tell him in person, but by the time he came home for Christmas break his father would already be here. I tried calling, but of course he didn't answer. This was a text message waiting to happen.

Mom: Your father is coming home.

Son: y

Mom: We've reconciled.

Son: srsly?

Mom: Seriously. What do you think?

Son: idk

Mom: I know it's unexpected.

Son: meh

Mom: What?

Son: whatever

That wasn't so bad. Emboldened by Mikey's lackluster response, I called my mother in Las Vegas.

"Hi, Mom," I said.

"What's wrong?" My mother always knew when something was up.

"I've got good news and bad news," I said. "Or bad news and bad news, depending on how you look at it."

"What's wrong?" she repeated.

"I got laid off."

"Oh, honey, I am so sorry. What is wrong with those people?"

"I should have looked harder for another job." I paused. "I'm looking now."

"What's the good news?"

"I hope you'll see it as good news."

"What's wrong?"

"Michael and I have reconciled."

"Oh, for Christ's sake," she said.

I laughed. "He got a job here and is on his way right now."

I could hear the wheels turning in my mother's mind. "It's a good position?"

"It's a good position."

"Hmph." My mother paused. "So maybe he's your blessing in disguise."

News travels fast among siblings. I didn't have to tell my older children; Mikey told them for me. By the time we all got together at a diner for dinner, they were ready to discuss their mother's folly as if I weren't even there.

Mikey: It's the yoga. When Mom became a yoga teacher, she completely changed. All she talks about now is love and forgiveness and redemption. She really believes in all that stuff.

Mom: I'm right here, you know.

Greg: You're totally wrong, Mikey. I don't think Mom's changed at all. This proves it. She's just repeating her old patterns. She's stuck.

Mom: I can hear you.

Alexis: Mom's getting old and we're all gone and she's all alone and miserable. She just wants to be happy. Give her a break. What do you care what she does?

Mom: Thanks, honey. I think.

With the big reveal safely behind me, I took my old, deluded, stuck yoga self home to meditate upon my past patterns and future follies. Five days, 2,727 miles and two new tires later, my blessing in disguise rolled up to the garden fence that fronted our little cottage in his beloved F-150 truck.

He kissed me. I laughed.

It was our déjà vu Christmas all over again.

Love Never Dies

Norma Jean Thornton

———•◦✕◦•———

Returning from a meeting in the middle of December and listening to a poignant rendition of "White Christmas" on the radio, I took a detour to look at Christmas lights. Suddenly I found myself driving by the restaurant where my husband and I had had our first date over forty years ago. As I slowly drove home alone through the rain, memories of the past took over.

If this were only nine years ago, a fire would be roaring in the fireplace because he knew it made me happy, and I'd be walking into a nice, warm, toasty house. Tonight, I blink through tears, knowing I'll have to light the pinecones and wood for myself when I get home. *But do I really want a fire?* Watching the flames no longer warms me the way it did then, and it hurts my heart.

In the past, I'd pull into the driveway and see two pairs of tiny, shiny eyes staring out at me from the small arched windows, just as they do tonight: two of our cats sit in the windowsills in the den and peek through curtains, waiting for me to come inside. He said they seemed to know exactly when I was due home from work, because every day at the same time, that's where they'd be.

The cats are still looking out the window, waiting for me each time I come home, but there's no fire to greet me, to warm my heart and soul, and no husband with a welcome-home bear hug.

I go inside, and the memories continue flooding back as I feed the cats. My thoughts wander back to that last Christmas season, and our final three days together, especially our last night.

Even though he was as excited about each present as the kids were and enjoyed Christmas, every year he would lightly grumble and grouse and complain about everything, including the stockings that were filled with goodies. He'd always mumble *"The Grinch had it right!"*

This was a second marriage for both of us, bringing a total of six kids to the family, so at Christmas eight stockings were always hung. However, one Christmas, one stocking was missing. Although I had filled his, I didn't hang it that year, waiting for his response. When he couldn't find it, he asked hesitantly, "Where's my stocking?"

I commented: "I thought you didn't want one."

Early in our relationship, he had found that rather than actually apologizing for anything minor, all he had to do was give me that apologetic look and pout, the way a little kid would, and it worked every time...melted my heart and always got a smile from me.

This time, like a shy little boy with his lower lip in that deliberately exaggerated, yet endearing pout and those pleading green eyes in the way that always tugged at my heartstrings, he sheepishly responded: "You know I don't really mean that."

He was right; he didn't mean it. But each year after that, we played the game, and he had to hunt for his stocking, as though it were an Easter egg, and he loved it.

But his last year, it was different… In the beginning of December, he was brought home by ambulance from his latest, and final, stay in the hospital. Complications of the cancer that was ravaging his gorgeous body had kept him there for six weeks this time.

As the attendants wheeled him through the house to his newly set-up hospice bed, he kept repeating, "I really didn't mean to be the Grinch and spoil Christmas. I really didn't. I'm so sorry."

He wasn't a Grinch and never could be, but he loved the Grinch, and had called himself that every year—another little game we played. The kids had even bought him a stuffed Grinch one year.

We all knew he didn't mean it, but now it bothered him more and more each day, especially since I hadn't done a thing yet for Christmas. Every other year by this time the house would smell good from homemade candy and cinnamon-spiced pinecones and be overdecorated with poinsettias, garlands and wreaths, with stuffed teddy bears, snowmen, Santas and elves sitting everywhere.

He would already—grudgingly, yet willingly—have put up the tree and added the lights, while I was busy making hot chocolate, playing Christmas music and pestering him to sing along with me, to keep him motivated, until it was my turn with the tree, to decorate it. His only job was to put the tree up and gladly take it down.

Suddenly, on the morning of December 10, he blurted out, "I don't want Christmas to be any different than before.

Promise me you won't change anything; do everything just like you've always done."

Completely confined to the bed, he feverishly focused on how Christmas should be, and hurriedly continued to tell me what he wanted done. Christmas 2005 would be his doing, even though he knew his time was quickly fading, and he wouldn't be there by Christmas Day.

"Be sure to have turkey, with your cornbread and wild rice dressing, mashed potatoes and gravy, and your sweet potatoes. And this time, don't forget the cranberry sauce!

"All the salsa, dips and chips, and everything else you always fix. Don't leave out anything…be sure to have beans and your bean dip. Everybody loves that.

"I want the tree decorated in red, white and green; same with the wrapping paper. Use paper plates and plastic forks… and this time, throw them away after dinner; don't wash 'em and save 'em like you always do.

"And make lots of candy, with nuts…especially the peanut butter fudge."

His hospice bed had been set up in the den, his favorite room, close to his TV. It was also near where we always put the Christmas tree, so I shoved my way through stuff that had been piled in the shed, to find the fake tree. While two of our boys worked on putting it up, I made a quick trip to Walmart for paper products and decorations.

Not wanting to be away from him one second longer than I had to, I rushed through the store, throwing everything red, white and green that I could find into the cart.

When I got back to the house, I dropped everything at the foot of his bed. I sat next to him and pulled each item from the bags. He tried to show interest, but he was so ill he couldn't even raise his head from the pillow and listlessly nodded his approval. He halfheartedly watched as four of the older granddaughters decorated the tree with red and white lights, red and white garlands, and red, white and green glittery ornaments.

I hastily dug through the myriad of Christmas stuff from years past to find his favorite ornament and added it to the tree: we had bought it in Hawaii in 1996. It was Santa and Mrs. Claus kissing on a surfboard. Santa was dressed in a red and white surfing outfit; Mrs. Claus in a white muumuu with red and green poinsettias and a red poinsettia lei around her head. He always said it reminded him of us.

The daughters set out the red poinsettia table centerpiece and white sparkly place mats with a red-and-green poinsettia design and red cloth napkins. Matching salt-and-pepper shakers and coasters were added to the table, along with fat red candles.

Everything would be as normal as possible for him, under the circumstances, with me on autopilot. I pulled the Christmas stockings out and hung his at the foot of his bed, and a granddaughter found his stuffed Grinch. When we put it next to him, he accepted it with a tentative, little lopsided grin.

He was adamant about having a clock and a light beside him at all times those last three days. His last night, just as the sun went down, and every thirty minutes or so afterwards, he asked, "What time is it?" He asked the time more frequently as the night went on. At 10:15 p.m., December 11, he frantically said, "It's time—quick, everyone come here… Hurry, hurry… Come on, little girls. Hurry!"

My sister, all six of our kids and four of the fourteen grandkids were there. He told each of them how much he loved them, how important each of them was to him and how proud of them he was. He kissed them all, and there wasn't a dry eye on any of us.

After his turn with the kids, he turned to me and said, "Come closer!"

I scooted as close as possible to him, but he kept saying "Closer!"

Crying silently, I crawled into bed with him, trying to get as close as I could. But he angrily said, "You're not the real Normie... Where's my Normie?... I want my Normie." His vision was all but gone by that time, and his eyes were clouded over. As his pain meds were rapidly increased, he was going in and out of consciousness, and it was impossible to tell whether it was him or the meds talking.

I kept repeating, "It's me, Honey." I finally straddled him on the bed, and I leaned down, holding his face in my hands, and kissed him. "What do I need to do to prove I'm me?"

I had on a lightweight button-up pajama top, and he put his hands to my chest, his fingers fumbling as he unbuttoned the thing, and said, "Ahh...that's my Normie." He took me in his hands and nuzzled his face into me.

He had rarely called me Normie in the past—maybe two or three times. I have no idea why he did then.

Everyone had already gone into the living room, allowing us to be alone, although they were still close enough to see and hear what was happening. I whispered, "Honey—all the kids are in the other room and can see what you're doing!"

He loudly said, "That's their problem!" as he moved his hands all over me and nuzzled me more.

Sometimes there's nothing one can do but laugh, even at the most horrible of times. That time brought a nervous laugh from everyone.

He kept repeating, "I love you, I love you. I'm so sorry I'm leaving you. I'm not going to be here to protect you."

Heartbroken, and knowing it was little consolation, I tried to reassure him: "Don't worry about that… Just remember, I love you with all my heart and always will."

He stayed with us for another five hours, going in and out of consciousness. He didn't ask for the time again, but at midnight, three hours before he died, he suddenly said, "Would you marry me again?"

Of course, I said, "Yes!" not realizing he meant right then, at that moment. I thought he was asking if I would do it all over again.

To my surprise, he hurriedly told me, "Give me a ring, quick, give me a ring!"

I took the wedding ring that had been my mother's from my left index finger, expecting him to put it back on that finger, but when I offered it, he said, "Give me the right finger—your ring one!"

During his last conversations with everyone that night, his voice was high-pitched and rushed, his sentences short, choppy and erratic. It was obvious that medication played a big part, but he was fighting to stay in control, even through the haze of mind-muddling drugs and the cancer. Because his actions had been so unpredictable, and we thought that his vision was completely gone, I was amazed that he had realized that it wasn't my ring finger. As he lay in bed, I held out the correct finger for him, without taking my original wedding set off. Without a word, and with his hands shaking, he took my hand and placed the ring on my finger.

I kissed him and said, "I love you." He closed his eyes and, less than three hours later, he was gone. My husband proposed twice, thirty years apart, and put a ring on my finger each time. There may not have been a second wedding ceremony, but it double-sealed the bonds from the first. Both rings will stay on that finger forever.

★ ★ ★ ★ ★

About the Contributors

---•◦✕◦•---

A Miracle Under the Christmas Tree

Jennifer Aldrich

Since the first time she slipped on her grandmother's high-heeled shoes and I. Magnin jacket, Jennifer Aldrich has imagined herself into dozens of rich fantasy lives. A hopeless Anglophile, she regularly attends fancy dress parties and takes tea at four o'clock daily. She lives in Northern California with her husband, another hopeless Anglophile, and their son, whom they are raising imaginatively.

Elaine Ambrose

Elaine is the co-author of *Menopause Sucks* and *Drinking with Dead Women Writers*. Her short stories and feature articles appear in several anthologies and magazines; and she owns Mill Park Publishing. She organizes Write by the River writers' retreats in Idaho and creates a sassy blog called *Midlife Cabernet*. Find more details at www.ElaineAmbrose.com.

Dee Ambrose-Stahl

Dee has been writing since she was a small child. She still resides in her hometown and teaches English at the middle school she attended. She has served as both reviewer and contributor for Holt, Rinehart and Winston. Her fiction and photography have appeared in specialty corgi magazines. When not writing and teaching, she enjoys breeding, raising and showing Pembroke Welsh corgis.

Ruth Andrew

Ruth is a freelance writer living in Spokane, Washington. Her previous short stories and articles have appeared in newspapers, lifestyle magazines and anthologies, including *My Mom Is My Hero* and *My Dog Is My Hero*. She is working on her first novel. You may read more about her at www.ruthandrew.com and beeconcise.wordpress.com.

Jo Anne Boulger

Jo Anne Boulger resides in Pebble Beach, California, where she keeps busy with various volunteer endeavors, painting and writing. She is a widow with four children and eleven grandchildren, and a first great-grandchild due in December of 2012.

Ruth Campbell Bremer

Ruth is a freelance writer, blogger and aspiring novelist. Her stupefying brilliance can be found at www.insightfulish.com.

David Scott Chamberlain

David has a communications degree from University of Southern California, masters in communication from California State University at Los Angeles, masters in educational multimedia from the Univerisy of Arizona, and works for NetApp. His mother Barbara has begun a series of mysteries set in Carmel—the first is *A Slice of Carmel*. She is currently the president of Northern California Pen Women, and she enjoys writing, storytelling and giving seminars on creative writing and storytelling.

Candy Chand

Candy has authored seven books. She lives in Northern California and can be reached at PatCan85@hotmail.com.

Harry Freiermuth

Rev. Harry Freiermuth is a member of the Central Coast Writers branch of California Writers Club, who specializes in short stories and has written a historical fiction novel. He is a retired Roman Catholic priest of the diocese of Monterey in California.

Kathleen (KM) Gallagher

KM is a writer, entrepreneur and pet travel specialist. She is the author of *SoleMate: The Runner's Companion for Taking Life in Stride*. Currently she is working on a series of winery guidebooks, *Sip + Slobber: A Dog's Companion to California's Dog Friendly Whineries*. KM also serves as president of StoryBiz, a content strategy firm that uses storytelling to build brands. She holds undergraduate degrees in history and philosophy and a masters in business administration from Northeastern University Graduate School of Business. KM, along with her dogs, splits her time between Texas and California.

Jeanne Gilpatrick

Jeanne lives in Oakland, California, with her dog Charlie.

She won a twenty-five-word essay contest at age twelve and has been writing ever since. She recently completed a young adult novel and is sharpening her pencils in anticipation of retirement. You can reach Jeanne at: jeannejo2@att.net.

Pat Hanson

Pat Hanson, Ph.D., is a veteran health educator, writer and public speaker living in Monterey, California. She lectures nationally on aging positively, and is a columnist for the magazine *Crone: Women Coming of Age* (www.cronemagazine.com). Visit her website at www.invisiblegrandparent.com.

BJ Hollace

BJ is a published author, editor and speaker who takes the ordinary and turns it into an extraordinary story. Her passion as a writer is to touch the hearts of her readers and empower them to follow their own dreams. Currently, she is working on a novel series and coaching first-time authors.

Rosi Hollinbeck

Rosi specializes in children's writing. Her work has been featured in issues of *High Five, Highlights,* and *Stories for Children* magazines, and her children's short story, *Helen's Home Run,* won first place in the 2011 Foster City International Writer's Contest, Children's Division. Her middle-grade novel, *The Incredible Journey of Freddy J.,* was a finalist in the Grace Notes Publishing Discovering the Undiscovered contest. She also has a story-poem that will be included in the 2012 British anthology *Fifty Funny Poems for Children.* She regularly writes reviews for the *Sacramento Book Review;* and her blog, rosihollinbeckthewritestuff.blogspot.com, has nearly a thousand readers a month.

Paul Karrer

Paul has been published in the *San Francisco Chronicle, Christian Science Monitor, Education Week, Teacher Magazine,* and interviewed on NPR. His essay "A Letter to My President, The One I Voted For," went viral. He is a fifth-grade teacher and union negotiator in Castroville, California.

Julaina Kleist-Corwin

Julaina is the Creative Writing Instructor for the City of Dublin, California. She has won first place awards in short story contests and been published in several anthologies by the San Francisco Writers Conference and Las Positas College. She is a field supervisor for intern teachers. You can find her blogging at timetowritenow.blogspot.com, or her website julaina. homestead.com. Her son Adrian Toryfter, was an audio designer for Diablo Valley College theater, where he had a fatal accident backstage.

April Kutger

April is an award-winning author of fiction and nonfiction. When she's not writing, April volunteers as a basic skills tutor and swims on a masters team. Christmas Eve with her three children and ten grandchildren is her favorite day of the year.

Liza Long

Liza is a teacher, writer, musician and single mother of four (mostly) delightful children. She bought her 1925 Model M Steinway grand piano at a thrift store. Her anthology *Little White Dress: Women Explore the Myth and Meaning of Wedding Dresses* won a 2012 Bronze Ippy Award in Women's Issues. She blogs at www.anarchistsoccermom.com.

Ingrid E. Lundquist

Ingrid is founder of the Book-in-Hand Roadshow and author of the *Dictionary of Publishing Terms: Words Every Writer Needs to Know.* After an international award-winning career as an event designer/producer, she rediscovered her first love—writing and art. She is owner of TLC Publishing, an imprint of The Lundquist Company, her event firm. She writes articles for event industry publications and is author of *Results-Driven Event Planning: Using Marketing Tools to Boost Your Bottom Line.* She travels on a whim and is an accomplished photojournalist. See www.TheBookInHandRoadshow.com and www.FiveWeeksInFlorence.com and www.ingridlundquist.com.

R. Bob Magart

R. Bob Magart is a freelance writer, a former businessman and a father of five. He makes his home between Montana and Washington and is an avid outdoorsman and cyclist. He was born on Christmas Day, 1952.

Laura Martin

Laura is a freelance writer and photographer whose work has appeared in *Sacramento* magazine, *Solano* magazine, *Via* magazine, the *San Jose Mercury News,* the *Boston Globe,* the *San Francisco Chronicle, Susurrus,* and other publications throughout Northern California. She is an Amherst Writers and Artists affiliate and leads writing workshops throughout Sacramento. "A Sears Catalog Christmas" is part of a working collection of creative nonfiction stories, entitled *The Last Night on Jackson Street,* about growing up in the small sawmill town of Weed, California.

Valerie Reynoso Piotrowski

Valerie is an award-winning writer, poet and fundraiser. She and her husband, John Piotrowski, reside in El Dorado Hills, California, with their three beloved dogs, and are active in philanthropic support of a number of community and charitable causes. They own a high-end spa franchise, Elements Therapeutic Massage Studio, in Folsom, California.

Louise Reardon

Louise is a fourth-generation Californian from the Central Valley, a mother, a wife and a teacher. After teaching for fifty years and volunteering almost as long for causes like food banks and equal housing, Louise is now enjoying her senior years.

Cheryl Riveness

"Living on an island in the Pacific Northwest is a writer's dream," Cheryl says. "It's a wonderful creative environment. Although I have lived in many places, my heart has always been here." You can follow Cheryl at www.theislandposts.com.

Jennifer Basye Sander

Jennifer is a *New York Times* bestselling author, former Random House senior editor and the mother of two amazing sons. She teaches publishing skills and nonfiction writing, and runs writing retreats in Lake Tahoe and on her great-grandfather's farm in Washington state. Learn more about her retreats at www.writebythelake.com or www.writeatthefarm.com.

Jack Skillicorn

Jack was born in 1933 in Watsonville, California, where he grew up, worked and attended Monterey Peninsula College. He studied, played football, dropped out and joined the USAF. He served during the Korean conflict for four years, then returned to the USAF during the Vietnam conflict, after which he returned to college for a bachelor degree in accounting. Jack was first published in the *California County,* Journal of the County Supervisors Association of California with an article called "Who Said You Could Run a County Like a Business?" In retirement he began writing stories for grandchildren and family.

A Kiss Under the Mistletoe

Dawn Armstrong

A charitable blog correspondent, Dawn wanders the world in search of time travel, danger, eternal love, all of which contribute to the scenes and content of her inspirational books and novels. Dawn's first book, *Sensations: A Little Book of Love…* , spreads hope around the globe. Don't miss her exciting new paranormal romance, *Knower*. To learn more, visit her at www.littlebookoflove.net and www.theknower.wordpress.com.

Jennifer Bern Basye

A *New York Times* bestselling author and former Random House senior editor, Jennifer is the mother of two amazing sons. She teaches publishing skills and nonfiction writing, coaches writers, and runs writing retreats in Lake Tahoe and on her great-grandfather's farm in Washington state. Learn more about her retreats at www.writebythelake.com or www.writeatthefarm.com.

Sheryl J. Bize Boutte

Sheryl is a Northern California writer and management consultant. More of her short stories, poetry and commentary can be seen at www.sjbb-talkinginclass.blogspot.com/.

Ruth Bremer

Ruth is a freelance writer, blogger and aspiring novelist. Her stupefying brilliance can be found at www.insightfulish.com.

Kathryn Canan

Whenever the family cabin in Montana is buried in snow,

Kathryn Canan and her husband live in California with two psychotic cats. She is a freelance writer, Latin tutor, and early music teacher and performer. She has recorded CDs of medieval and Renaissance music with Briddes Roune and the New Queen's Ha'penny Consort. Her master's thesis on Anglo-Saxon medicine has made her one of the few experts in diseases caused by malevolent elves.

Cherie Carlson

Cherie Carlson has lived in Northern California for 37 years. The joys of her life are her four children and nine grandchildren, to whom she is "Ranna." A full-time caregiver to her husband, she is also a part-time Realtor. In her spare time she is working on a homeschooling blog and a parent curriculum for homeschoolers.

Melissa Chambers

Melissa Chambers comes from a family of writers. She has taught elementary school for more than 25 years and loves teaching Writing Workshop to her wonderful third grade class. An animal lover since she was given a Banty chick at age two, she has been involved in animal rescue for 10 years. Currently working on a novel, she is also collaborating with her husband on a book of short stories about the many special-needs Chihuahuas they have known and loved.

Scott "Robby" Evans

Scott (aka Robby) Evans is happily married and has three sons. He teaches writing at the University of the Pacific in Stockton, CA. His new, somewhat romantic psychological thriller, *Sylvia's Secret,* was published by Port Yonder Press in 2013. It is the third in a series of "literary" murder mysteries.

Neva J. Hodges

Neva belongs to California Writers Club Tri-Valley Branch and was membership chair for three years. She has been published in the Oakland Senior Anthology and the local newspaper for a real-life story. Currently she is writing short stories and a novel.

Julaina Kleist-Corwin

Julaina is a creative writing instructor for the City of Dublin, California. She has won first place awards in short story contests and published in several anthologies by the S.F. Writers Conference and Las Positas College, and is a field supervisor for intern teachers. You can find her blogging at timetowritenow.blogspot.com or her website at julaina.homestead.com.

Chels Knorr

Chels Knorr is an editor, writer and student. Her favorite things include traveling, walks with her dog, Goose, a competitive game of Scrabble and chocolate chip waffles. Sometimes she posts ramblings at chelsknorr.com.

Dena Kouremetis

Consumer journalist, author and would-be shrink Dena Kouremetis loves to examine life from a midlife perspective. She is a professional blogger for *Forbes Magazine* and a national Lady Boomer examiner for Examiner.com. She has authored, co-authored and contributed content to dozens of books, and loves to speak to groups about how our online presence says volumes about us. She welcomes visits to her website at www.communic8or.com.

Charles Kuhn

Charles Kuhn is an accomplished writer in the areas of mystery, nonfiction and adventure. He has published short stories in various magazines, self-published and writes for local writers groups, including the poetry group for the local Sacramento Multiple Sclerosis Association. Mr. Kuhn and his wife reside in Citrus Heights, CA.

April Kutger

April Kutger, an award-winning author of fiction and nonfiction who, when she's not writing, volunteers as a basic skills tutor and swims on a Masters team. Christmas Eve with her three children and ten grandchildren is her favorite day of the year.

Lelia Kutger

Lelia Torluemke Kutger Fettes was born in 1917 in St. Louis, MO, the granddaughter of German immigrants. She met Joseph Kutger when she was working as a telephone operator in Fort Dix, NJ. They married in 1942. While going through an old box of papers many decades later, she found the telegram she received telling her that her husband was missing in action. It inspired her to collaborate with her daughter about what she went through during the war.

Suzanne Lilly

Suzanne writes lighthearted stories with a splash of suspense, a flash of the unexplained, a dash of romance and always a happy ending. Her debut novel was *Shades of the Future* in 2012 followed by *Untellable* in 2013. Her short stories have appeared in numerous places online and in print. She lives in Northern

California where she reads, writes, cooks, swims and teaches elementary students. To find out more visit her author page at http://www.suzannelilly.com, her blog at http://www.teacherwriter.net, her Facebook page at www.facebook.com/SuzanneLillyAuthor and follow her on Twitter @SuzanneLilly.

Paula Munier
Paula Munier is a writer, teacher and content strategist who's authored or co-authored a number of books, including the acclaimed memoir *Fixing Freddie: A True Story about a Boy, a Mom, and the Very, Very Bad Beagle Who Saved Them* and *5-Minute Mindfulness: Simple Daily Shortcuts to Transform Your Life.* She lives in New England with her ex-husband, a relationship best described by her Facebook status: It's Complicated.

Marsha Porter
Marsha Porter mastered the art of the 500-word essay when such compositions were the punishment du jour at her parochial grade school. She has since published over 200 articles and an annual movie review guide. Her short stories have won numerous awards.

Christina Richter
Christina and her husband Mark have been married 26 years and live in Northern California. Her two daughters are off to college but they still love to surprise her with special Christmas presents. Christina is a writer; her current project is the history of the Roseville Fiddyment family, a gold rush era story that continues to this day.

Margaret H. Scanlon
Margaret is a longtime resident of Hamburg, New York.

Jack Skillicorn
Jack Skillicorn was born in 1933 in Watsonville, California where he grew up, worked and attended Monterey Peninsula College. He studied, played football, dropped out and joined the USAF during the Korean conflict for 4 years, then out 4 years, then returned to the USAF during the Vietnam conflict, and then back to college for a BS in Accounting. Jack was first published in the *California County* journal of the County Supervisor's Association of California with an article called, "Who said you could run a county like a Business?" In retirement he began writing family stories for grandchildren and family.

Judy Stevens
Judy Stevens enjoys blowing the dumb blonde stereotype out of the water with a masters degree in education, and as the mom of five, Judy voices her opinion whenever possible. Writing is a passion. She started writing with an eye to the future and authoring a parenting book.

Illia Thompson
Illia Thompson, a graduate of Antioch College in Ohio, teaches memoir writing throughout the Monterey Peninsula and presents private journaling workshops. She received Honorable Mention in Writer's Digest Poetry Contests and has been published in poetry magazines. Her books include *Gracious Seasons,* about her journey through the last year of her husband's cancer, as well as *Heartframes,* collected poetry. Her most recent book, *Along the Memoir Way,* holds poems

followed by blank pages, a workbook for memories. She resides in Carmel Valley, California.

Norma Jean Thornton

Her baby sister called her Nonie, her great granddaughter calls her GumGum. Norma Jean Thornton, aka Noniedoodles and Granny-GumGum, is a rhyming, art-doodling, writing granny from Rio Linda, California, with four cats. She has self-published two books through lulu.com: *Nonie's 1st Big Bottom Girls' Rio Linda CookBook* and *Doodles & Rhymes: Noniedoodles, Volumes 1, 2 & 3*. As Granny-GumGum, Norma also writes children's truth-based animal stories, a variety of fun rhymes, and as The-Granny, is working with her cat, The-Windy, on *Nosie Rosie's Diary: The True "Tails" of a Very Special Kitty*. Norma Jean writes mainly nonfiction-Heinz-57-stuff, dabbling in everyday humor and more rhymes...then there's this rare, serious, emotional true story, "Love Never Dies." You can reach her at nooniedoodles@yahoo.com.

Pam Walters

Pam Walters spent 25 years as an ad agency copywriter. Since then, she's self-published *Become The Person You Were Created To Be* and *The Out Of Work Coloring Book*. Pam lives in Carmel, CA.

Jerry White

After a career in the military and in real estate, Jerry now teaches in the Earth Science department of a community college.

Teri Wilson

Teri Wilson grew up as an only child and could often be

found with her head in a book, lost in a world of romance and exotic places. As an adult, her love of books has led her to her dream career—writing for Harlequin Love Inspired and HQN. When Teri isn't traveling or writing, she enjoys knitting, painting and dancing, although she still hasn't quite mastered the tango. Teri lives in San Antonio, Texas, with her family and four sweet dogs, and loves to hear from readers! Visit her at www.teriwilson.net and be sure to look for her next book, *Unleashing Mr. Darcy,* coming from Harlequin HQN in January 2014.